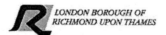

AN INKY BUSINESS

AN INKY BUSINESS

A HISTORY *of* NEWSPAPERS *from the* ENGLISH CIVIL WARS *to the* AMERICAN CIVIL WAR

MATTHEW J. SHAW

REAKTION BOOKS

Published by
Reaktion Books Ltd
Unit 32, Waterside
44–48 Wharf Road
London N1 7UX, UK
www.reaktionbooks.co.uk

First published 2021

Printed and bound in Great Britain by
TJ Books Ltd, Padstow, Cornwall

A catalogue record for this book is available from the British Library

ISBN 978 1 78914 386 7

Contents

Preface 7

Introduction 11

1 Origins 20

2 Reporting Parliament 52

4 Colonial Papers 75

4 News and the American Revolution 90

5 The French Revolution 113

6 Scandal 147

7 The Creation of the Modern Press 175

Afterword 211

REFERENCES 215

FURTHER READING 230

ACKNOWLEDGEMENTS 232

PHOTO ACKNOWLEDGEMENTS 233

INDEX 234

It is true that we have not studied the newspapers, as the biologists have studied, for example, the potato bug.

– ROBERT E. PARK (1923)

Preface

This is a book about the making and printing of news. As such, it is a history of ink, paper, printing press and type, and of the men and women who made and read newspapers in Britain, continental Europe and America from the time of the English Civil Wars to the Battle of Gettysburg in the United States over two hundred years later. But it is also an account of what news was, how the idea of news became central to public life and, at the same time, how newspapers were much more than simple carriers of information: they helped to define communities and offered entertainment, advice, untruths, advertisements and obituaries. At times – for example, in *ancien régime* France – newspapers were seen as a threat to the very existence of the state; for similar reasons they were seen as a vital part of civil society, a pillar in the construction of the new American republic whose undermining might bring the entire edifice to the floor. Newspapers also ranged from purveyors of high seriousness to carriers of scurrilous gossip. They attracted the ire of moralists or were charged with being ponderous and tedious publications, full of pomposity and having the magic ability to send grown men to sleep in their clubs. Given their variety, there are good reasons for treating the various forms of newspaper publications throughout these two centuries less as a clear progression of a format than a sometimes contradictory and independent set of developments. But in the face of such thickets of confusion some sort of path needs to be cut, and a historical approach will not only help to show how newspapers came to be, but how they differed in responses to local needs or characteristics.

As well as taking a historical and critical approach, this book puts forward a number of hypotheses. One is that the making of news is a very geographical business. Centre, periphery; colony, metropole – all these aspects of society profoundly affected the way newspapers developed and were distributed, made and read, and also what the meaning of news was. Local or national papers now have a very distinct set of meanings, but it is one that changed over time, and was worked out in different, if comparable, ways across Europe and America. It views the press as an international innovation, with copy, personnel and ideas moving across the seas and borders with regularity. The period covered – from the English Civil Wars to the American Civil War – is broad, but limits the focus of this book to the period of the 'hand press' rather than the industrial age of paper production, although technical innovations such as stereotyping and the telegraph were in place by the mid-nineteenth century. Such an account is by necessity an aerial view, rather than a close examination of the ground. However, rather like a newspaper, the narrative attempts to liven the journey with human interest stories and occasional editorializing or opinion pieces. In attempting to tell a macro-level story, it focuses at each stage on a micro history, in which a smaller level of analysis aims to reveal something of the larger picture. And, of course, much is left out, as is inevitable for such a huge topic.

Another notion that informs this book relates to the idea of news and the role of reading. People gather their information from all kinds of places: today it may be from the television, Facebook, Twitter or even conversations around the proverbial water-cooler. For past generations, though, it may instead have been the sermon, the song or the play. These formats, places and modes of communication share common features, and newspapers relate, compete and feed off all these other modes of information transmission. It would be a mistake to carve off newspapers into their own separate space, not least because newspapers dealt with so much more than 'news'.

Any account of information, news or reading is also an account of difference, privilege and exclusion. We may today, drawing on the ideology of the American Revolution and the crusading press of the nineteenth century, see newspapers as an important means of democratizing information. But news also had its cost. Literacy was often exclusionary. Newspapers as a genre played with the idea of those 'in the know' and those outside the inner circle. At times of revolution, war or revolt, information really was power, and its control a vital aspect of governance. Our current obsession with 'fake news', the worrying revelations or hints about how money, power and technology shapes and controls the press and flows of what is believed to be genuine information, has dark early-modern echoes. We are also entering a time when the notion of what the 'news' is is being dramatically reshaped by protean forms of media and a politics taking its cues from reality television, social media and old-school propaganda. It seems apposite to revisit how news and reporting, and the role it played in civic society, came into being, for good or ill.

Finally, and perhaps as a counterweight to news' tendency to reduce everything to a story or an angle, this account is about real people and things: inky hands; the trundle of the newspaper barrow; the rustle, cost and afterlife of paper, from the chamber pot to the ubiquitous fish counter. News has its material history: newspapers are nothing if not texts about, made in and consumed with the world. And, we should remember, journalists – and their readers – are people, too: with noble aims as well, although, as the English eighteenth-century writer Dr Johnson noted, sometimes seeming to be 'without a Wish for Truth, or Thought of Decency'.[1]

AN ENGLISHMANS DELIGHT OR NEWS OF ALL SORTS.
NOON GAZETT
Morning Herald,
Morning Chronicle,
Morning Post,
Gazetteer,
St. James Evening
London Evening
Lloyd's Evening
Public Ledger,
Public Advertiser,
Sunday Cronicle.
All Englishmen delight in News
In London there's enough to chuse
Of morning papers near a Ream
Fill'd with every kind of theme
At Noon theres such a duced Clatter
Strangers must wonder what's the matter
And E'en that day the Lord hath blest
Is now no more a day of rest
Forth from the Press the Papers fly
Each greedy reader to supply
Of battles fought, and numbers slain,
Of Towns besieg'd, and prisoners ta'en.
Engagements both by Sea and Land
Eccho from Aldgate to the Strand
Hail! happy land, sure none's so blest
With News to comfort every breast.
Published as the Act directs 30 Decr. 1780 by W. Richardson No. 68 high Holborn.

An Englishman's Delight; or, News of All Sorts, 1780, satirical print. The consumption of news is associated with English metropolitan identity.

Introduction

Like most books, this one was written over a number of years. Before my research and writing began in earnest, the idea of a newspaper was a fairly fixed thing in my mind: inky collections of text in columns on large, crunchy pieces of paper that appeared, thanks to an invisible army of scribblers, printers and deliverymen, both in letterboxes and on newsagents' shelves every morning. Someone from a century before would have been familiar with the whole process. I was aware, of course, of some changes to the industry – hints that things may not be as stable as they appeared. As a teenager in the rural southwest of England, I worked, like many, as a part-time paperboy for one of the new free newspapers that proliferated in the 1980s, bringing news of the latest deal on new tyres at a local garage or a litter of kittens for sale in the ten-pence-per-word classified advertisements. I then graduated to a proper daily paper round, taking care to avoid impressment to the smaller crew of Sunday boys and girls, as on that day newspapers turned into large and heavy compendia of supplements, enough to bring on youthful sciatica. Then, in March 1986, the launch of Eddy Shah's *Today* brought some changes to the route (households taking the *Daily Mail* or *Express* on the round were the most likely to try this new mid-market tabloid). The new paper – with great fanfare – added a novel dash of colour to the black, white and red contents of my heavy newspaper bag, thanks to the latest computer typesetting and colour-offset printing technologies, and was printed outside of inner London, rather than on Fleet Street. Colour and digital technologies were innovations that made their way to the other papers, although not before the biggest media shake-up of the decade, that of the closure of old print shops in the face of severe union opposition and the move by News International to new facilities at Wapping. On the back of these technological and manufacturing changes, the 1980s and '90s were fat years for the papers and their proprietors. The old presses in Fleet Street were deserted for more efficient and self-consciously modern, high-tech (*Financial Times*) or even postmodern (*Telegraph* at One Canada Square in 1991) offices and print-works in places such as the London Docklands, then rising in the east of the city on the remains of the former port that was the heart of Britain's political and commercial empire. Advertising revenue meant that papers could almost be given away, and circulation remained strong despite the fears of an earlier generation of the impact of radio, cinema and television. The newspaper reading habit remained strong, and editors experimented with expanding the size of their papers. Lifestyle or opinion pieces increasingly dominated the contents of papers, as did scandal and celebrity in the red-top tabloids.

But real change, when it arrived, came swiftly. Following their introduction in Scandinavia, free daily papers were distributed in London at the very end of the twentieth century, challenging the established *Evening Standard*'s dominance in the capital. In the United States, the free *amNew York* began in 2003 and *Metro New York* arrived in 2004, while in France, Parisians could grab a copy of *20 minutes* or *Metronews* from 2002. Broadsheets shrank in size, as left-leaning Britons began to tuck 'Berliners' under their arms and squeeze ever closer on public transport (until this format was also replaced by the newly tabloid-sized *Guardian* in 2018). Local newspapers increasingly found themselves rolled up into larger conglomerations. And, of course, households hooked up to the Internet. Newspapers followed. In late 1994 the *Daily Telegraph* launched its first web edition, and by mid-1995, 150 papers worldwide had done the same. *The Times* and the *New York Times* began to publish online in 1996. By 1997, 1,600 titles published online around the world.[1] A paradigm shift was promised: following the advertising revenue model, news could be free on the web, and newspapers could flourish in the new world, safe in the knowledge that people on the whole would keep the newspaper habit, prefering the resolution and portability of the printed page.

None of this worked out as the proponents of the new world promised. Technology destroyed these safety nets, at the same time making journalism ubiquitous and apparently free, accessible anywhere and at any time on laptops, phones and tablets, and easier to get hold of when compared with queuing in a newsagents that is more interested in selling bars of chocolate than providing a compelling hub of news delivery. Two papers closed each week in the United States at the start of the Great Recession in 2009, while advertising revenues fell by 65 per cent over the decade.[2] In Britain *The Guardian* revealed that it lost some £44 million between 2011 and 2012 (in 2019 the paper reported a small operating profit thanks to moving to a model that relies on the generosity of its readers). It is now not impossible to imagine a world without newspapers; for many – the young in particular – it is a world that they already know. Beyond the economic forces confronting the industry, now is also a moment when the 45th president of the United States of America can label two of the country's foremost papers, the *Washington Post* and *New York Times*, as purveyors of 'fake news' and call journalists 'enemies of the people'.[3]

But before we get to that point, it may be as well to look again at how we came to have newspapers, and why we might do well to value them, as well as understanding their limitations. This book is about how news, in its printed form, came into being – and also what it was for. It begins in the mid-sixteenth century, during the tumult of the English Civil Wars, and follows the development of what we now think of as newspapers up until the period of the Crimean War and the American Civil War – a point at which the modern newspaper industry, with all the apparatus of a modern paper (telegraphy, journalists, editors, distribution channels and even press barons), was clearly in place. Our focus will be the English-speaking press in Britain and America, which inevitably leads to a tendency to focus on metropolitan hubs, particularly New York and London, but these will also be seen in the light of the importance of other, more local presses. Indeed, the geography of the press provides an important tool for understanding its importance, and the very close relationship between paper and place. Newspapers provided a way of enunciating community, giving voice to city, county or region. They also offered a link for those readers to other places, providing a window on the wider world and, as such, negotiating the local, national and international. The growth of newspapers overlapped with the development of nationalism and the nation state; they were, as we shall see, very much an instrument of that nation-building process.

To an extent, this book deliberately avoids firmly staking out the territory of what exactly is a newspaper, a printed product that has always been a volatile and mutable format.[4] It argues that newspapers cannot be wrenched from their context, whether of gossip, magazines, theatre or the other rituals of daily life of which papers played, and play, their part. This said, it is also concerned with how a particular format that was recognized as such came into being. Newspapers, of course, meant different things at different times to different people in different places. One recent definition of the newspaper suggests it can be defined as something 'periodic, mechanically reproduced, available to all who pay for it; also content must be varied, general, timely and organized'.[5] For many texts that might have been classed as a newspaper, some or even none of these will be particularly true. Early papers appeared erratically or in short runs; perhaps more importantly, even if they were printed with regularity, they only appeared in the hands of their far-flung readers according to the vagaries of a distribution system that had grown in a relatively haphazard fashion. Often, the news was so stale as to be barely news at all. The content of these papers can appear jumbled to modern eyes, rather than organized, with paragraphs laid out in the order in which they were received by the printer.

The story told in these pages is largely one of development towards a defined and recognizable end product, but it is written with a sense that things did not have to happen in that way. The newspaper form was not inevitable, or necessarily distinct from other forms not just of news, but of writing. Newspapers were often not that concerned with 'news', but contained much more besides, from adverts to poetry and selections of pamphlets or essays. Unlike the sustained focus of books, or the unifying themes of magazines, newspapers are a magpie format, able to absorb and juxtapose nearly anything that may amuse, entertain or inform their reader. Cartoons, adverts, recipes, letters, opinion, reviews, poetry, short stories, statistics, humour and even spot-the-ball competitions have all fallen within newspapers' purview over time. Any attempt to define what a newspaper is, and what it seeks to do, needs to encompass its protean and miscellaneous nature.

Newspapers also have a particularly physical, if ephemeral, presence in the world. We fold them, roll them under our arms, carefully cut out sections to keep or send, and pin them to walls. With a few notable exceptions, few histories of newspapers, and still fewer histories of journalism, considered papers as physical objects, playing a role in society as material objects as much as information sources or texts.[6] While books may furnish a room, they rarely help out with a fish and chip supper, dry sodden shoes, line clothes drawers or form a floor for a rabbit hutch. Newspapers catch the drip of paint, protect glasses and china during transit and dissolve to be moulded anew as children's *papier-maché*. Less helpfully, newspapers are forever to be seen blowing along the street, in corners of coffee shops, cluttering the backs of seats on tube or metro trains or caught in melancholy fashion in wire fences. But they are (or at least until relatively recently were) an omnipresent component of our modern lives. While books are sold in specialist stores, and still seem out of place in a section among the supermarket shelves, newspapers are happily hawked on street corners, given away at railway stations and sold by vending machines on U.S. street corners. Unlike books, which find themselves corralled on shelves and often limited to private or indoor spaces, newspapers are part of our everyday world. In many ways, they are as much quotidian paper objects as they are printed carriers of textual information. This difference, the physicality, ubiquity and ephemeral nature, distinguishes them from the grander form of the printed book. As my younger self was very aware when I loaded up my newspaper bag before heading on my round, newspapers are physical things. Their history needs to take into account their – often heavy – materiality, and the physical connection that they have to the world. Print shops, street hawkers, newspaper boys and newspaper women, who dominated the London street-selling trade for much of the seventeenth century, are all part of the trade's history, as much as hacks, proprietors and their readers. The history of the fourth estate is as much about this messy, complicated reality as it is a search for the growth of objective reporting of the news. The story of the newspaper is, then, as much about people, the societies that they lived in and how the newspaper changed those societies as it is about individual titles.

The idea of a fourth estate – that is, the realm of public opinion, with as much a say in society as the other three estates of the aristocracy, the clergy and commoners – first rose to prominence during the eighteenth century: a 'very large and powerful Body', suggested the writer Henry Fielding in 1752.[7] The creation of a news-reading public and the development of journalism as a form of career helped to create a space for the discussion of public affairs, creating an alternative to the royal courts and parliaments. As such the press helped to create a public sphere, a supposedly rational space for debate, along with other sites of discussion, such as the periodical, reading room, salon and lecture hall. Newspapers not only formed a reading public, but helped to create a critical public with the potential to challenge the status quo. Unsurprisingly, governments paid close attention to controlling the press, and only gradually allowed newspapers to be printed. In many countries, publications that most resembled what we would now term a newspaper were the equivalent of the *Annual Register*. Other papers were banned. Even when the press was allowed, censorship continued to restrict what could be published, threatening rebellious writers and printers with fines or imprisonment. The battle between authority and the growing power of the press remains a constant tension throughout this book.

As well as being an alternative, and potentially more inclusive, democratic space for discussion, the public sphere that newspapers helped to create also gave rise to a sense of that space as an important aspect of society. It was – or could be – a rational space, offering enlightenment and improvement for those willing to participate. As the philosopher Immanuel Kant argued, the 'public use of reason must at all times be free, and it alone can bring about enlightenment among men'. There was, then, a moral imperative behind the dissemination and discussion of news. And, with revolutionary political potential, those who participated in it could also begin to claim that because it was a public, national and rational sphere, the basis of political authority lay with it, rather than in tradition or established forms of government. Newspapers, with their reporting on contemporary events, also implied change, suggesting perhaps that people might make their own circumstances, rather than simply inherit them. Although the press did many things, its defining characteristic was and is about openness, about doing things in public. Unlike news sent via letter, which tended to have a limited audience in mind, a newspaper is meant to be read widely, and assumes a reading public. How the public was seen changed how the press was seen. The press might also be engaged in the work of influencing the public.

Since the publication in English of a work by the German philosopher and sociologist Jürgen Habermas, *The Structural Transformation of the Public Sphere,* in 1989, historians and communications theorists have revisited the role that the press played in the creation of such a public sphere. Habermas began to work on the concept of the public sphere after the Second World War, and it reflects his concern about the failure or corruption of democratic states. In the flourishing coffeehouse and newspaper culture of Britain in the eighteenth century, he saw something of an ideal public sphere in which rational, public debate could take place and create an alternative form of legitimate society. However, during the nineteenth and twentieth centuries, the life in this rational, democratic space was stifled by commercial and state control, leading to the decline in truly democratic politics. Habermas has been criticized for his failings as a historian (his sample of coffeehouses, for example, was cursory at best, his chronology sketchy and the details of actual change difficult to pin down) and for his politics: Habermas's public sphere is bourgeois and overwhelmingly male. The rational society his work argued for has been criticized for those that it would exclude. But his influence remains remarkably strong, not least among those seeking to explain the cultural and political transformations of the French Revolution, and the more general influence of the press. Historians have also claimed that he underestimated the importance of coffeehouses and newspapers during the late seventeenth and eighteenth century in England, arguing that public debate was even more prominent than he suggested.

Habermas, of course, was not the first to identify the role of the press in forming public debate: newspapermen were very keen to promote this idea of themselves, as we will see in later chapters. During the Stamp Act Crisis of 1765 in America, for example, newspaper printers depicted themselves as a voice of reasonable people in the face of despotism. In 1923, several decades before Habermas, the former journalist and Chicago School sociologist Robert E. Park also saw newspapers as a space for communal debate. In an article on the 'Natural History of the Newspaper', he examined the role of the modern newspaper – a product he considered to be a very debased vehicle, arguing that 'the motive, conscious or unconscious, of the writers and of the press in all this is to reproduce, as far as possible, in the city the conditions of life in the village.'[8] For Park, the newspaper functioned as the village square for the twentieth-century urbanite, with its mutual exchange of gossip and latest 'local' tidings. The newspaper business profited from the human need for community, offering a form of connection in an often atomized and increasingly urban society. By creating the idea of a reading community, newspaper editors, journalists and politicians also formed a potential political actor, one that could help shape public opinion in powerful ways.

The public created, or envisioned, by the press could take many forms. Early news sheets would have been read by very few. Many of them were aimed at a distinct audience, especially one defined by religious affiliation. In London, newspapers were often closely associated with a party or politically involved benefactor; their readership might similarly be partisan. By the nineteenth century, newspapers and periodicals were produced for a wide range of groups, reflecting church or religious affinities; trades and guilds; villages, towns, cities, counties and regions; the military; science, medicine and engineering. Even gender could provide the basis for certain papers, with women not only being sold but producing periodicals (usually weekly or monthly).

Such an approach made commercial sense, since it could count on a known audience with a thirst for information on a particular topic or laced with a certain slant, but these publications could also have another motive. They could shape or promote opinion, as well as form bonds within a community. And, whether intentionally or not, they had the potential to create a community. On a national level, national papers spoke for the nation. Readers regularly taking papers in the morning might grasp a sense of a wider imagined community almost ritually doing the same thing at the same time. For the political scientist and historian Benedict Anderson, this consumption of these 'daily best-sellers', date-stamped with a moment in time and suggesting a community of others, was seen as a critical component in nation-forming and the growth of nationalism. Other identities were also possibly reinforced or given shape by the press, not least local identity, which could be opposed or complicated national consciousness. And those reading papers in colonies could find themselves being tied to the metropolis by regular reports of goings on in London or Paris. Given the nature of travel and the slow and piecemeal practice of news gathering, the temporal imprint of papers could be disjointed. Rather than suggesting a nation taking in the news over breakfast at the same time, it could be a reminder of distance and separation, of province and region, or of conflict as much as community. Careful reading of newspapers points to inequalities in power, and to the potential of information to control or contest it.

1
Origins

Our story might begin in Drogheda, a town in eastern Ireland some 50 kilometres (30 mi.) north of Dublin. It had the misfortune to occupy a strategic spot on the mouth of the River Boyne during the civil wars of the mid-seventeenth century. By 1649, following the overthrow of English rule, the Irish Catholic Confederation controlled most of Ireland. In August that same year, however, Dublin and the port of Rathmines had been regained by the English in a surprise attack by the Parliamentarian commander Colonel Michael Jones. Once the seaport was secured, Oliver Cromwell was able to land an army of 12,000 along with siege artillery in an attempt to reconquer Ireland. Drogheda, whose 6 metre (20 ft) walls and fort were defended by over 3,000 royalists, became the first town assailed in Cromwell's campaign. Demoralized and lacking ammunition, the defending forces began to melt away. On 11 September, after offering terms of surrender that were refused, his forces overwhelmed the high walls and stormed the town. On Cromwell's orders, and in line with the standards of the day, the remaining garrison and Catholic priests among them were given no quarter and were killed, along with many of the townsfolk. The commanding officer, Arthur Aston, had his brains beaten out with his wooden leg by the besiegers, who believed it contained gold pieces (some accounts suggest they later found two hundred coins in his belt). The numbers are unclear, but perhaps 3,000 royalist troops who refused Cromwell's summons were killed in hot and cold blood, and three hundred of the garrison were executed after surrendering to Cromwell's mercy, some within the church in which they were sheltering. The ranks were decimated in the Roman fashion, and many survivors deported to the West Indies. The heads of sixteen royalist officer corpses were decapitated, sent to Dublin and put on pikes on the roads into the city.

Although arguably not unusual by the standards of seventeenth-century warfare on the Continent, if not in Britain, the massacre at Drogheda remains very much a live issue, contested by historians and those on either side of the Irish question. Indeed, the paragraph above, as neutral and as objective in intention as it is, will undoubtedly contain enough to anger either side. Cromwell himself justified the killing in three ways. The behaviour of the attackers could be justified by the laws of war. It could also, he claimed, be seen as 'a righteous judgment of God upon these barbarous wretches who have imbrued their hands in so much innocent blood', even though many of those killed had not taken part in the confederate rebellion against the English; Drogheda had never been a confederate town. Finally, he argued for the killings as a compassionate act in the long run, as they would terrorize other towns into immediate surrender (only four other towns did refuse to surrender after Drogheda, although this included the massacre at Wexford a month later). For the royalist side, the actions of Cromwell's armies presented them with a propaganda coup. Royalist presses quickly set to work in Britain and Ireland, printing and disseminating the news that 2,000 of the 3,000 dead were civilians, and reporting in detail the horrors of those put to the sword. The anonymous 'A Bloody Fight in Ireland', for example, which was printed in Smithfield, London, in 1649, reported 'news come of the certain taking of Drogheda' via the master of a boat from Dublin, who 'could not stay to bring over any Letters, himselfe being a testimony sufficient'.

Yet the terrible stories of murder, killing and massacre in Ireland were sadly far from unique. While such sectarian violence and the treatment of the defeated defenders at Drogheda and Wexford offered a startling comparison with the interpretation of the laws of war on English soil (despite the many atrocities committed by Royalist and

Parliamentarian alike), they were familiar to anyone who had read or heard about the horrors of the Thirty Years War. A dispute between the Catholic and Protestant powers within the Holy Roman Empire became a central European war, attracting intervention from Denmark and Sweden and growing into a clash between the Bourbon and Habsburg powers. Between 1618 and 1648, disease, dearth and conflict reduced the population of Germany by more than a third. The male population was halved.

Pamphlets – short and quickly printed accounts – offered English readers a window into the horrors unfolding across the Channel, as well as Protestant theological reflections on their cause. As one told its readers, 'Behold here, as in a Glasse, the mournefull face of a sister nation, now drunke with misery.' Central Europe, England and Ireland were not alone in the religious and political tumults of the early and mid-seventeenth century. France underwent a series of rebellions by members of the aristocracy and their followers, known as the Fronde; she was also violently divided between Catholic and Huguenot. News of 'much fear' and the 'execution of eminent persons', as one 'Letter from Paris' recounted, was collected and printed in pamphlets. North America offered some respite from such strife, at least in the thoughts of a few, high-minded settlers, such as the Pilgrim Fathers. But for most, and certainly for the indigenous peoples of that land, the New World was a land of violence, imported or freshly encountered, disease, exile and enslavement.

Our story of news begins, then, within a Europe and America divided, suffering from pestilence, war and violence. The nature of the state, the balance of power between monarch, nobility and subject, the true interpretation of scripture and the meaning of religious tradition were all in question. Print, manuscript and oral debate offered a clamour of voices, often fervent in their views, but giving little room for compromise. It was a world that was confused, argumentative and desperate for some sort of meaning or authority to be imposed. While the medieval world-view might be described as relatively static, with shared views about the natural state of affairs, the jolts caused by the overthrow of old certainties meant that the world needed to be freshly described, with new tidings and interpretations offered up to an eager public. Change, and the speed of change, gave rise to the need for regular updates: for what we now call news.

'News', as we call it today, had of course always been sought. The ability to produce information about current events required a certain amount of organization and technological ability, as well as creating an information hierarchy among those with access to news and those excluded from it. From the start, the production of news was also tied to official propaganda: from AD 206 to 221 the Han Dynasty in China distributed government news sheets known as *tipao*, a form of imperial bulletins issued by local and central government destined for consumption by bureaucrats. Either handwritten or printed by engraved wooden blocks, sadly no early *tipao* survive, but their echo can be felt. As a format they continued into the early modern period, and even into the nineteenth century, as 'reports from the capital'. Information and the carriers of information were closely linked to the centres of power.

In the West, written news took epistolary form. The letter, written on rolls of papyrus paper, established itself as a routine means of public and private communication in the Greco-Roman world and carried news of goings-on across the Roman Empire. Romans could also discover the latest official news from *Acta diurna* ('Daily Acts' or 'Daily Records'), once these initially secret bulletins were made public under Julius Caesar. Lasting until the age of Constantine, the *Acta* initially reported the outcomes of legal proceedings, but expanded to include more general public announcements, as well as notable births, marriages and deaths, and imperial or senatorial decrees. Again, no physical *Acta* survive, despite being archived after being displayed in public spaces, such as the Forum, on whitened boards (album) or inscribed on metal or stone. We do, however, know a little of how the *Acta* were used from other texts that survive, including accounts of slaves reading the *Acta* out to their master for the amusement of those at the table. There are also hints of what we might call the first journalists: a substantial number of *actuarii* working for the senate who gathered and prepared the information.

Others made a business out of reporting on the *Acta* and disseminating them to the provinces. News even spread beyond Italy, making use of Rome's vast network of roads and maritime commercial networks. From the time of Augustus, and probably long before, official couriers travelled the roads by horse or carriage, stopping at regular staging posts. It is estimated that news could usually travel at 40 kilometres (25 mi.) a day, with 80 being possible if the news was especially urgent. In theory, this system, which represented an enormous expense, was limited to official correspondence, particularly confidential information. Merchants also had their own means of sharing information along the roads and across the seas, sharing financial news, such as the cost of corn, with their colleagues. Other forms of correspondence made their way across these networks, bringing news to the furthest reaches of the empire, along with 'tydings' passed on by word of mouth. From the fragments of numerous wooden writing tablets found at Vindolanda, a Roman military camp in modern-day Northumberland, England, we can grasp a little of how the empire's communication networks knitted the known world together. Remarkably preserved by the chemical properties of the soil, these wooden tablets are covered in inked script, written by a broad cross-section of garrison society, from the governor and his wife to more lowly members. They reveal something of the extent of literacy at the time, and of its close connection to the workings of imperial power. The creation of a postal system, with the vast cost involved, enabled the projection of Roman Imperial might even to this cold, windswept edge of civilization. The control of communication meant the control of power.

Medieval Europe placed similar importance on epistolary communication, and the written transmission of information played a crucial role in shaping the influence of the main pillars of power: the Church, the State and, increasingly, merchants. It took centuries to replace the distressed communication networks of the Roman Empire. The Church remained wedded to the written word through a largely literate priesthood, and through the scriptoria of monasteries the institution continued to hold some of the knowledge of the classical world. Furthermore, a network of bishoprics and monasteries formed permanent nodes in a communications network, where letters could also be copied at scriptoria and copies deposited at libraries en route to their destination. Although cloistered, monks took a lively interest in the world and began to record the stories of their times, perhaps most famously in the Anglo-Saxon Chronicle. We can think of this, anachronistically no doubt, as a slow-moving ticker tape, recording the few events deemed noteworthy that year – tidings of floods, Vikings or religious signs.[1]

Monasteries and other religious settlements were often placed at key geographical points, and even if originally placed at deliberately remote spots, they often became destinations in themselves. The popularity of pilgrimages, in which the devout would travel to shrines of particular saints, ensured a steady flow of travellers who could carry news by word of mouth and also courier letters. The numbers could be great: in 1300, after Pope Boniface VIII declared a plenary indulgence for pilgrims to the Holy Basilica in Rome, around 200,000 made the journey. Rome also served as the administrative centre for Christendom, bringing thousands of petitioners and office seekers, many of who would write home during their often long sojourn in the city. The papacy also generated its own correspondence and had a small team of around forty papal couriers who could be trusted with confidential despatches. This select body was augmented by sending less confidential correspondence with those returning from visits to Rome or Avignon (the latter becoming the seat of papal administration from the fourteenth century). Such systems steadily grew into a formidable, if expensive, communications and information network, able to bring in and circulate the news that it wished. That said, letters could still take weeks or months to arrive – or even be sent, as for reasons of economy they tended to be bundled up together.

Church, State and commerce were often interlinked. During the thirteenth century, Glastonbury Abbey (in Somerset in the west of England) was one of the richest in the land. Although still largely surrounded by marshes, it was linked to the wider world by the River Brue. The abbey employed one particular tenant to keep up an eight-man boat in order to ferry the abbot, his men, kitchen, huntsmen and dogs from the abbey to his summer house in Meare to the east of the main abbey. His duties also included carrying the abbot's letters to Bleadney and Panborough, where the abbot kept a vineyard and wine depot.

Secular authorities in the patchwork of kingdoms, principalities and empires that constituted Western Christendom also desired the ability to discern what was going on, but although they attempted to emulate the reach of the papacy, the expense of such systems ensured that information parity eluded them. News of the rulers' wishes could be sent downwards among their subjects with relative ease, but communication between states was trickier, as was news gathering. Like the papacy, royal families relied on private teams of couriers to carry letters and messages: an expensive business. Isabella, wife of the Prince of Wales and future Edward II, employed thirteen messengers, two of whom were mounted, largely to keep in contact with her family overseas.

The official business of state generated an enormous amount of correspondence ranging from tax matters to official writs. By the fourteenth century sheriffs of English counties could expect to receive several thousand writs each year. Italian city-states developed sophisticated systems of financial record-keeping and generated a wealth of paper chits and letters, helping trade to flourish as well as spreading information between their courts and senates.

News gathering, if we can call it that, was also driven by political demands. Smaller states, such as the Italian city-states mentioned above, were driven by the need to understand what their neighbours were up to, while communicating with their own citizens was much more straightforward. As such, the tools of diplomacy – notably resident emissaries at foreign courts, as well as sophisticated cyphers to encrypt letters – were first put into place by the Italians. An important duty for such proto-ambassadors was the collection and reporting of news back to home state. Elsewhere, competition for land and commercial advantage also gave reason for monarchs to be well informed. A premium was placed on foreign intelligence from as far away as the Levant. The letter-books of King James II of Aragon (1264–1327) reveal an extensive network of correspondents across his native Italy and beyond. The many thousands of letters reveal a steady stream of reports on commercial and political developments. In Northern

Europe the dynastic wars of the fourteenth century gave an impetus to create better information networks, as well as a means of undertaking negotiations with other states or dynastic families. Effective monarchy depended, at least in part, on the creation and maintenance of a proper pool of trained couriers and the cultivation of a network of correspondents. Information became a necessary component of the wielding of power.

These networks, then, helped to enable an early form of news, which remained a protean form of intelligence. They mixed the oral with the literate and were largely limited to closed circles of connections. Trusted couriers carried confidential messages from the pope or a king, which they communicated verbally, but they would also carry letters of introduction, along with other written correspondence. Those without their own network of couriers would also try to include their own written messages in the official letters carried between the courts of Christendom. Such networks remained highly unreliable, dependent on the weather, the vagaries of shipping and the condition of mud-soaked roads, paths and byways. War and disease, notably the Black Death, amplified the desire for news and information while destroying the very networks that helped disseminate it and draining the royal coffers that paid for a cadre of messengers. Such events also generated rumours and gossip, increasing the amount of information but severely damaging its reliability. Within the courts of Europe, systems had to be developed to filter this information.

During the English Wars of the Roses (1455–87), many subjects were reluctant to believe the latest news, such as of victory or defeat, or the death of a protagonist, until they saw physical evidence. Eyewitnesses could also quash rumours: following the killing of the Earl of Warwick for treason, King Edward IV displayed his body at St Paul's Cathedral, forming a body of witnesses who could give the lie to the rumours which soon circulated that the earl was still alive. In order to attempt to disseminate official pronouncements, official town criers were employed in London and other English cities, a communication system that continued well into the seventeenth century.

But news, as the accounts of the massacre at Drogheda remind us, was often as much about the manipulation of opinion as it was of objective reporting. In the medieval period, the opinion that mattered was largely restricted to a very limited circle. This was recognized by the dauphin Charles in early fourteenth-century France, whose party circulated manuscript letters to drum up support among the Anglo-Burgundian alliance following the assassination of John, Duke of Burgundy (in which plot the dauphin was probably involved). Such letters reached a very small audience, of course, but testify to the belief in the propagandistic power of the written word.

News and News Sheets

Literacy remained an elite skill, but the growth of cities and the merchant class greatly increased the number of those with access to the written world. From the sixteenth century there was a religious impetus to read: the Protestant Reformation placed special emphasis on the individual and their relation to the religious texts contained in the Bible. The Catholic response was also to emphasize schooling and the catechism, the better to refute heresy and misbelief.

Such was the context for what is often seen as the birth of the newspaper. There are several claims to the title of the 'first newspaper'. Venice can claim the monthly *Notizie scritte* (Written Notices), which sold for one gazzetta and gave birth to our word 'gazette'. These handwritten news sheets, also known as *avvisi*, carried political and financial news far beyond the Venetian lagoon and were sent or copied to courts and cities across Europe. Far to the east, as Marco Polo might have known, the Ming Dynasty was already publishing official and private news for limited circulation. In the German lands, a merchant called Fugger received intelligence from his large network of correspondents and repaid the favour with his handwritten news sheet. He also spiced up his product with fiction and gossip.

None of these were printed; nor were they regularly issued and dated. The primary claim to all of these lies with the Strasbourg-printed *Relation aller Fürnemmen und gedenckwürdigen Historien*, begun by Johann Carolus in 1605. Four years later, *Avisa* began to be published in Wolfenbüttel. Then, in 1618, the *Courante* began in Amsterdam – again, a trading city. Proto-newspapers, known as

Adriaen van Ostade, *Reading the News at the Weavers' Cottage*, 1673, pen and brown ink, watercolour.

'courants', were distributed far and wide along these trading networks, and the first English-language paper started here in 1620. Two years later, in May 1622, Nicholas Bourne (or Nathaniel Butter; the publisher is known from the paper's title page as 'N. B.') and Thomas Archer had the idea to publish *Weekly Newes from Italy, Germanie, Hungaria, etc.* Their innovation found a ready audience, despite a legal bar on reporting British affairs, and was soon published with an issue number on its mast head. France had its *Gazette* from 1631. *Ordinari*

Post Tijdender, which still continues in online form as *Post-och Inrikes Tidningar*, began in Sweden in 1645. By the mid-seventeenth century the capitals of Europe were, in emulatory fashion, all furnished with a form of publication that we might today recognize as a weekly (or thereabouts) paper. America had its first English-language newspaper in the form of the Boston *Publick Occurrences both Forreign and Domestick* for one issue in 1690. Newspapers worked their ways into the daily lives of people across Europe, creating a point in the week to pause and reflect on the wider world, connect with others and discuss the news. The physical presence of paper and type became a quotidian affair, part of everyday life, and not just limited to the elite but disseminated across society, something captured in images such as Adriaen van Ostade's *Reading the News at the Weaver's Cottage*, one of several works depicting newspaper readership in Dutch society. Perhaps costing the same as a couple of pints of beer, and possibly a couple of weeks or a month old, a paper could be enjoyed just as much in modest surroundings, or shared with others at a pub, as it could be in a wealthy home.[2]

But was this new? And in what way was it 'news' rather than information? Histories of newspapers have, since the great Victorian accounts of the birth of the fourth estate, delighted in recounting the tale of the genesis of the new printed, serial genre; in this Big Bang of the newspaper universe, there must surely be some experimental data of worth in locating the first, the origin of all this inky business. Unlike the Big Bang, the press, by necessity, derived from a much longer and more complex history. News and information could be disseminated through a variety of media, from handwritten news sheets such as the Venetian *gazzetta* to letters and word of mouth. The invention by Johannes Gutenberg of moveable type in the mid-fifteenth century, combined with the gradual spread of printing technology, offered a powerful new avenue for the exchange of information, although the new forms of text continued alongside traditional scribal and handwritten modes of communication and dissemination. Across Europe, the Americas and Asia at this time we can see numerous vast networks of communication and exchange of ideas, intelligence, argument, secrets and gossip. Politics, trade and military life all depended on such flows of information, as, in its way, did education, extended family life and even religious devotion. Printed texts paid homage to this. Lamentations from Germany, for example, reprinted a 'Copie of a Letter sent by the Ministers of Germany to the Dutch Church in LONDON' along with a selection of other letters.

Print and manuscript were only one form of such interchange. Orality provided another. News, as the historian Joad Raymond reminds us, is 'communicated by word of mouth'.[3] The first printed forms of news reflected this close relationship. The types of material most closely rooted in oral culture – sermons and plays, ballads, pamphlets and cheaply printed chapbooks aimed at a wider readership – circulated widely: for example, between 600,000 and several million ballads are estimated to have been circulating in the second half of the sixteenth century; the low prices of small pamphlet or chapbooks put them within reach of even a English day labourer. In the early sixteenth century, opposition to the Reformation of the English Church found its voice in ballads, which combined contemporary events with polemic. The textual counterpart of the sermon, lecture or street-corner argument, the pamphlet similarly mixed news with opinion. In Catholic Europe, propaganda – in its original meaning, 'that which is to be propagated' – offered in printed form the advice, argument or strictures of the Tridentine clergy.

Such publications, of course, differ from the post-nineteenth-century ideal of objective reporting. Their often-extreme biases or fabrications were integral to their composition, purpose and reception. The use of traditional tropes creates a timelessness that differs from the the regularity and immediacy we find in modern 'news'. Ballads wrapped events in the narrative of what Raymond describes neatly as 'timeless and providential patterns that lay behind particular events'. Yet they still feed a desire for updated information: the desire for news, for 'tydings'. We can also detect the opposite urge, the desire for 'newslessness', for example in a letter from Jean-Louis Guez de Balzac in 1653, a man famed for his news correspondence in the 1620s and '30s: 'Truly, if you wanted to make me happy, you would ban everything that goes by the name of *relation*, *gazette*, *ordinaire*, *extraordinaire*, and so forth.'[4]

Early publication also took place within a very different legislative context. There was no freedom of the press, and governments and their censors closely monitored what could or could not be published: in 1487, for example, Henry VII had issued an edict against 'forged tidings and tales'. In 1557 the Stationers' Company received their Royal Charter, and thereby controlled who could be a printer and what they could print within England and her dominions. The Company only issued licences to those known to have 'skill, ability and good behaviour'. The normal, and necessary, mode of operation for government was secrecy. Yet it was recognized that news did not have to be completely stifled, and there was even support for the notion that proper information could help promote political and religious allegiance. Henry VIII's annulment of his marriage to Catherine of Aragon, for example, saw a sophisticated polemical campaign to support this move and for the break with Rome. During the reign of Elizabeth I, sympathy for Protestantism in France, and the realization that there was an eager market for such products, led the government to allow an influx of translated French news publications. In 1592, for the first time, some of these were published as numbered serial publications. Rather than standing as individual texts, focusing on one point in time, such a process helped to create the expectation of more news, and perhaps encouraged more consumption of texts. The text's form reflected news' concern with the passage of time and with the present. Serials also encouraged the process of collecting, even the search for completion – an instinct that bore fruit in extraordinary collections of newspapers, such as those gathered by the Reverend Charles Burney and now held by the British Library. The creation of this body of material was by no means inevitable but was closely linked to the history of print in Europe in the 1600s.

In 1665, in an attempt to escape the terrible plague afflicting London, the English Parliament departed for the relative safety of Oxford. Although the city in which it made its temporary home lacked a university press, it was also exempt from the regulations on printing that restricted the trade to London, and on 16 November 1665 the first issue of the *Oxford Gazette* emerged from the hand-press of the printer Leonard Lichfield.[5] An inauspicious start, perhaps, but this is the usual date given for the publication of the first newspaper published in England. Other forms of printed news had existed before, but this was the first to be published following the form of what we would call a newspaper. While other titles might make a claim to be the first English paper, the *Gazette* in its *Oxford* form has the surest hold on this title, in terms of the nature of its content, its physical form, and its periodicity and longevity – in the form of the *Annual Register* it is still published today as an official record of royal, legal and political business. It became the formal record of the Crown, carrying extensive amounts of news, and through its selection and presentation of news could also influence public opinion and the political winds.

If we are to count the *Gazette* as the first English paper then Reverend Walter Blandford, the vice-chancellor of Oxford and rector of Witney in Oxfordshire, was the first person to receive notice in an English newspaper in an account of his election as Lord Bishop of Oxfordshire. It was not a dramatic start for such a claim to Fleet Street fame: apart from his royalist sympathies and his pastoral support for the Duchess of York, a dying Catholic convert, Blandford has left little impression on the archival record. As the short notice in the *Oxford Dictionary of National Biography* of 1885 recalls, he 'published nothing'. The paper continues with a list of names of persons appointed sheriff in England and Wales, a useful piece of information, and then a longer run of news from home and abroad, in no particular order, other than perhaps receipt by the printer. Assurances of the veracity of the information is given, such as 'I lately received from a good hand in *Rochel* . . .' The origin of news from letters is clear. Elsewhere the focus is on trade, such as the arrival and departure of merchant ships at various ports around England, war – particularly with the Dutch – and pestilence, with news from Chester that 'This City and County (thanks be to God) remains in good health, without the least infection.' The foot of the final page carried the mournful toll from London, the 'Weekly Bill' of mortality, with 1,050 dead from plague; a decrease, at least, of 428.

The title – *Gazette* – was unusual for an English news publication, of which there had been many short-lived examples during the Civil War and Interregnum when the Star Chamber's restrictions on the reporting of news, except events abroad and natural disasters, had lapsed definitively.[6] More typically, '*currant*' or '*mercury*' were preferred as masthead titles, while the term '*gazette*' implied a handwritten newsletter, an expensive and labour-intensive form of news media usually only available to nobility or rich merchants. The choice of name underscored the intentions of the newspaper, 'published by authority', which promised access to the official news of state.

The publication also took advantage of a lull in the fortunes of the bi-weekly news sheets *News* and *The Intelligencer*, which were published by Roger L'Estrange, whose ownership of letters patent gave him a theoretical monopoly on the printing of 'diurnals and books of public intelligence'.[7] L'Estrange concerned himself more with his role as censor, suppressing materials he deemed opposed to the Restoration of the monarchy and which promoted religious dissent. He remained in London during the government's move to Oxford and the sheets, which had become little more than anti-dissenter propaganda, closed in January 1666.

L'Estrange's Oxford competitor had been founded by Joseph Williamson, under-secretary to the Southern Department, the arm of government concerned with domestic and foreign policy, and as such had special access to a stream of information gathered by the department. Some of this material was already creamed off by entrepreneurial clerks, such as Henry Muddiman, a former schoolteacher who became a journalist and publisher covering the proceedings of the Rump Parliament in late 1659. Muddiman distilled his information into manuscript newsletters, which he distributed to private subscribers for about £5 a year, thereby taking advantage of his ability to use the 'Letter Office of England', the post office of its time.[8] Jealous of Muddiman's financial success and growing reputation, Williamson copied his business model but replaced manuscript newsletters with a printed news sheet.[9]

The *Gazette* offered its readership a number of novel features, along with its claims to accuracy and official approval. Its size, pagination and use of typography represented a departure from the news sheets or newsbooks that had been produced in England before then, and instead borrowed from European design cues. Given the practical difficulties and complications in making and distributing a newspaper, such details were – and continue to be – important, affecting the way information and news was shaped by the publishers and consumed by the readership. Before the *Gazette*, most printed news publications were a single page or, more commonly, a book or booklet. Comprised of a single sheet printed and folded into eight before being stitched and cut (a format known as *octavo*, about the same size as a small, squarish modern-day paperback), news publications such as the *Mercurius politicus* resembled a book, with a title page, a blank page on the verso and the text beginning on the third page. The *Gazette* instead was a folded sheet of paper, modelled perhaps on the continental layouts begun by the Amsterdam paper *Courante uyt Italien, Duytslandt, &c* of 1618, arguably the first Dutch newspaper. The *Gazette* published on a weekly basis until 1669. Its layout also perhaps borrowed from the experience of its printer, Lichfield, in producing Bibles, deploying two columns to aid reading and to make the most efficient use of the space. Again, this format, like the title, gave credence to the paper's claims of authority by echoing the appearance of Holy Writ.

Unlike the pamphlets or booklets of earlier news publications, such newspapers could devote more of the paper to print than those folded into eight or four pages, making them more economical to produce. As such, the newspaper format offered an efficient means of paper-based communication. The use of columns and smaller font sizes was also a method used by printers of the Bible to pack in as much text as possible. Early Dutch bi-fold papers, such as the *Courante* or the *Tijdinghen,* contained between 1,700 and 2,000 words, while pamphlets could only squeeze in around 800–1,000 words per issue.[10] By the end of the seventeenth century typefaces had shrunk in size and a Dutch paper might contain as many as 3,500–4,000 words per issue. But while such methods were economical in terms of paper, they placed special demands on the printer, who had to deal with smaller-sized type and to lay text out in two frames to make the columns. Lichfield's Bible printing had given him the expertise in working in such a format.

The format also had implications for the ephemerality or permanence of the newspaper. Pamphlet news publications were typically designed to be collected and bound so that they could be used as reference material, as Samuel Pepys records in his diaries of 1660–69; to aid in this, they were numbered at the top, and even included what printers refer to as signature statements (marking each issue or bundle of folded papers as 'A', 'B', and so on, to aid correct binding in sequence). In general, folio newspapers lacked these features and were less likely to be preserved, seemingly destined for a short, ephemeral life. The *Oxford Gazette*, however, used signatures and was numbered, suggesting that an eye was being kept on its importance and permanence by its printer. A market certainly existed in Dutch society for bound collections of papers, with several booksellers advertising collections of bound newspapers in the seventeenth and eighteenth centuries.[11] British papers continue today to follow the habit of numbering their issues, if not including signatures at the bottom of their pages.

Space was also saved by the brevity of the title. In contrast, news books, with a page devoted to the title, could afford the space given to lengthy titles, such as *Mercurius Politicus, comprising the sum of foreign intelligence, with the affairs now on foot in the three nations of England, Scotland, and Ireland, for information of the people from May 1660*. The *Oxford Gazette* was considerably shorter. It also, somewhat unusually, used a mixture of upper and lower-case, again saving space, and used a typeface new to England, in a size known as canon – Lichfield used a light version known as French canon, and the London edition used a larger Dutch canon. The format was copied by other London papers, and the *Gazette* soon used a font made by the printer, globe maker and type-founder Joseph Moxon. The paper made liberal use of italics for emphasis, and also helped the reader to pick out proper nouns easily on the page. The tag 'Published by Authority' was set in bold type underneath, with lines above and below drawing attention to this statement of both legitimacy and authority. At the foot of the final page, the place of publication and the printer offered further assurances about the publication's provenance: '*Oxford Leonard Lichfield*, Printer to the University, 1665.'

By using a column-based format and a hierarchy of typefaces, Muddiman's *Gazette* helped to shape the expectations of what a newspaper looked like, one that we still recognize today. It managed to convey a striking amount of information on its two sides of paper, information that was both potentially useful (if, say, the reader was seeking a sheriff to petition or was wondering how likely a shipment of timber ordered from the Baltic coast was to arrive) and interesting. The text makes it clear that the editor has derived the news from information gleaned from shared letters, which at once gave a claim to the news' veracity and provided the newspaper with a tone of voice that encouraged a sense of shared purpose and community between the editor and the readership. Finally, geography played a part in the physical shaping of the paper. Domestic and foreign news were separated into sections, with foreign news arranged by place of origin. The newspaper, from the start, offered a window onto the world.

On 7 November 1665 Pepys took to his diary as usual: 'This day the first of the Oxford Gazettes come out, which is very pretty, full of newes, and no folly in it.' The diarist was referring to the republication of the *Gazette* in London a few days after the Oxford edition by the manager of the king's printing house there, Thomas Newcombe (sometimes spelled Newcomb). Pepys's diary is a constant reminder of the ongoing search many undertook for news, recording gossip, accounts and letters, and recorded a visit to Westminster Hall earlier that year, and paying for his 'newes-books' (18 July 1665). He clearly continued to take the *Gazette*, recording in his diary the next year, 'This day, in the Gazette, is the whole story of defeating the Scotch rebells, and of the creation of the Duke of Cambridge, Knight of the Garter' (6 December 1666). (Here, Pepys is using 'story' in the sense of history or perhaps an account, rather than 'news story', or item of news, which is an American term from the late nineteenth century).[12] When Parliament returned to the capital from Oxford in February 1666, as the plague abated, Newcombe became the sole printer, publishing bi-weekly on Mondays and Thursdays.

Muddiman edited only two of the London editions before Joseph Williamson replaced him with Charles Perrot. Williamson provided much of the editorial direction. A competitor soon appeared under Muddiman's direction: the *Current Intelligence*, which in format very much resembled the *Gazette* and was published on the same days.

The two papers soon entered into a typographical war, with each emphasizing the line 'Published by Authority' with blackletter: old-English-style type typically used for official proclamations.

The *Gazette* soon had more news than it may have wished for. If the previous autumn and winter had been exceptionally cold, then the summer of 1666 was particularly dry. On the night of Sunday 2 September, a fire broke out in the home of Thomas Farriner, a baker on Pudding Lane. Such events were not unusual in a city lit, warmed and baked by naked flames, and although alarming for the inhabitants of the house, who had to escape through an upstairs window, were met with the usual response. Residents on the street called the alarm while others ran to fetch water from pumps, lead or wooden pipes, or the Thames, along with pikes to attack the fire. As the fire took hold, neighbouring buildings should have been pulled down to create a fire break; however, apparently unconcerned, Lord Mayor Thomas Bloodworth refused to grant permission for this action, commenting 'Pish! A woman could piss it out.' The fire spread. Within the baker's house, the maid succumbed to the fire, and what became known as the Great Fire of London claimed its first victim.

The 'lamentable and dismal fire' went on to consume most of the City of London, from Fleet Street to the edges of the Tower of London, coating what remained in inches of soot, destroying houses, churches and ancient company halls. Stuart London was tightly packed, with most of the buildings constructed from timber. As night turned into day, the fire spread quickly, consuming more of the city. Rather than fight the flames, people fled. The conflagration began to create its own weather, with gusts of flames and sparks spreading the fire towards St Paul's Cathedral to the west of Pudding Lane and the Tower of London to the east. By Monday, the fire threatened Southwark on the southern side of London Bridge. Within three days four-fifths of the ancient city had been destroyed by the inferno. As many as 100,000 people were rendered homeless, and more than eighty churches were razed, along with St Paul's Cathedral, the Royal Exchange and the Guildhall.

The flames not only consumed buildings but paintings and tapestries, and evaporated thousands of gallons of wine, beer and other liquor. Many thousands of books and manuscripts also joined the pyre in perhaps one of the most terrible, and neglected, losses of the Great Fire. As one historian of the fire notes, 'never since the burning of the great library at Alexandria had there been such a holocaust of books.'[13] As the flames jumped from building to building, urgent action was taken to attempt to save precious codices. The Stationers' Company's books had been carried down to the west crypt, the peculiar site of the ancient parish of St Faith's under St Paul's, in the hope of escaping the flames. Partly abetted by the wooden scaffolding that surrounded the building during Christopher Wren's restoration work, the fire also spread to the cathedral itself, melting 6 acres of lead on the roof, which crashed into the crypt and poured onto the streets with, as the diarist John Evelyn noted, 'the very pavements glowing with fiery redness, so as no horse nor man was able to tread on them'. The books 'were all consumed, burning for a week following'.[14]

The city's new newspapers were not spared. The *London Gazette* was able to carry news of the conflagration shortly after it broke out. On the final page of the paper there is a short report showing that news reached the printer just before going to press. Then there is a break of a week. When the *Gazette* was able to be published again, it began with an account of the 'sad and lamentable incident' of the fire. Such was the importance of the event that it filled the entire front and back page of the *Gazette*. Despite the appearance of the paper, the printer had not been spared the fire, and Newcombe's press and much of its stock were destroyed when the flames reached him. He decamped to fresh lodgings on the Strand by the river, where he made use of a different typeface to print the paper, since his own type had either melted or was still in transit. Physically altered in appearance as a consequence of the fire, the paper then carried news around the country, bringing the first reliable report of the disaster that had befallen England's capital.

The repercussions of the fire were not limited to the printer and editor, but severely affected the many sellers of the newspaper since they were now out of work, and most likely had lost their homes. As a result of their distress and consequent appeals to the government something of the structures of newspaper distribution can be uncovered

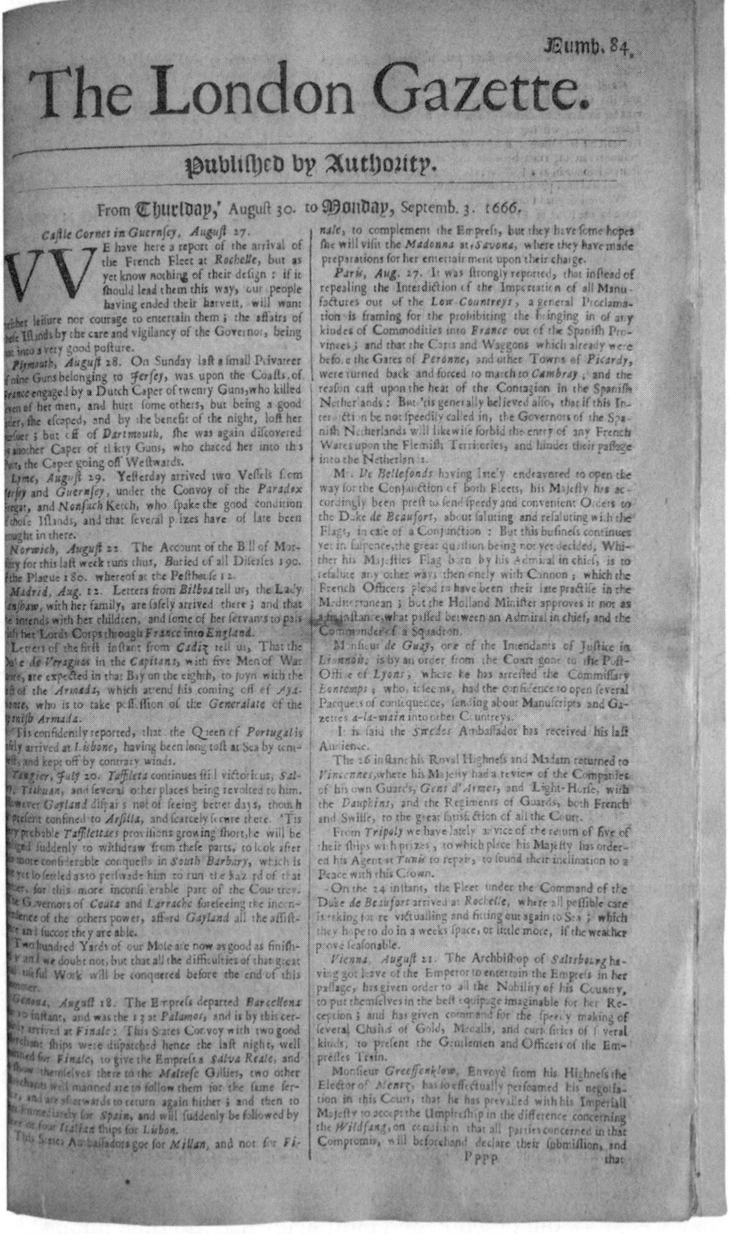

Numb. 84.

The London Gazette.

Published by Authority.

From Thursday, August 30. to Monday, Septemb. 3. 1666.

Castle Cornet in Guernsey, August 27.

WE have here a report of the arrival of the French Fleet at *Rochelle*, but as yet know nothing of their design: if it should lead them this way, our people having ended their harvest, will want neither leisure nor courage to entertain them; the affairs of these Islands by the care and vigilancy of the Governor, being put into a very good posture.

Plymouth, August 28. On Sunday last a small Privateer of nine Guns belonging to *Jersey*, was upon the Coasts of *France* engaged by a Dutch Caper of twenty Guns, who killed seven of her men, and hurt some others, but being a good sailer, she escaped, and by the benefit of the night, lost her pursuer; but off of *Dartmouth*, she was again discovered by another Caper of thirty Guns, who chaced her into this Port, the Caper going off Westwards.

Lyme, August 29. Yesterday arrived two Vessels from *Jersey* and *Guernsey*, under the Convoy of the *Paradox* Fregat, and *Nonsuch* Ketch, who spake the good condition of those Islands, and that several prizes have of late been brought in there.

Norwich, August 22. The Account of the Bill of Mortality for this last week runs thus, Buried of all Diseases 190. of the Plague 180. whereof at the Pesthouse 12.

Madrid, Aug. 12. Letters from *Bilboa* tell us, the Lady *Fanshaw*, with her family, are safely arrived there; and that she intends with her children, and some of her servants to pass with her Lords Corps through *France* into *England*.

Letters of the first instant from *Cadiz* tell us, That the Duke *de Veraguas* in the *Capitana*, with five Men of War more, are expected in that Bay on the eighth, to joyn with the rest of the *Armada*, which attend his coming off of *Ayamonte*, who is to take possession of the *Generalate* of the *Spanish Armada*.

'Tis confidently reported, that the Queen of *Portugal* is safely arrived at *Lisbone*, having been long tost at Sea by tempests, and kept off by contrary winds.

Tangier, July 20. *Taffileta* continues still victorious, *Salley*, *Tituan*, and several other places being revolted to him. However *Gayland* dispairs not of seeing better days, though at present confined to *Arsilla*, and scarcely secure there. 'Tis very probable *Taffilettaes* provisions growing short, he will be obliged suddenly to withdraw from these parts, to look after his more considerable conquests in *South Barbary*, which is not yet so setled as to perswade him to run the hazard of that matter, for this more inconsiderable part of the Countrey. The Governors of *Ceuta* and *Larrache* foreseeing the inconvenience of the others power, afford *Gayland* all the assistance and succor they are able.

Two hundred Yards of our Mole are now as good as finished, and we doubt not, but that all the difficulties of that great and useful Work will be conquered before the end of this Summer.

Genoua, August 18. The Empress departed *Barcellona* the 10 instant, and was the 13 at *Palamos*, and is by this certainly arrived at *Finale*: This States Convoy with two good Merchant ships were dispatched hence the last night, well manned for *Finale*, to give the Empress a *Salva Reale*, and to shew themselves there to the *Maltese* Gallies, two other Merchants well manned are to follow them for the same service, and are afterwards to return again hither; and then to sail immediately for *Spain*, and will suddenly be followed by three or four *Italian* ships for *Lisbon*.

This States Ambassadors goe for *Millan*, and not for *Finale*, to complement the Empress, but they have some hopes she will visit the *Madonna* at *Savona*, where they have made preparations for her entertainment upon their charge.

Paris, Aug. 27. It was strongly reported, that instead of repealing the Interdiction of the Importation of all Manufactures out of the *Low-Countreys*, a general Proclamation is framing for the prohibiting the bringing in of any kindes of Commodities into *France* out of the Spanish Provinces; and that the Carts and Waggons which already were before the Gates of *Peronne*, and other Towns of *Picardy*, were turned back and forced to march to *Cambray*; and the reason cast upon the heat of the Contagion in the Spanish Netherlands: But 'tis generally believed also, that if this Interdiction be not speedily called in, the Governors of the Spanish Netherlands will likewise forbid the entry of any French Wares upon the Flemish Territories, and hinder their passage into the Netherlands.

Mr. *De Bellefonds* having lately endeavored to open the way for the Conjunction of both Fleets, his Majesty has accordingly been prest to send speedy and convenient Orders to the Duke *de Beaufort*, about saluting and resaluting with the Flags, in case of a Conjunction: But this business continues yet in suspence, the great question being not yet decided, Whither his Majesties Flag born by his Admiral in chief, is to resalute any other ways then onely with Cannon; which the French Officers plead to have been their late practise in the Mediterranean; but the Holland Minister approves it not as a fit instance, what passed between an Admiral in chief, and the Commander of a Squadron.

Monsieur *de Guay*, one of the Intendants of Justice in *Lionnois*, is by an order from the Court gone to the Post-Office of *Lyons*, where he has arrested the Commissary *Bontemps*; who, it seems, had the confidence to open several Pacquets of consequence, sending about Manuscripts and Gazettes *a-la-main* into other Countreys.

It is said the *Swedes* Ambassador has received his last Audience.

The 26 instant his Royal Highness and Madam returned to *Vincennes*, where his Majesty had a review of the Companies of his own Guards, *Gens d'Armes*, and Light-Horse, with the *Dauphins*, and the Regiments of Guards, both French and Swisse, to the great satisfaction of all the Court.

From *Tripoly* we have lately advice of the return of five of their ships with prizes, to which place his Majesty has ordered his Agent at *Tunis* to repair, to sound their inclination to a Peace with this Crown.

On the 24 instant, the Fleet under the Command of the Duke *de Beaufort* arrived at *Rochelle*, where all possible care is taking for re victualling and fitting out again to Sea; which they hope to do in a weeks space, or little more, if the weather prove seasonable.

Vienna, August 21. The Archbishop of *Saltsbourg* having got leave of the Emperor to entertain the Empress in her passage, has given order to all the Nobility of his Countrey, to put themselves in the best equipage imaginable for her Reception; and has given command for the speedy making of several Chains of Gold, Medalls, and curiosities of several kinds, to present the Gentlemen and Officers of the Empresses Train.

Monsieur *Greeffenklow*, Envoyé from his Highness the Elector of *Mentz*, has so effectually perfoamed his negotiation in this Court, that he has prevailed with his Imperiall Majesty to accept the Umpireship in the difference concerning the *Wildfang*, on condition that all parties concerned in that Compromis, will beforehand declare their submission, and

Pppp that

London Gazette, 3 September 1666, with news of the fire arriving in the final paragraph.

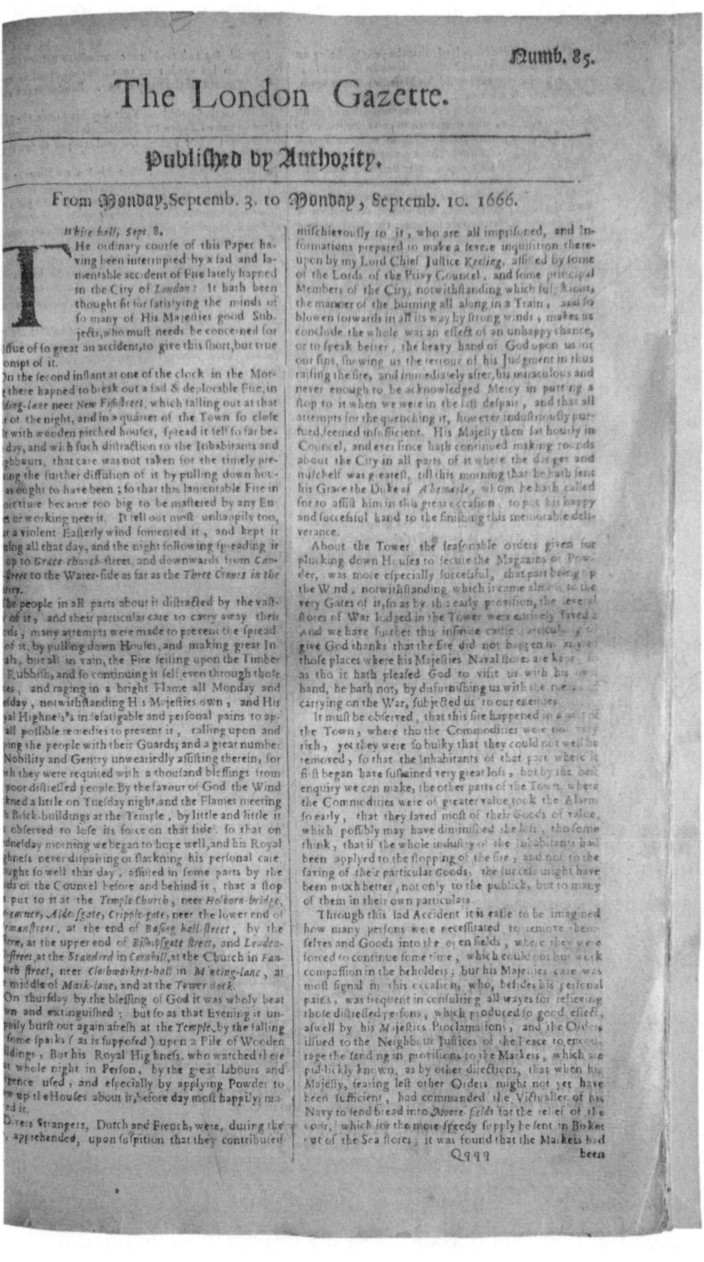

Numb. 85.

The London Gazette.

Publiſhed by Authority.

From Monday, Septemb. 3. to Monday, Septemb. 10. 1666.

White-hall, Sept. 8.

THe ordinary courſe of this Paper having been interrupted by a ſad and lamentable accident of Fire lately hapned in the City of *London*: It hath been thought fit for ſatisfying the minds of ſo many of His Majeſties good Subjects, who muſt needs be concerned for [...]ſſue of ſo great an accident, to give this ſhort, but true [...]ompt of it.

[...]n the ſecond inſtant at one of the clock in the Mor[...] there hapned to break out a ſad & deplorable Fire, in [...]*ding-lane* neer *New Fiſhſtreet*, which falling out at that [...] of the night, and in a quarter of the Town ſo cloſe [...]t with wooden pitched houſes, ſpread it ſelf ſo far be[...]day, and with ſuch diſtraction to the Inhabitants and [...]ghbours, that care was not taken for the timely pre[...]ing the further diffuſion of it by pulling down hou[...] as ought to have been; ſo that this lamentable Fire in [...]ort time became too big to be maſtered by any En[...]s or working neer it. It fell out moſt unhappily too, [...]t a violent Eaſterly wind fomented it, and kept it [...]ning all that day, and the night following ſpreading it [...]p to *Grace-church*-ſtreet, and downwards from *Can*[...]*ſtreet* to the Water-ſide as far as the *Three Cranes in the* [...]*ntry*.

[...]he people in all parts about it diſtracted by the vaſt[...] of it, and their particular care to carry away their [...]ds, many attempts were made to prevent the ſpread[...] of it, by pulling down Houſes, and making great In[...]ahs, but all in vain, the Fire ſeiſing upon the Timber [...] Rubbiſh, and ſo continuing it ſelf, even through thoſe [...]es, and raging in a bright Flame all Monday and [...]ſday, notwithſtanding His Majeſties own, and His [...]yal Highneſs's indefatigable and perſonal pains to ap[...] all poſſible remedies to prevent it, calling upon and [...]ing the people with their Guards; and a great number [...] Nobility and Gentry unweariedly aſſiſting therein, for [...]ch they were requited with a thouſand bleſſings from [...] poor diſtreſſed people. By the favour of God the Wind [...]kned a little on Tueſday night, and the Flames meeting [...] Brick-buildings at the Temple, by little and little it [...] obſerved to loſe its force on that ſide, ſo that on [...]dneſday morning we began to hope well, and his Royal [...]ghneſs never diſpairing or ſlackning his perſonal care, [...]ught ſo well that day, aſſiſted in ſome parts by the [...]ds of the Councel before and behind it, that a ſtop [...] put to it at the *Temple Church*, neer *Holborn-bridge*, [...]*-corner*, *Alde-ſgate*, *Cripple-gate*, neer the lower end of [...]*manſtreet*, at the end of *Baſing-hall-ſtreet*, by the [...]*tern*, at the upper end of *Biſhopſgate ſtreet*, and *Leaden*[...]*-ſtreet*, at the *Standard* in *Cornhill*, at the Church in *Fan*[...]*ch ſtreet*, neer *Clothworkers-hall* in *Mincing-lane*, at [...] middle of *Mark-lane*, and at the *Tower dock*.

On thurſday by the bleſſing of God it was wholy beat [...]wn and extinguiſhed; but ſo as that Evening it un[...]pily burſt out again afreſh at the *Temple*, by the falling [...] ſome ſparks (as is ſuppoſed) upon a Pile of Wooden [...]ldings; But his Royal Highneſs, who watched there [...]t whole night in Perſon, by the great labours and [...]gence uſed, and eſpecially by applying Powder to [...]w up the Houſes about it, before day moſt happily ma[...]ed it.

[...]ivers Strangers, Dutch and French, were, during the [...] apprehended, upon ſuſpition that they contributed miſchievouſly to it, who are all impriſoned, and Informations prepared to make a ſevere inquiſition thereupon by my Lord Chief Juſtice *Keeling*, aſſiſted by ſome of the Lords of the Privy Councel, and ſome principal Members of the City, notwithſtanding which ſuſpicions, the manner of the burning all along in a Train, and ſo blowen forwards in all its way by ſtrong winds, makes us conclude the whole was an effect of an unhappy chance, or to ſpeak better, the heavy hand of God upon us for our ſins, ſhewing us the terrour of his Judgment in thus raiſing the fire, and immediately after, his miraculous and never enough to be acknowledged Mercy in putting a ſtop to it when we were in the laſt deſpair, and that all attempts for the quenching it, however induſtriouſly purſued, ſeemed inſufficient. His Majeſty then ſat hourly in Councel, and ever ſince hath continued making rounds about the City in all parts of it where the danger and miſchief was greateſt, till this morning that he hath ſent his Grace the Duke of *Albemarle*, whom he hath called for to aſſiſt him in this great occaſion, to put his happy and ſucceſsful hand to the finiſhing this memorable deliverance.

About the Tower the ſeaſonable orders given for plucking down Houſes to ſecure the Magazins of Powder, was more eſpecially ſucceſsful, that part being up the Wind, notwithſtanding which it came almoſt to the very Gates of it, ſo as by this early proviſion, the ſeveral ſtores of War lodged in the Tower were entirely ſaved: And we have further this infinite cauſe particularly to give God thanks that the fire did not happen in any of those places where his Majeſties Naval ſtores are kept, ſo as tho it hath pleaſed God to viſit us with his own hand, he hath not, by diſfurniſhing us with the means of carrying on the War, ſubjected us to our enemies.

It muſt be obſerved, that this fire happened in a part of the Town, where tho the Commodities were not very rich, yet they were ſo bulky that they could not well be removed, ſo that the Inhabitants of that part where it firſt began have ſuſtained very great loſs, but by the beſt enquiry we can make, the other parts of the Town, where the Commodities were of greater value, took the Alarm ſo early, that they ſaved moſt of their Goods of value, which poſſibly may have diminiſhed the loſs, tho ſome think, that if the whole induſtry of the Inhabitants had been applyed to the ſtopping of the fire, and not to the ſaving of their particular Goods, the ſucceſs might have been much better, not only to the publick, but to many of them in their own particulars.

Through this ſad Accident it is eaſie to be imagined how many perſons were neceſſitated to remove themſelves and Goods into the open fields, where they were forced to continue ſome time, which could not but work compaſſion in the beholders; but his Majeſties care was moſt ſignal in this occaſion, who, beſides his perſonal pains, was frequent in conſulting all wayes for relieving thoſe diſtreſſed perſons, which produced ſo good effect, aſwell by his *Majeſties* Proclamations, and the Orders iſſued to the Neighbour Juſtices of the Peace to encourage the ſending in proviſions to the Markets, which are publickly known, as by other directions, that when his Majeſty, fearing leſt other Orders might not yet have been ſufficient, had commanded the Victualler of his Navy to ſend bread into *Moore-fields* for the relief of the poor, which for the more ſpeedy ſupply he ſent in Bisket out of the Sea ſtores; it was found that the Markets had

Qqqq been

London Gazette, 10 September 1666, with a smaller typeface for the title.

in the careful records made in the State Papers. Newspaper sellers and distributors were crucial to the business of newspapers; without them, men and women such as Pepys would never had received their twice-weekly fix of news. Distribution is as much a vital link in the chain of newspaper production as methods of gathering information and printers to prepare and then print their pages. While the *Gazette* had begun in a similar fashion to the manuscript newsletters and printed new sheets, distributed by post to subscribers, it soon tapped into and developed a network of wholesalers and street hawkers. The density of the population of London, the number of literate residents with an interest in political and mercantile affairs, and an existing network of booksellers ranging from street hawkers to established shops and warehouses enabled newspapers to be sold to whomever might want and benefit from a copy. Pepys, as we saw earlier, travelled to Westminster to acquire his copy of the *Gazette* from his usual bookseller there, Mrs Mitchell. Much of the supply of printed materials was controlled by wholesalers, who then passed on their wares to any number of stationers, booksellers such as Mitchell and, perhaps most importantly for the future newspaper trade, street hawkers, who could roam the city advertising their wares with their cries, a system that was later known as the 'London Plan'. Many of these wholesalers were women, and were given the name 'Mercury Women', or 'Mercuries', from the Roman god associated with communication and messages, and are recorded as supplying street hawkers with 'News papers and pamphlets'.[15] But the Great Fire disrupted their supply of materials and scattered many of their customers, despite the widespread desire for news. For the hawkers, the consequences were terrible. 'Those poor People' or 'miserable Creatures', as these vendors were sometimes called in the State Papers, worked in very precarious conditions on the margins of society, and were often homeless or elderly. Many were also blind or physically disabled.

The fire cost them what little they had. One woman complained that following the conflagration she had 'noe more cloathes than she had on her back', and asked the Post Office, who supplied her with the papers, to improve her pay to compensate. As autumn approached, the temperature dropped, and the hawkers, such as one Mrs Andrews, complained that the job required her to spend hours outside in the cold; she wanted better pay to compensate, and could threaten to withdraw her labour if not satisfied. The reports survive because the government was using the hawkers as a means of controlling the press and spying on its production, and, under L'Estrange, had received bonuses as compensation. Andrews informed her contact at the post office that after the fire, the *Gazette*'s printer, Newcombe, 'careys himselfe more strangly then others' and had managed to 'set himself up in the Churchyard'. With little choice, their work continued, with the Mercury Women risking 'hazard their halts if not their Liues' entering the burnt city to collect their papers, where the 'stench of ye earth is much offensiue & unholesome'.[16]

While the fire was at first nothing but a disaster for the London book trade, destroying presses and print shops, displacing the population and disrupting business, it enabled something of a shake-up in the press and some lifting of government control. Following the destruction of the Cathedral and the many print shops that surrounded it, the press was no longer densely concentrated around St Paul's and instead had set up shops in a number of different locations. This geographical dispersal meant that it became more difficult for the government to both supervise and suppress the press. The need to turn a profit also incentivized printers to try their hand at more lucrative enterprises, and they were tempted to print previously forbidden books and other texts. Mercury Women and hawkers offered an effective way to distribute such material. The marginal nature of the hawkers' existence meant that they were keen to sell whatever they could and, as legal records show, quickly began selling suppressed materials after any brush with the law or repeated periods of detention in prison. The number of urban working-class women seeking employment meant that their number was also quickly replenished – and, because hawkers had such a close relationship with their customers and interacted with them regularly, they could prompt their Mercury Women suppliers to provide them with materials that they knew would sell.

The Great Fire did not extinguish the *Gazette*, but instead ensured it rose as something of a phoenix during the rebuilding of the city. The *London Gazette*, as it was now known, confirmed a market not just for news, but for a product resembling the European *courants*, and the newspaper joined the news-book, the broadside, the newsletter and a host of oral forms used to disseminate news, gossip and opinion. The number of newspapers increased from the 1660s, and by 1712, spurred by the lapsing of the Licensing Act in 1695 (which did not remove censorship, but made the risk of publishing worthwhile), London could boast a dozen papers and had seen a plethora of titles founded, including Benjamin Harris's *Domestick Intelligence* (1679–89) and subsequent *Intelligence Domestic and Foreign* (1695) and *London Post*, the *Athenian Gazette* (later *Mercury*, 1690–97), the *Gentleman's Journal* (1692–4), *Lloyd's News* (1696–2013), *Dawk's News-letter* (1696–1716), the *English Spy* (1698), the *Daily Courant* (1702–97 in various forms of the *Gazetteer*), the *Weekly Review* (1704–13) and in 1706, the first evening paper, published three times a week, the *Evening Post*. And for four weeks in early 1693, the publisher of the *Athenian Mercury* issued the *Ladies Mercury*, the first periodical aimed at 'the female sex', which asked its readers to 'send their Questions to the Latin Coffee House in Ave Maria Lane, to the Ladies' Society there'.[17] Norwich and Bristol established the first provincial papers in 1701 and 1702 respectively, and in 1706 the *Worcester Post-man* began to publish regularly, after an erratic programme of publishing from 1690. Still published in 2020, it claims the title of 'the world's oldest newspaper'. Edinburgh gained its *Gazette* in 1699 and its *Courant* in 1705. By 1811 London could boast 52 papers, and a further number of Sunday papers such as the *British Gazette and Sunday Monitor*, which broached sabbath prohibitions. News could now be considered its own commodity, its very existence creating a growing desire for its consumption.

Increasingly, it was consumed alongside another addictive commodity: coffee. In 1677, alarmed by 'subversive discussion' allegedly taking place in James Row's coffee house in Parliament Close, the Edinburgh Privy Council closed what was then a novelty in the Scottish city. Offering a place not only to drink coffee but to mingle with 'gentleman, mechanic, Lord, and scoundrel', these new social spots offered a chance for the politically minded to meet, discuss the latest events and share pamphlets, papers and other forms of news and gossip. The Edinburgh Privy Council was concerned about the gathering of dissenting conventicles on the government's doorstep. When, three years later, the coffee house again opened its doors, the Scottish Council demanded that all 'Gazettes and News-Letters read in Coffee-houses' should be reviewed by the Bishop of Edinburgh or a council official to erase 'false and seditious news and slanders'.[18]

This conflict between authority and the perceived cacophony of dissenting voices was, of course, not simply a Scottish phenomenon, but an example of a European innovation that had been imported to Oxford in 1650 and London in 1652, and expanded across the country in the turbulent months and years following the death of Oliver Cromwell. By the 1680s coffeehouses had sprouted in most of the major towns and cities of the land, including Cambridge, Bristol, Gloucester and Great Yarmouth. In Scotland a coffeehouse had opened in Glasgow in the same year as James Row's in Edinburgh, with Dundee and Aberdeen following in the early 1700s. By the end of the 1670s, the Commonwealth of Massachusetts could point to its own coffeehouse in Boston. In 1660 in Dublin, Ireland, The Cock Coffee House began serving; within forty years, Cork, Limerick, Kilkenny, Clonmel, Wexford and Galway had coffeehouses of their own. Their patrons also consumed news alongside their bitter coffee, whether in Devizes, Hereford, Oxford or Norwich.

These coffeehouses, both provincial and metropolitan, could trace their origins to Istanbul coffee shops, and thence to Venice and the west in the seventeenth century. They provided a space for the consumption of invigorating drinks based on coffee beans (and sometimes other beverages), and created a site for discussion, business and gossip. British travellers, notably a culturally and intellectually curious subset described as the 'virtuosi', encouraged their re-creation in London, Oxford, Edinburgh and elsewhere. This phenomenon followed developments in France, where coffeehouses also began during the same period. These new quasi-public places provided a space for the dissemination of news or political and philosophical discussion, alongside the more down-to-earth consumption of coffee, everyday conversation and the pursuit of business. Cafés that opened in Marseille, Lyon or Paris played an increasingly central role in those cities' social and intellectual life. And, as the historian of the coffee house Brian Cowan notes, 'No coffeehouse worth its name could refuse to supply its customers with a selection of newspapers.'[19] Such places were unlikely to survive without a decent set of subscriptions to newspapers. In 1683 the printer Nathaniel Thompson estimated that proprietors had to spend four or five shillings a week on papers to feed their customers' demands, a sum amounting to around £13 a year (equivalent to around £1,500 today) – although other estimates run somewhat lower.[20]

Coffeehouses offered a distinctive and novel social space. Unlike traditional inns, taverns or ale-houses, they could not point to a long history of serving food and alcoholic drinks, or offering hospitality to travellers. While coffeehouses similarly offered shelter and drink, the substance their owners plied was at first an unnecessary luxury, an innovation that had been imported from the east. Coffee was an expensive, bitter product that needed expertise in production to produce a palatable drink. Those drinking coffee at first were at the cusp of a new wave of fashion, stimulated by the Eastern associations as much as caffeine stimulation. For such men – and, initially, it *was* men rather than women – coffee was linked to the Grand Tour and the exotic. Coffeehouses emphasized this cosmopolitan Eastern connection: no fewer than 37 London coffeehouses used a variant of the name the 'Turk's Head', along with several in Oxford. In Paris, the grandest café – Procopio Cutò, opened by Francesco Procopio dei Coltelli in 1686 – offered a range of spices and other products, all served by waiters dressed in exotic garb. Consumers of news from far-flung places – as well as courts, intrigues and excitements closer to home – were reminded of their cosmopolitan links through the substance of their drink, the café' atmosphere and the content of their papers.

While the fashion for stimulants such as coffee and, later, tea helped spur the success of the coffeehouse, or café, it was fuelled as much by the desire for news as it was for a refreshing drink. News came in different forms, of course. Coffee houses offered a focal point for the merchant or political classes to gather, and the reading and

Publish'd According to Act of Parliament Septr. 18. 1762

The GRUMBLERS of GREAT BRITAIN;

A New Humorous POLITICAL SONG.

By a GRUMBLETONIAN.

TUNE. *The Roast Beef of England.*

I.

GOOD People attend (if you can but spare Time)
To a Grumbling Poet, who grumbles in Rhyme,
To sit down in Silence—is now deem'd a Crime.
O the rum Grumblers of England!
And O the Old English Grumblers!

II.

When Statesmen miscarry and Things go awry
The Coffee-House Grumblers their Rancour let fly,
And snarl, snap and worry—yet know not for why.
O the rum Grumblers, &c.

III.

Muckle Glee fills the Heart of brave *Sawney* the *Scot*,
Because he has slily the upper Hand got.
The *Englishman* grumbles—because he has not.
O the rum Grumblers, &c.

IV.

Some *Grumblers* possess'd of more Money than Sense,
Complain of the Land-Tax, the War and Expence,
That *Conquest brings Ruin*—they plead for Defence.
O the rum Grumblers, &c.

V.

The poor People grumble about the Strong Beer,
Our Soldiers and Sailors too grumble for Fear,
Of losing the *Dollars*—they hope to bring here.
O the rum Grumblers, &c.

VI.

The *Pittamites* grumble at *Hogarth*'s new Print,
With Countenance crabbed, they just take a Squint,
And swear from * *John Bull*—he has pilfer'd the Hint.
O the rum Grumblers, &c.

VII.

Old *Formal* exclaims thus against the Qee–n's Ass,
" What Pity the Author unpunish'd should pass?"
" Let them grumble, cries *Hal*—while I add to the [Mass."
O the rum Grumblers, &c.

VIII.

Thus grumbling and growling from Morning till Night
The Nation remains in a terrible Plight;
For Grumbling will never—set Matters to right.
O the rum Grumblers, &c.

IX.

Then let us not into such strange Madness fall,
And loudly for *Peace*, and no *Peace* rave and bawl;
But pray for a Good One—or else none at all.
O the rum Grumblers of England!
And O ye Old English Grumblers!

* *John Bull*'s House in Flames. Vol. 1. 13

D Bedford sailed for France Sept. 3. to Treat for Peace. Sept 15 1762

Sold by W. TRINGHAM, Engraver in Castle-Alley, Royal Exchange, and at the Print-Shop under St. Dunstan's-Church. And by all the Print and Pamphlet-Shops.

[Price SIX-PENCE.]

The Grumblers of Great Britain, 1762, a satire on attitudes towards the Seven Years War peace negotiations, with anti- and pro-government newspapers in 'Bedford Coffee House', a reference to the Duke of Bedford's mission to Paris.

discussion that took place within them formed a key point within the information networks that spread through cities, towns and across the seas. Word of mouth, ranging from gossip to informed disclosure or paid informants, was a valuable currency in such a setting, and could be traded for status, favours, information in return or perhaps just a drink and supper. Handwritten letters and notes could be passed, copied and traded within the smoky shade of coffeeshops. However, increasingly, print became associated with such places, and their customers expected to find newspapers alongside their drinks, which included gin and tea after the opening up of the Canton trade from 1717. The costs of news were a significant factor to coffeehouse proprietors. In 1728, for example, a group of coffeehouse owners complained that 'when a news-paper is first set up, if it be good for any thing, the coffee-men are, in a manner, obliged to take it in. And a paper once received into a coffee-house is not easily thrust out again.' Demand was not limited to British papers, but given the nature of international trade it required decent coffeehouses to take papers from France and the Low Countries. The proprietor Isaac Branch, for example, paid Edmund Jones £4 a year for a supply of 'French News' (about £420 today, or forty days' wages for a skilled craftsman).[21]

The natural scientist and architect Robert Hooke had an addiction to such coffeehouses. His first diary notes visits to at least 64 London coffee houses between 1672 and 1680, sometimes visiting a coffeehouse three times in a day. In the coffeehouse, such as Garraway's in Cornhill, Hooke found a venue to explore his interests in science, painting and exploration. He could discuss these subjects with fellow-coffee drinkers or consult prints, paintings, books and newspapers; the latter providing him with useful bits of information, such as an account of 'certain men walkin[g] the water' in a 'high Dutch gazet'. As Cowan notes, 'nuggets of curious information such as this were the common currency of virtuoso conversation.'[22] Newspapers offered excellent grounds for such prospecting. Coffeehouses were sometimes associated with a bookseller, who made their wares available. In his diary Samuel Pepys noted buying a book on architecture from an Exchange Alley coffeehouse, which he later judged 'not worth a turd'.[23] We should also include chocolate-houses, offering a different drink and perhaps a more distinguished and cultivated air than their coffeehouse brethren.

This – Pepys's view aside – is perhaps the romantic view of the coffee shop and the world of information of which newspapers were part: as a hub of cosmopolitan free thought, offering a public sphere open to all, with access to the latest news. Many were dismissive of the coffeehouse. The writer and diarist John Evelyn – a man who, in his book *Fumifugium* (1661), derided the smoke and filth to be found in the city – makes no mention of ever visiting one, and tended to be dismissive of the coffeehouse and its visitors, noting that they were 'impolite, permissive'.[24] Although often seen as democratic, they could be relatively exclusive places, pitching themselves socially above the ale-house or tavern, with its association with drunkenness, rowdy behaviour and sex workers.

Coffeehouses and their clientele were not all equal. In London those clustered around the Royal Exchange, Cowan suggests, 'specialized quite quickly and developed to serve the business and social needs of London's merchant and governing elite' and offered the contemporary equivalent of a businessman's office space. Coffeehouses clustered around Covent Garden and Westminster served a similar purpose, offering services to the gentry and courtiers in those areas. But another tier of coffeehouses simply served a local population, offering drink, newspapers and other services to the neighbourhood. Coffeehouses were a place to collect (for free) and send mail, write letters and meet business partners or friends.[25] Other houses plied a riskier trade, such as Tom and Moll King, who were able to retire to an estate near the village of Hampstead but whose coffeehouse was a notorious venue for 'late-night rakish carousing and prostitution' in the 1720s.[26] Coffeehouses focused on clientele defined by geography, whether association with an English county, Scotland, France or Germany, or for merchants that focused on a particular trade: Virginia, Jamaica, the East Indies or New England. Coffeehouses marshalled news from these places, together with relevant notices and broadsides. Even placards were pasted. In Edinburgh, for example, arrival and departure times of ships from the port of Leith were regularly posted around the coffeehouses, much to the annoyance of the town council, which sought to make a profit on the monopoly of such information. Restoration coffeehouses 'soon became known as places "dasht with diurnals and books of news"'.[27] Coffeehouse owners also supplemented their income by publishing a paper or by circulating a more exclusive, or sensitive, newsletter in manuscript form. One merchant, for example, acquired updates from a clerk of the House of Commons in 1664, and sold access to it at his shop on Bread Street.

As centres of newsgathering – or gossip – coffeeshops also attracted journalists and newsletter writers, who gathered (and exchanged) material over drinks, turning gossip and insider information into news stories. The philosopher and author Lorenzo Magalotti noted that English coffeehouses gathered 'various bodies or groups of journalists where one hears what is or is believed to be new, be it true or be it false'.[28] Coffeehouses might be seen to be as much a nexus of disinformation as they were of truth.

In these ways, newspapers and their places of creation, dissemination and consumption were integrated into the changing life of the city, whether in Paris, London or Edinburgh. Some 2.5 million papers were sold in England in 1713, for example.[29] They were part of its trials and tribulations and offered a link to a wider world. They not only recorded these travails and excitements, but experienced them; and in the case of the *London Gazette* in the Great Fire even physically changed with the use of a new typeface. Such early newspapers, their makers and readers, we should remember, were part of a close-knit community, creating a written, discursive space, but also very much part of the real, physical and urban world. And from these metropolitan centres, the papers themselves and the news that they contained rippled out into other provinces, towns and villages. Very much from their inception, all the elements of creating a newspaper, from gathering information, editing and repacking it, and then distributing it (and responding to reactions from readers) were part of how papers were created. In business terms, subscriptions and cover prices were present from the birth, and were soon joined by advertisements – such 'advices' and 'notices' of real estate, shipping, medical remedies, books and pamphlets for sale and lost or found announcements that for years formed the bedrock of many newspaper business models; by

1705, the *London Gazette* cost around £9 to print (equivalent to about £960 today), and could bring in £8 in advertisements.[30] Newspapers' origins, from within the political machinery of the government's Southern Department, also point to their political ties, and their potential for political controversy. While ploughing their own course where they could, papers were also under the influence of political power and intrigue. The *Gazette* in particular became a political pawn, both in terms of the patronage its publication could offer and the influence such an organ could hold over a broader public. It was a political plum, which tended to tame it over time. In 1712, for example, as part of yet another political scheme, Jonathan Swift manoeuvred to make Charles Ford 'Gazetteer', noting that 'It is the prettiest employment in England of its bigness'; alas, the recipient did not appreciate the prize: 'yet the puppy does not seem satisfied with it . . . He thinks it not genteel enough.'[31] As editor, Ford proved timid, overseeing a decline in news and an increase in what one historian of the paper describes as 'verbiage of praise from governors of colonies, mayors and councils, justices, sheriffs, chancellors, freeholders and anybody disposed to express to the Crown its gratitude for the way the country was being governed'. The press, for all its potential to challenge or hold power to account, very quickly fell under its control. The choices an editor made could easily blunt a paper's teeth, whether out of decorum or for political favour. As Ford noted, 'I had writ a good deal more of the Queen's illness, an account of her birth etc., But I could not find out Mr L[ewis, the under secretary] and had no body to consult with, and therefore chose to say too little, than anything I doubted might be improper.'[32] As newspapers took firmer root in British society, this relationship between the press and the government became a central concern.

2
Reporting Parliament

The British became exceptionally proud of their constitutional system as the eighteenth century went on. At the heart of this political settlement, which followed the convulsions of the Civil Wars and the 'Glorious Revolution' of the seventeenth century, lay Parliament, a venerable political instrument that carefully held in check the powers of both monarchy and people, upheld the rule of law and preserved the sacred principle of property ownership. Within the chambers of the Palace of Westminster, which had absorbed its Scottish counterpart in 1707, men of power and influence came to legislate and debate the matters of the day. But outside the debating chamber, who knew what they were saying, and how? 'Strangers', as male and female visitors to the House of Commons were known, had long been permitted in the House, sometimes venturing as far as the debating floor itself, but mostly limited to what was called the Strangers' Gallery. Although not initially intended for the public, by 1621 this structure was in general use. Such was its importance that when Parliament fled temporarily to Oxford in 1625, the office of works felt compelled to construct 'a kind of terrace loft' in the Divinity School.[1] By the eighteenth century, visitors could also gain entry to the House of Lords. Here, relatives of peers were given special seating, while others stood, as a parliamentarian observed, 'below the bar, with an intolerable crowd of other persons, and with risk of having their pockets picked'.[2] Access to parliamentary debate was not just a consequence of general curiosity, offering an entertaining afternoon or evening listening to oratory and argument, but represented what was understood to be an important and ancient constitutional right. Entrance, however, was still limited, either by a ticket provided by an MP or, more usually, by bribing the doorman.

But while strangers – and even pickpockets – could attend debates, and even involved themselves via shouts and cheers, journalists were forbidden from reporting proceedings, even after restrictions on the press were loosened more broadly. Parliament jealously guarded its privilege to speak freely without being reported in the pages of the press. Peers and MPs wished to be free to discuss matters of the day without fear of libel or other civil or criminal repercussions, as well as external political meddling. Affairs of state, or so the argument went, were to be freely discussed without appealing to a wider public or couched in coded language to avoid unwelcome scrutiny. Neither did the government wish foreign powers to be able to learn about its deliberations in an unfiltered fashion. Within such a context, transparency in public affairs was not deemed a virtue, but instead was seen to threaten the serious business of government. Reporting on Parliament could be a perilous activity for printers, who risked fines, imprisonment or worse.

This said, official records of Parliament had begun in 1510, and unsanctioned accounts had long circulated among the well-connected. Publishers began selling reports in the early seventeenth century, and this was soon followed by Parliament's first efforts to suppress them in 1628. In 1640, following the recall of Parliament by Charles I, a new form of weekly publication, labelled 'diurnals' (misleadingly, perhaps, since the name derived from the Latin for 'dailies'), answered the public's need to discover the latest news from Parliament. Initially taking the form of manuscript newsletters, by 1642 more than twenty diurnals were being published by royalist or parliamentarian printers to ensure that their side of the story got out.[3] This flurry of what we might just about recognize as a newspaper did not last: as Parliament felt increasingly threatened by royalist propaganda, a series of parliamentary Acts proscribed the freedom of the press with increasing severity, and this form of publication was largely stamped out.

By the start of the eighteenth century the only paper authorized by government was the *London Gazette*, which was distributed to subscribers by the Royal Mail rather than placed on general sale. Despite such official limits on parliamentary reporting, news of debates and government activities remained central to the many newsbooks and manuscript reports that circulated among the elite and wealthy. The information superhighway of the day was clearly a two-speed one. For the wealthy, political information flowed with relative ease, lubricated by money, cronyism and cultural capital, while for the rest, a potholed, misleading and sometimes dangerous route was on offer, one that privileged gossip and rumour over hard fact. Increasingly, publishers and authors sensed a wider market, one consisting of those willing to purchase what became known as 'registers' or 'annuals', an annual publication that promised its reader a true and authentic record of the year's political, social and religious events, often with claims to having access to special information. These, as we will see, offered the first tears in this cloak of privilege and secrecy that surrounded parliamentary proceedings. In the following pages, we will look at a handful of characters who began to tear this away over the course of a century or so: a former soldier (if that is indeed what he was), a city printer and a rakish politician, equally infamous for his womanizing as he was for his calls for freedom of the press.

David Jones and *A Compleat History of Europe*

We begin with the soldier. Very little is known today about the life of David Jones, a Welsh-born writer active from the 1680s, except that he may have served in the English Army and that he was the son of a Welsh non-conformist minister. Jones came to wider public attention in 1697 when he published a collection of letters purporting to reveal the 'private minutes between France and England', which was based on his inside knowledge gleaned as a secretary-translator for the marquis de Louvois. *The Secret History of White-hall* resembled many such works that sought to profit from the public's desire to peek into the corridors of power, and as such competed with many other supposedly secret court memoirs that appeared after the relaxation of press censorship in 1685. Perhaps making use of funds that the *Secret History* provided, Jones followed his first publication with *A Compleat History of Europe*, an annual that appeared on an eclectic schedule from 1702 to 1713, and then on an intermittent schedule until 1720. After this, nothing further is heard from him. For the *Compleat History* Jones garnered as much as he could from the European papers and other annuals, but he also used various sources to include parliamentary accounts from the preceding year alongside maps of military campaigns, lists of office holders and obituaries of officials. He included not only the English Parliament but the Scottish Parliament, before the two were combined, and in 1710 provided an account of the Stannaries of Cornwall and Devonshire of 1703. As such, its coverage broke new ground in terms of parliamentary reporting without attracting the fierce attentions of the censor.

It should be stressed that these were neither newspapers nor the news as we would recognize them today, and we should be wary of viewing or judging them in the light of subsequent parliamentary journalism. Jones began his work lamenting the fortunes of the new century, which had the 'saddest prospect, that was perhaps ever known, of destructive and bloody wars'. The publication placed its relations in a certain relationship to time, reflecting on what was new and saving the past from disappearing. He sought to place events in their historical perspective, and through the 'collecting and digesting' of numerous 'original papers' save for others that would otherwise be 'in a few Weeks time almost irretrievably lost'.[4] Jones re-edited the texts over the years, and from 1713 he escaped the present and began to cover the recent past instead, publishing volumes for the seventeenth century. The *Compleat History* was also published annually, so the news his publication contained was of the stale variety, yet despite all this the success of the publication points to a readership eager to discover political information, particularly, the preface to 1705 edition noted, 'Domestick Concerns, about which People are generally most sollicitous'. Jones also placed a great weight upon accuracy – or at least the 'aura' or impression of accuracy. His preface explained that the work was one of a 'gentleman', providing the publication with a claim to authority, and he emphasized the 'no small Pains' that he had taken to ensure his information was correct. He not only made use of published materials, but entered into 'Conversation with many Foreigners' to be 'better inform'd' and to correct errors in his text. This, it seems, was not just advertising, since at least one letter exists showing that he and his publishers corresponded with the great and the good asking for information and confirmation of reports. Along with gathering together such materials from courts across Europe, Jones also provided details of parliamentary debates – allowing him to be credited as something of a pioneer of parliamentary reporting, if that concept does not obscure his intentions. From what we can tell, the accounts were made by someone, perhaps even Jones himself, who attended parliamentary debates at Westminster in person and made a summary account, either from memory or from surreptitious note-taking.

Abel Boyer

Jones did not have the field to himself for long, and a more responsive form of political reporting soon followed on the heels of his annual *Compleat History*. In 1711 a new monthly periodical, the *Political State of Great Britain*, began to be published in London, where it was printed by John Baker at the sign of the Black-Boy in Paternoster Row and sold for a shilling. It initially borrowed text from Jones, but the frequency of its publication changed its temporal dynamic, making it more of a newspaper than an annual record. The *Political State* published debates from both houses, but avoided prosecution by printing after sessions had adjourned and claiming it was printing 'history' rather than current affairs. It seemed to have been welcomed by the political class: some editions went to three printings. Although parliamentary privilege was being abused, it seems that the paper was published with a certain amount of acquiescence, or even the assent, of the governing class of the day. Many politicians provided their speeches verbatim to the publisher, and other accounts were received via clerks and messengers of both Houses, who sat in the gallery during debates.

Often attributed to Daniel Defoe, the editor of this bold new news source was in actuality a French-born Huguenot, Abel Boyer, who had moved to England in 1689 after completing his studies in the Low Countries. He worked as a tutor and undertook translation and editorial work, and had a limited success as a playwright before lexicography proved to be his literary winning ticket. In 1702, making the most of his royal connections, Boyer published his *Dictionnaire royal francois et anglois* at The Hague. The royal association was something of a stretch: Boyer claimed it was composed for the late Duke of Gloucester, whom Boyer had tutored, and was published with the encouragement of Princess Anne. The project proved to be remarkably successful and formed the basis for many subsequent dictionaries over the next century. Through his talents and hard work, Boyer thus made himself known as a useful and well-educated toiler on 'Grub Street' (as the eighteenth-century writer Samuel Johnson later defined it: 'originally the name of a street . . . much inhabited by writers of small histories, dictionaries, and temporary poems, whence any mean production is called grub street'). Boyer's politics placed him in sympathy with the Whig faction, which had established their prominence in English politics following the 'Glorious Revolution' of 1688, and these connections allowed the possibility of his newspaper, the *Political State*. Like Jones's *Secret History*, it announced its conceit on its title page; rather than purported letters between a secretary and his noble employer, Boyer's paper made use of his Dutch background and advertised itself as a 'monthly letter to a friend in Holland'. Furthermore, the journal also claimed to be 'impartial'. And, as in *Secret History*, the *Political State* contained lists and updates of Establishment affairs – military, ecclesiastical and court – and included cribbed records of parliamentary debates. Similar devices were used to escape prosecution. Speakers in the House of Lords were identified by a single letter, for example, while members of the Commons were identified by name; according to Boyer, this was with their agreement. The *Political State*, then, is the first, unofficial, regular public reporting on Parliament, albeit, it seems, with some quasi-official nodding through. Boyer only once found himself in trouble during his 26 years of editorship, when he and his printer were imprisoned by the House of Lords for six days in the spring of 1711 for publishing parliamentary news. Apart from this incident, Boyer seems to have found his enterprise to be a profitable one, since it continued for a number of years.

Who read these publications? The answer lies partly in the process of their creation, since the physical efforts required to print and distribute a newspaper or journal should not be underestimated. The labour, skill, materials and logistics that underpinned newspaper production were reflected in the cost of the product and affected who could afford to buy them. Compared to France or, later in the century, the United States, Britain held some advantages in terms of its geography and its centres of printing and political power. Westminster was just a short water-taxi ride, or a 45-minute walk, from the heart of the nation's printing world, the warren of streets and buildings surrounding the churchyard of St Paul's Cathedral. Here lay printing expertise born from the production of books, pamphlets, forms, posters and other ephemeral jobbing work, access to capital and a growing pool of hacks able to turn oral reports into printed copy. In terms of the material demands of printing, London offered a well-developed network of manufacturers of paper and ink, and much of the paper made from recycled scraps of rags and waste papers. Booksellers and hawkers offered a means of distributing the newspaper, while an efficient postal network allowed it to reach the four corners of the kingdom and, indeed, the nascent empire beyond. But the cost of buying or subscribing to these newspapers was not insignificant, and we can assume that only the relatively wealthy class of British subjects would have seen fit to buy such papers: merchants, landowners, clergy, well-to-do officers and the nobility. Of course, many others may also have had access via coffeehouses, where such papers were available to read by patrons, or as the paper was resold or passed on. We should also not assume that readers were exclusively male.

We can also be certain that the paper and its readers were well connected. Boyer certainly believed that he was within striking distance of admission to the Establishment. The editor of the *London Gazette* – the official record of affairs of state – was a plum position following the death of the incumbent, and Boyer believed it would soon be his. However, his alignment with Whig politics scotched such ambition. He was twice overlooked for the appointment, despite writing to friends that he believed the post was his for the taking.

His disappointment is a reminder of the nature of politics in eighteenth-century Britain and the hierarchical nature of news. Despite boasting the broadest franchise and perhaps the most democratic form of government of its day, power remained firmly in the hands of the elite. While perhaps 4 per cent of the adult male population could participate in the ballot, real politics took place in the dining and drawing rooms of a select group of ministers and power brokers. Politics was a matter of patronage and court society, a state of affairs that was reflected in – and helped to shape – newspapers. It was also an oral affair, something undertaken via spoken debate and discussion, whether in public or private, while patronage was something that also took place in public, with those finding favour granted physical proximity and 'face time', as politicians would call it today. By 1714 Boyer was known as much for his manuscript newsletter as his printed publication, underscoring the close connections between print and the circulation of handwritten and copied materials, as well as the different levels of access to information that such different forms of dissemination allowed. Within this hierarchy the handwritten remained at the apex as it represented the most privileged kind of news, one that excluded those without knowledge of the newsletter itself as well as the means to pay for it.

Such hierarchies of access to information reflected and helped to create the complex social and political dynamics of the Stuart and Hanoverian courts and politics. Political favouritism bestowed different levels of insider information, access to the places where such information could be shared, and public recognition. Those in favour, as Lord Waldegrave (a great-grandson of James II) recalled in his memoir, found themselves 'caress'd in the most public manner; and were honor'd with all the nonsense of gracious smiles, mysterious Nods, and endless Whispers, in every corner of the Drawing Room'.[5] More practical favours might then follow, such as official positions, pensions or other sinecures, or perhaps a beneficial introduction for a marriageable offspring. In return the beneficiary would owe loyalty to their patron. Memoirs and letters of the day were full of such hopes, speculation and social successes and failures, on which family fortunes could be built or threatened. Published guides to manners and social behaviour helped to codify this culture and offered a preparation for those seeking entry into society. And while power was concentrated in the person of the king, his ministers and Parliament, the latest gossip spread out into wider society. The Georgian court, that of the king and his ministers, exerted its power within a web of wider social connections and events. The latest events were discussed at card parties or dinners, while plans for the next day were hatched at coffeehouses, with agents or supporters of ministers and other great men. News and politics were represented in the reports of the day, typically letters and memoirs, as 'clamour'. Pamphlets and newspapers used the language of 'we hear', reported 'what is said', and informed their readers of 'clamours and alarm'.

In this way, political news was presented as gossip and intrigue. Only the elite were able to break through this miasma of rumour and disinformation and unlock the real meaning of what was being reported. Although Boyer offered a record of debates for posterity, the dozen or so London newspapers of the day avoided more up-to-date reporting, being well aware of the legal repercussions that would follow. Provincial papers sometimes included stories that were gleaned from circulating newsletters, but here, too, Parliament applied legal force and prosecuted reports of its affairs. The House of Lords zealously protected its members' privacy, bringing prosecutions against papers that advertised a biography of one peer in 1721, while the publisher of James Read's *Weekly Journal; or, British Gazetteer* was dragged into court for unwittingly printing news of charges being made against a member of the House of Lords.[6]

Other weekly periodicals, including the *Gentleman's Magazine* (from 1731) and the *London Magazine* (from 1732), attempted to print parliamentary news by making use of a legal loophole and publishing during Parliament's recess. The House of Commons disagreed with this reading and on 13 April 1733 confirmed that such reporting was prohibited. In response, the magazine created a set of mythical parliaments whose debates were remarkably like those taking place in Westminster. Parliament indulged them in this subterfuge until 1747, when the House of Lords imprisoned two printers for publishing reports on the trial of Lord Lovat for treason. The *Gentleman's Magazine* stopped publishing its reports at this point, while the *London Magazine* ceased attributing speeches to individual members and provided only summaries of debates. These were so dull and uninformative that the magazine dropped them in 1757 owing to what they might have rightly believed to be a lack of interest by their readers.

John Wilkes

But fashions – and political winds – change, and parliamentary reporting soon became one of the most politically charged issues of the day, through a mixture of heightened political conflict, competition between papers and the skilled manipulation of one of the foremost editors and provocateurs of the age – or indeed, any age. In 1757 changes to the Stamp Act taxing printed papers were sloppily drafted, a mistake that would cost Parliament greatly. Publications of six or more pages were now liable for three shillings per edition, rather than a halfpenny or penny per copy – a greatly reduced charge (which ultimately led to the legal classification of newspapers).[7] New papers were founded to capitalize on this opportunity, including the daily *Public Ledger* in 1760 and three tri-weekly papers – the *London Chronicle* in 1756, *Lloyd's Evening Post* in 1757 and the *St James' Chronicle* in 1761 – and the numbers of individual editions soared. Competition between these newspapers led their editors to revisit the attractions of parliamentary reporting, and news of the political affairs of members of the Lords and Commons began to find its way into their pages. In response the Commons complained in 1760 that four papers contained 'printed Accounts of the Proceedings of this House, in contempt of the Order, and in Breach of the Privilege of this House'. Summoned to the House, the printers confessed and were released only after they were reprimanded by the Speaker. In 1762 the printer of the *London Chronicle* was summoned to the custody of the Serjeant at Arms for publishing a speech by the Speaker. These were warning shots across the bows of the newly fitted-out presses and proper parliamentary reporting ceased until 1768.

New weekly papers, such as the *Weekly London Journal*, which was launched in 1762, continued to put pressure on this system of control. Often short-lived, such papers could represent more radical views. One of these was the inflammatory *North Britain*. Printed in London, again in 1762, its title was a satirical allusion to what its editor saw as the malign influence over the king by the Scottish minister Lord Bute, and it sparked a political explosion, bringing mobs onto the streets and challenging the privilege of Parliament and king. The man who chose to light the touchpaper was its editor, John Wilkes, reputed to be one of the ugliest men in Christendom (not that he cared, since he made up for his looks with his ample charm and quick wit). It is impossible to tell the story of the expansion of press freedom without considering the role of this controversial, mercurial figure, a man 'gigantic in Vice, and whose Life and Manners were a Scandal to Society'.[8] Born in Clerkenwell, London, as the second son of a malt distiller, the family quickly recognized his intelligence as a child, and marked his younger brother out as the future manager of the distillery. Rather than destine him for a life in 'trade', his parents gave young Wilkes's education special attention, sending him to a school in Hertford in 1734. He was soon excelling in both Greek and Latin. His other interests became apparent when he attended the University of Leiden a decade later, in 1744, where, according to a later boast to the Scottish writer James Boswell, he spent his time in taverns and brothels. In 1747, before he could complete his studies, his family summoned him back to England for a marriage that they hoped would cement the family fortunes: his wife was to be Mary Mead, a devout daughter of a wealthy widow who brought with her a healthy dowry – as well as ten years' seniority to Wilkes. The marriage clearly constituted a great mismatch between an ambitious rake and a pious, quiet, country gentlewoman.

Wilkes soon shared his time between Aylesbury, Buckinghamshire, where he served as a country magistrate, and the fashionable parts of London, where he won election to the prestigious Royal Society in 1749 and the fashionable dining club the Sublime Society of Beef Steaks (motto: 'Beef and Liberty'). In Buckinghamshire he joined what became known later as the Hellfire Club, notorious for its drinking, womanizing and club motto *Fais ce que tu voudras* (Do what thou wilt). Here he became friendly with the rake's rake (and son of an archbishop) Thomas Potter, who convinced Wilkes that he would choose him as his joint candidate for the second of the two Aylesbury parliamentary seats. Wilkes was taken in by the suggestion, but in the end was given the ill-regarded position of county sheriff, and Potter was elected with another candidate. Continuing to seek parliamentary office, and the social standing that came with it, Wilkes contested an election at Berwick-upon-Tweed, at the far end of the country. Despite encouragement from the prime minister, the Duke of Newcastle, Wilkes lost, and incurred not only the great cost of contesting the election but the disapproval of his wife. Appalled by this and the costs of his fashionable lifestyle, they had a trial separation in 1756, a state of affairs which became permanent the following year. Wilkes agreed to pay Mary £200 per annum and retained the Aylesbury estate and the charge of their daughter, Polly.

Wilkes gained parliamentary success the following year, taking Potter's seat after his move to another constituency when he was given office in a new ministry under William Pitt. Great things were expected of him in Parliament, not least by his new patron Pitt, but Wilkes remained silent in the chamber and failed to win a series of government posts, including Lord of Trade, ambassador to Constantinople and governor of Quebec. He retained his seat at the 1761 election, using the expensive, but not unusual for the day, method of offering £5 to three hundred of the five hundred voters to avoid a contest. He returned to Parliament as a follower of Pitt, now out of office, and spoke several times, although Horace Walpole noted in his diary that he 'spoke coldly and insipidly, though with impertinence; his manner was poor, and his countenance horrid'.

While his parliamentary career, such as it was, confirmed that his brilliance did not lie in public oration, at the age of 36 it became apparent that it lay in his pen. First publishing an anonymous pamphlet in March 1762 (*Observations on the Papers relative to the rupture with Spain*), he founded the political weekly the *North Briton* that June. He had a political target in mind, as the title hinted: the ministry of the Scottish Lord Bute, whom Wilkes and his fellow contributors believed was leading the takeover of England. Much of the paper focused on the negotiations of the Treaty of Paris, which ended the Seven Years War, the terms of which, the paper believed, 'saved England from the certain ruin of success' through its generosity towards a defeated France. The paper credited Bute's political success to an erotic liaison with the king's mother.

The paper soon had a very respectable circulation of around 2,000 – and generated a large circle of enemies. In October of the same year, Wilkes fought a pistol duel with Lord Talbot, the Lord Steward of the Royal Household, but the government found no legal means of silencing the paper. Then, following the resignation of Lord Bute in April 1763, the paper launched an attack on the king's speech during the closing session of Parliament. *North Briton*, number 45 (23 April), denounced the 'ministerial effrontery' that obliged George III to give his 'sacred name' to such 'odious' measures. With that, a legal firestorm began, as the Grenville ministry saw their opportunity to charge Wilkes with seditious libel. They issued a warrant against the 'authors, printers and publishers' and arrested Wilkes and his associates – despite them not being identified by name in the general warrant. Claiming parliamentary privilege, Wilkes was released, to the general applause of a crowd that had gathered, along with shouts of 'Wilkes and Liberty!' Wilkesite mobs took to the streets, becoming a feature of London life for the next dozen years. Wilkes launched legal counter-actions.

The case rumbled on for several months, the subject of great popular agitation and national discussion. The House of Commons debated the issue, and Wilkes was drawn into another duel in November, this time receiving such a serious wound from Samuel Martin MP's pistol that he claimed he was unable to participate in further legal or political discussions. In December he fled to Paris. In January 1764 the House of Commons confirmed that Wilkes was the publisher of *North Briton* and expelled him from the House, without

THE NORTH BRITON.

NUMB. XLV.* SATURDAY, APRIL 23, 1763.

The following advertisement appeared in all the papers on the 13th of April.

THE NORTH BRITON makes his appeal to the good sense, and to the candour of the ENGLISH nation. In the present unsettled and fluctuating state of the *administration*, he is really fearful of falling into involuntary errors, and he does not wish to mislead. All his reasonings have been built on the strong foundation of *facts*; and he is not yet informed of the whole interior state of government with such *minute precision*, as now to venture the submitting his crude ideas of the present political crisis to the discerning and impartial public. The SCOTTISH minister has indeed *retired*. Is HIS influence at an end? Or does HE still govern by the *three* wretched tools of his power †, who, to their indeliable infamy, have supported the most odious of his measures, the late ignominious *Peace*, and the wicked extension of the arbitrary mode of *Excise*? The NORTH BRITON has been steady in his opposition to a *single*, insolent, incapable, despotic minister; and is equally ready, in the service of his country, to combat the *triple-headed, Cerberean* administration, if the SCOT is to assume that motley form. By HIM every arrangement *to this hour* has been made, and the notification has been as regularly sent by letter under HIS HAND. *It therefore* seems clear to a demonstration, that HE intends only to retire into that situation, which HE held before HE first took the seals; I mean the dictating to every part of the king's administration. The NORTH BRITON desires to be understood, as having pledged himself a firm and intripid assertor of the rights of his fellow-subjects, and of the liberties of WHIGS and ENGLISHMEN.

Genus ORATIONIS *atrox, & vehemens,* cui opponitur *lenitatis & mansuetudinis.*

CICERO.

" THE *King's Speech* has always been considered by the legislature, and by the " public at large, as the *Speech of the Minister* §. It has regularly, at the be- " ginning of every session of parliament, been referred by both houses to the consi- " deration of a committee, and has been generally canvassed with the utmost freedom, " when

---

* The passages included within the inverted commas are the *only* passages, to which any objection is made in the INFORMATION filed in the *King's-Bench* by the *Attorney-General*, against the publisher, Mr. *George Kearsly*.

† The earls of *Egremont* and *Halifax*, and *G. Grenville*, esq.

§ Anno 14 G. II. 1740. Duke of Argyle.

The King's Speech is always, in this House, considered as the Speech of the Ministers. LORDS Debates, vol. 7. p. 413.

Lord Carteret.

When we take his Majesty's Speech into consideration, though we have heard it from his own mouth, yet we do not consider it as his Majesty's Speech, but as the speech of his Ministers. p. 425.

Anno 7 G. II. 1733. Mr. Shippen.

I believe it has always been granted, that the speeches from the Throne are the compositions of ministers of state; upon that supposition we have always thought ourselves at liberty to examine every proposition contained in them; even without doors people are pretty free in their marks upon them: I believe no Gentleman here is ignorant of the reception the speech from the throne, at the close of last session, met with from the nation in general. COMMONS Debates, vol. 8. p. 5.

Anno 13 G. II. 1739. Mr Pulteney, now Earl of Bath.

His Majesty mentions heats and animosities. Sir, I do not know who drew up this speech; but whoever he was, he should have spared that expression: I wish he had drawn a veil over the heats and animosities that must be owned ONCE *subsisted upon this* [h]*ead; for* I AM SURE NONE NOW SUBSIST. Vol. 11. p. 96.

North Briton, issue XLV, 23 April 1763.

a vote. Four days later, the Court of the King's Bench convicted him of publishing the paper, and after he failed to respond to summonses to attend, he was declared outlawed.

Wilkes did not exactly lie low. Among the effects taken from him under a general warrant by Philip Carteret Webb and Lovell Stanhope was a manuscript for 'An Essay on Women', an obscene parody of the poet Alexander Pope's *Essay on Man* begun by Potter and based on his affair with the wife of Dr Warburton, and enlarged by Wilkes with lines such as, 'Just a few good Fucks, and then we die.'[9] Suspecting that this would then be published and used as a means to prosecute him, Wilkes alighted on a bold scheme to draw the sting from the threat. He published an announcement in the *Public Advertiser* that 'Speedily will be published by Philip Carteret Webb and Lovell Stanhope, Esqrs, *An Essay on Woman*.' Since they were terrified of being linked to the manuscript, it was quickly returned to its author, as Wilkes intended. But rather than leaving it at that, Wilkes made use of his printers, who were now short of work after the cessation of the *North Briton,* to run off a dozen or so copies of *An Essay on Woman* for his Hellfire Club friends. Although it was to be strictly limited to his drinking and womanizing companions, stray pages made their way into the hands of a hostile printer, McFaden, and thence to the government. His enemies added some extra lines about the Holy Trinity, and Wilkes was now charged with blasphemy. Lines were read out in the Lords, to general mirth, and helped to boost Wilkes's popularity among the denizens of the streets on London. Indeed, the scheme was 'so gross and scandalous', as Horace Walpole recorded in his *Memoirs of the Reign of George III*, that 'the whole world almost united in crying out against the informers.'

In early 1768, after making the most of Paris and European society, encompassing trips to Italy and, it was said, amorous liaisons, notably with the 'nimble-thighed' Italian opera dancer Gertrude Corradini, Wilkes returned to England in spectacular fashion. After a few weeks incognito, he stood for Parliament for the City of London. He lost the election but announced that he would now challenge the sitting members of the county of Middlesex – the seat representing London and its environs. Wilkes and his supporters ran a formidable and organized campaign. With large pro-Wilkes crowds effectively intimidating his opponents' supporters, he won the seat in a three-way race by 1,292 to 827 and 807. The House of Commons quickly decided to expel him, just as Wilkes again faced trial for the *North Briton* Affair. The affair became a sensation, and a political lightning rod for street politics over the next few years, with Wilkes gaining a huge personal following on the streets of London as well as among radical, reforming and opposition political factions. Between 1768 and 1774 the Commons twice annulled the vote, while Wilkes was returned by the electors three times; he sneaked into court in disguise, only to be freed by a mob, and, in one incident dubbed the 'Massacre of St George's Fields', troops fired on his supporters, killing at least six people. Wilkes was also incarcerated in King's Bench Prison, although it was a rather lax and luxurious confinement. He eventually took his seat in 1774, but secured election as an alderman of London in 1769 (with several other Wilkesites securing places over the next twelve months). He was supported by the Society of Gentleman Supporters of the Bill of Rights (who also helped to settle his financial debts), and the City of London became his power base.

By February 1771, Wilkes had become a powerful radical figure – with a grudge against government – known throughout the land. Excitement surrounding the Middlesex election had significantly expanded supply of and demand for the political publications from the London press. Few of these resisted reporting on parliamentary debates. However, in February 1771 Parliament summoned two printers (Nathaniel Thompson, printer of the *Gazetteer*, and John Wheble of the *Middlesex Journal*) for this offence, and when they failed to appear, ordered their arrest. For Wilkes and his supporters, it suggested that the government would seek to suppress free reporting in the newspapers, and was an example of the use of general warrants to suppress political dissent.

In response, they concocted a plan. The City of London was responsible for issuing arrest warrants within its borders, and it was now under the control of Wilkes, as magistrate, and his allies. Printers were invited to seek refuge within its borders. The Commons issued further orders for arrest, and on 15 March attempted to arrest John Miller, publisher of the Wilkesite *London Evening-Post.* The magistrates refused to comply. In response, the Commons imprisoned the Lord Mayor and another alderman, and summoned Wilkes, who declined to attend – Parliament now considered him 'too dangerous to meddle with', and left him alone. Parliament was reluctant to override the City's privilege over the matter of reporting and conceded defeat. Newspaper reporting of Parliament remained illegal, but in practice it could continue from its City base. From July 1771, as the bibliographer Stanley Morison states, 'no consistent attempt was made to prevent the publication of parliamentary reports in any of the newspapers.'[10] In 1775, when Wilkes was Lord Mayor, he challenged the House of Lords to continue its own ban. The chamber avoided confrontation and acquiesced.

Wilkes, who continued to have a political career until his death in 1797, thus found himself the focus of a great social change. It was one that he had also, to a great extent, stirred up. His personal qualities and place in the social hierarchy played no small part in the affair. A man of ambition and a morality that had little place for false modesty, the cant of the status quo or undeserving privilege, who could 'never put on the mask of hypocrisy', he found himself within reach of success by dint of his parent's mercantile wealth, his brains, access to good schooling and a marriage of convenience.[11] However, like many, his limited access to the establishment (and his understanding of its corruption from his drinking and dining companions) did not bring satisfaction, but spurred him on to even more mischievous agitation. A novelist might also speculate on the links between his amatory adventures, desire for excitement and hot-headedness in explaining his long-standing desire to goad the system.

But there was more to Wilkes than just the desire for personal fame and fortune. He was also driven by a genuine desire for reform and a hatred of corruption and base stupidity. His brilliance as a journalist was not just to plug into a popular desire for reform, but also to align it with a more demotic genius for satire, scabrous attacks and sexual and scatological allusion. The press is never as alive as when it plugs into a pulsing, popular vein of outrage, sharp humour and blunt attacks on the hidden, privileged and self-serving systems of power. Wilkes's popularity on the street as well as in the pages of the press demonstrated how powerful and explosive 'news' could be. Neither was Wilkes working alone, although his personality and notoriety overshadowed the other crucially important players. Without support in the City, his coup would have been impossible; it must also have gone with the grain of opinion in Parliament, many members of which accepted the usual routes of reporting its business, such as Jones's and Boyer's earlier efforts. The affair points to the potential power of the news and of a more popular form of politics.

William Woodfall

Wilkes's celebrity was also built upon the by-then sophisticated and secure foundations of a popular print culture. The web of printers, financiers, patrons, sellers and provincial networks and papers and pamphleteers gave Wilkes and his campaigns a proper public platform. Chief among these was the journalist and publisher William Woodfall. The contrast between him and Wilkes was marked. One was impulsive, the other rigorous and more adroit at working with the established order. But both seized the opportunity to shake the status quo with vigour. Born in 1746, Woodfall was Wilkes's junior by two decades. The younger son of a London printer and proprietor of two papers, *The Advertiser* and the *London Packet*, Woodfall was initially apprenticed to a bookseller in Paternoster Row before setting his sights on an acting career and travelling to Scotland as an actor in Fisher's company. In 1769, when their father died, Woodfall's older brother, Henry Sampson, took over *The Advertiser*, while Woodfall gave up on his acting ambitions and took over the *London Packet* in 1772. He then moved to editing and printing the *Morning Chronicle* in 1774.

Although he was proud of his objectivity, Woodfall's political sympathies lay with the Whigs and the constitutional interests of the merchants of the City of London. The Middlesex election and the massacre in St George's Fields electrified the 'spirit of the nation'.

John Almon, a bookseller, printer and Wilkesite political journalist, claimed in his memoirs that he decided now was the moment 'to make the nation acquainted with the proceedings of Parliament' through parliamentary sketches that he printed thrice weekly in the *London Evening Post*. As reports they were short, but, Almon claimed, 'they were in general pretty accurate, and their accuracy was perhaps the cause of the printer's security,' since Parliament left Almon alone. Other papers, aware of the huge public interest in the Middlesex election, also followed Almon's lead, albeit more cautiously, and provided even briefer summaries of the debates on Wilkes, lists of speakers and occasional division numbers. The monthlies were more sanguine, including the influential *Gentleman's Magazine*, which published long reports thinly disguised as accounts of 'a newly established society' for young gentlemen. Woodfall took full advantage of the opportunity presented to report on parliament created by Wilkes in 1771, and his reputation for parliamentary reporting to maintain a commanding position among political reporters over the next decade. Parliamentary reporting became a central feature of the *Morning Chronicle*, and it proudly headed its 'Parliamentary Intelligence' in larger type than the main body font (and, later, with the debates divided up by sub-headings). When the House was in session, the masthead was also changed, with the date placed above 'Parliamentary Intelligence' rather than its old position above 'London'. Other newspapers, such as the *Morning Herald*, soon gave similar prominence to 'parliamentary intelligence' in their pages.[12]

Woodfall's success led to many stories of his prodigious memory, upon which he supposedly based his reports after sitting with his eyes closed, leaning on a walking stick and listening to the speeches, most notably during a visit to Dublin in 1784 to report on the Irish parliamentary debates. His powers of recall were such that they were described as 'supernatural' and surpassed the abilities of other contemporary shorthand reporters. Indeed, he attracted such celebrity from this ability that crowds are said to have followed 'Memory Woodfall', as he was nicknamed, on the street. Although he was trained as an actor, and no doubt possessed fine abilities of concentration and recall, he also had other methods upon which to rely. Another journalist, James Stephen, noted that Woodfall, as 'master of his own paper' and with the will to 'sacrifice all other considerations to its reputation for Parliamentary reports', waited until he had read all the other papers' reports before he sent his own to bed, in order to ensure that he missed nothing in his accounts. The *Morning Chronicle* appeared a few hours after its competitors but could thereby trade on its reputation for accuracy and completeness, as well as its purported objectivity. Woodfall's 1782 portrait by a pupil of Sir Joshua Reynolds, Thomas Beach, shows him at work, quill in hand. To his right sits a roll of paper, titled 'the Debates of the House' (the *Morning Chronicle* described Beach as 'illustrious and eminent . . . [a] natural genius').[13] In 1789 Woodfall sold his share in the *Chronicle* and founded the *Diary; or, Woodfall's Register*, which printed for the first time a report of the proceedings in both houses from the night before; selling for four pence, it only survived until 1793. Despite this, Woodfall had made a profound contribution to making the workings of parliament more open.

The failure of his paper is a reminder of the risks that smaller newspaper proprietors took, while major papers had become increasingly profitable. By the 1780s annual profits were around £2,000, and would triple or more in the case of *The Star* or the *Morning Herald*. Some, such as the *Morning Chronicle*, which Woodfall had at one point had a share, made £12,000 a year by the 1820s. And in 1803, Daniel Stuart sold the *Morning Post* for £25,000 after rescuing it from financial hardship. Towering over all these was *The Times*, which by 1819 was valued at £45,000. Provincial papers could also be remarkably successful, drawing on news found in London and other provincial papers, and finding both a ready readership and a large pool of advertisers in their local area. Newspapers also advertised themselves, with posters pasted across towns and the sound of newspaper sellers' cries were an intimate, and loud, part of cities and towns' aural landscapes. Some proprietors, such as Ann Ward of the *York Courant*, also found it congenial to live in London and engage a local editor to run their paper in its home town.[14]

Woodfall knew the benefits of being close to the centre of things, attempting to translate this access to political information to profit and public benefit. Woodfall regularly approached participants directly and appealed to speakers for their speeches for his paper, as his surviving letters reveal. For example, he wrote to tea merchant Richard Twining in December 1794, letting him know that he was 'preparing a Report of the Debate at the India House of Wednesday last' and that 'if it suited your wishes to convey what you said in the course of the Debate, though the medium of my Report, I will provide accordingly, having no object but an impartial communication of what passed.'[15] Even here, Woodfall was aware of the value of information, and notes that Twining may have had his own plans for publication. Woodfall often made use of such methods, pestering parliamentary speakers for notes of their speeches, writing to William Adam in 1784, for example, 'Can you help me by loosely throwing upon paper any points you recollect to be strongly put which have not appeared or have not been given in the papers already?'[16] It might be noted that this was not too onerous a demand on the speakers, as rather than spontaneous debate, speakers in both Houses tended to prepare their speeches in advance, often with a view to publication.

Woodfall made his methods plain in the preface to his report on the Dublin debates, *An Impartial Sketch of the Debate in the House of Commons of Ireland in 1785*, which he tellingly dedicated to 'The Publick'. *An Impartial Sketch* was, of course, a more authoritative publication than a newspaper, but it speaks both of his reputation and his methods. Woodfall, as the self-styled 'Reporter', informed his audience that he had 'spared no pains' to 'render his sketch as authentic as possible'. His reputation, and by extension a recognition of the role of the newspaper press in everyday life, was noted in number 86 of the Reverend Vicesimus Knox's influential and much reprinted *Essays Moral and Literary* of 1778 included a somewhat dismissive comparison of artistic and political women. The former's 'reading was chiefly confined to the poetry corner in newspapers', while the latter – who sometimes 'ventured to contribute a paragraph or two' – derives 'all of her learning' from a 'Say or a Woodfall' (the irony perhaps here

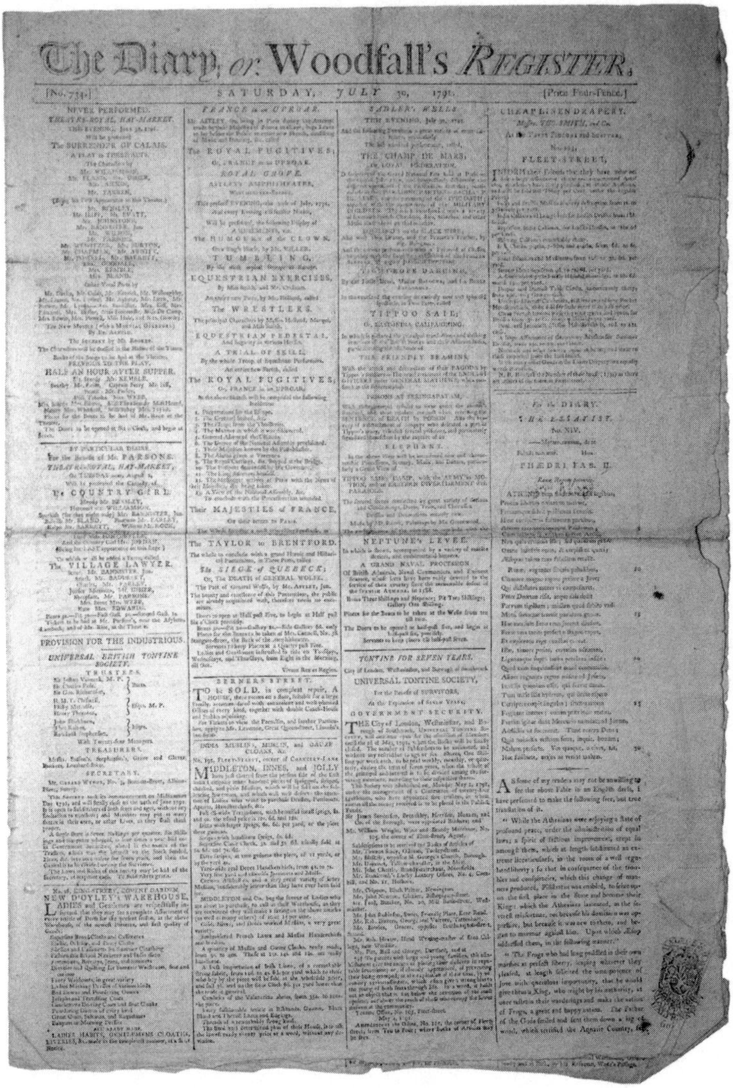

The Diary; or, Woodfall's REGISTER.

[No. 734.] SATURDAY, JULY 30, 1791. [Price Four-Pence.]

NEVER PERFORMED.

THEATRE-ROYAL, HAY-MARKET.

The SURRENDER of CALAIS.

HALF AN HOUR AFTER SUPPER.

The COUNTRY GIRL.

The VILLAGE LAWYER.

PROVISION FOR THE INDUSTRIOUS.

UNIVERSAL BRITISH TONTINE SOCIETY.

TRUSTEES.

TREASURERS.

SECRETARY.

NEW D'OYLEY's WAREHOUSE.

FRANCE in an UPROAR.

The ROYAL FUGITIVES;

ROYAL GROVE.

ASTLEY's AMPHITHEATRE,

TUMBLING.

EQUESTRIAN EXERCISES,

The WRESTLERS.

EQUESTRIAN PEDESTAL.

A TRIAL OF SKILL.

The ROYAL FUGITIVES,

Or, FRANCE in an UPROAR.

Their MAJESTIES of FRANCE,

The TAYLOR to BRENTFORD.

The SIEGE of QUEBECK;

Or, The DEATH of GENERAL WOLFE.

BERNERS STREET.

TO be SOLD, in compleat repair, A HOUSE,

INDIA MUSLINS, MUSLIN, and GAUZE CLOAKS, &c.

MIDDLETON, INNES, and JOLLY

SADLER's WELLS.

THE CHAMP DE MARS;

TIPPOO SAIB;

THE FRIENDLY BRAMINS.

PRISONS AT SERINGAPATAM.

NEPTUNE's LEVEE.

A GRAND NAVAL PROCESSION

TONTINE FOR SEVEN YEARS.

UNIVERSAL TONTINE SOCIETY,

GOVERNMENT SECURITY.

CHEAP LINEN DRAPERY.

FLEET-STREET,

For the DIARY.

THE ESSAYIST.

No. XIV.

PHAEDRI FAB. II.

As some of my readers may not be unwilling to see the above Fable in an English dress, I have performed to make the following free, but true translation of it.

Diary; or, Woodfall's Register, 30 July 1791.

being that 'Say' is most likely Mary Say, who published three newspapers in London). Knox also noted that 'the newspaper forms the whole library of the politician.'[17] The interconnections between journalism and politics were to have revolutionary consequences in France, America and beyond.

3
Colonial Papers

Modern-day newspapers are rarely the product of purely local forces. Most are owned by international corporations or overseas interests. As well as the financial underpinnings of the news industry, many of the personnel in the anglophone world are expats, with journalists often working on both sides of the Atlantic, whether freelance or on the payroll. Tellingly, perhaps, this seems less true of the connections between Britain and the Continent, with Robert Maxwell's *European* daily newspaper failing to find much popular traction in the 1990s. Newspapers are also concerned with foreign affairs and no national paper would today be considered complete without overseas news reporting, whether via a bureau or their own correspondents (although many have dramatically reduced their overseas commitments). More recently, digests of high-profile papers are included in their transatlantic, or cross-channel partners: for example, the *New York Times* partnered with the British *Telegraph* online and in print from 2004, while in 2010 the dissemination and analysis of some of the WikiLeaks diplomatic cables material were handled by a consortium of papers with a shared liberal outlook in Britain, Germany, France and the U.S. There were earlier precedents for such international connections. The influential North American journalist and editor James Gordon Bennett Jr began the *International Herald Tribune* in 1887 as the *Paris Herald* (which closed its Paris newsroom in 2016 when it was finally rolled into the *New York Times* International Edition). More informal exchanges existed long before these transatlantic interchanges, with papers happily reprinting the copy of their overseas cousins in the eighteenth century, reporting the latest news from foreign capitals, often with only minor changes and typically without permission or compensating the original papers. During the nineteenth century, papers and printers also made liberal use of the serial publications of novels and other stories that were closely tied into the popular consumption and publication networks used by newspapers. Part works by novelists, notably Charles Dickens and Anthony Trollope, were a matter of intense competition, to the extent that American publishers had runners at the Port of London ready to race the latest work across the Atlantic ahead of the competition and speed pirated editions into print.

In the 2010s both the UK *Daily Mail* and *The Guardian* focused on their U.S. online sites, with the *Daily Mail* finding great success in terms of page hits and advertising revenue. But news also travelled across the seas in the eighteenth century; indeed, one could argue that such cross-channel and trans-Atlantic connections were as strong in an age when transit by water was faster than muddy roads, and the news of Paris or London fashions or politics were crucial information in the reading rooms of Bridgetown, Philadelphia, New York or Boston. In the age of sail, one of the most valuable contributions that the press could offer to the commerce of the day was the exchange of information about shipping news and the current prices of far-flung commodities such as Baltic wood or Cuban molasses.[1] And as the ships criss-crossed the oceans and navigated rivers, carrying cargo and passengers, their holds could easily accommodate a few trunks of the most current newspapers that could be happily exchanged for specie, bills of trade or bottles of rum to take the edge off the month-long (or more) crossing. Just as trade was the thread which bound empires together and linked nations with others, so the news that traders carried helped imaginatively to link lands and peoples together. Ideas of Englishness or Americanness were in part created by the reading of papers, with news from other cities, counties or the metropolis helping to define identity for their readers. At the same time, newspaper printers' continuing interest in foreign affairs (notably, for Protestant America and Britain, the troubling affairs of Catholic countries) helped to define the 'other'.

News in the American Colonies

By the 1760s Colonial America was relatively well provided-for by newspapers. Nearly every colony had one or two of its own newspapers, along with overseas papers that ships brought from Europe as regularly as they could, weather permitting. As the printer of the *New-York Gazette; or, Weekly Post-Boy* James Parker noted, no doubt with some self-interest, newspapers were 'the Amusement we can't be without'. Benjamin Franklin believed that there were 25 papers in the colonies by 1770, and Boston, in which he had learnt his trade as a printer and editor, could boast a substantial proportion of all the papers produced in Britain's overseas empire.[2] Major ports such as Savannah, Philadelphia, New York or Boston also had new news arriving via sail each week, and like the British provincial press, local printers turned these 'fresh advices' into newspapers, acting as editor and publisher.[3] The Caribbean sugar and tobacco islands also offered another route for waterborne news to arrive, with papers in Barbados and Jamaica making particular use of these relatively fresh sources of news from Europe, as well as information on the trade in enslaved people from West Africa that underpinned these economies. Printers found that papers could be a successful business proposition: they brought in advertisers, they could be exchanged with other printers and suppliers for stock and materials, and they attracted the all-important 'job printing', such as posters, calling cards or printed forms, that constituted their financial life-blood.

Newspapers had a physical presence beyond the folder paper; both in the person of the printer and in his or her print shop, which acted as a place of exchange and a holder of letters and brought the printer a certain cachet in their community. Along with printing newspapers, printers and printing offices acted as community hubs. William Bradford, for example, could be found in Philadelphia at 'the Sign of the Bible where people may be supplied with this Paper at Ten Shillings a Year . . . and where Advertisements are taken in' at the 'Corner House of Front and Market Street'.[4] The papers themselves were easily transported, and with their relatively thick linen rag paper were robust enough to last well. Typically four pages in size, and printed in runs of several hundred to a few thousand, colonial newspapers carried numerous advertisements, the occasional letter and a few columns of international, colonial and local news. These snippets were arranged from oldest to newest, as the printer's metal type was laid out as news arrived. The printer might also retain a space for a short editorial. Such paragraphs proved to be an important vehicle for the formation and dissemination of political opinion as relations between Britain and America were tested from the 1760s.

We have seen in the previous two chapters something of how newspapers developed in Europe from the seventeenth century. At first, they were largely the tools of merchants and those with political interests. Increasingly, they also spoke to a broader public, and, as their numbers increased in terms of both titles and numbers of papers issued, they employed a growing number of workers from all social classes: secretaries providing official news, printers acting as editors and proto-journalists, ink-makers, journeymen, wives and widows composing and printing the pages, folders and packagers of the finished newspapers, wholesalers, booksellers and street hawkers. To this we can add the more specialist trades who created the type and machinery, and itinerant workers who gathered rags to create paper, as well as the beaters, wiremen and dyers of the paper-making trades. Franklin remarked in his autobiography that his wife, Deborah, 'assisted me chearfully in my Business, folding and stitching Pamphlets, tending Shop, purchasing old Linen Rags for the Paper-makers, &c. &c.'[5] In the Americas printers also owned slaves who worked on the papers, including Franklin, whose enslaved assistant Peter Fleet helped to print the *Boston Evening-Post* in the 1740s. A successful printer might also need a bookkeeper to deal with their accounts. Additionally, newspapers came into contact with the machinery of the state: paper and sometimes papers were taxed. They certainly attracted the attention of the censor. In such ways, newspapers, their producers and their consumers were tied into their local and national communities. The newspaper as an object, as well as its content, increasingly helped to form these identities.

News and newspapers played a vital role in the genesis and development of American self-consciousness.[6] Colonial society was at

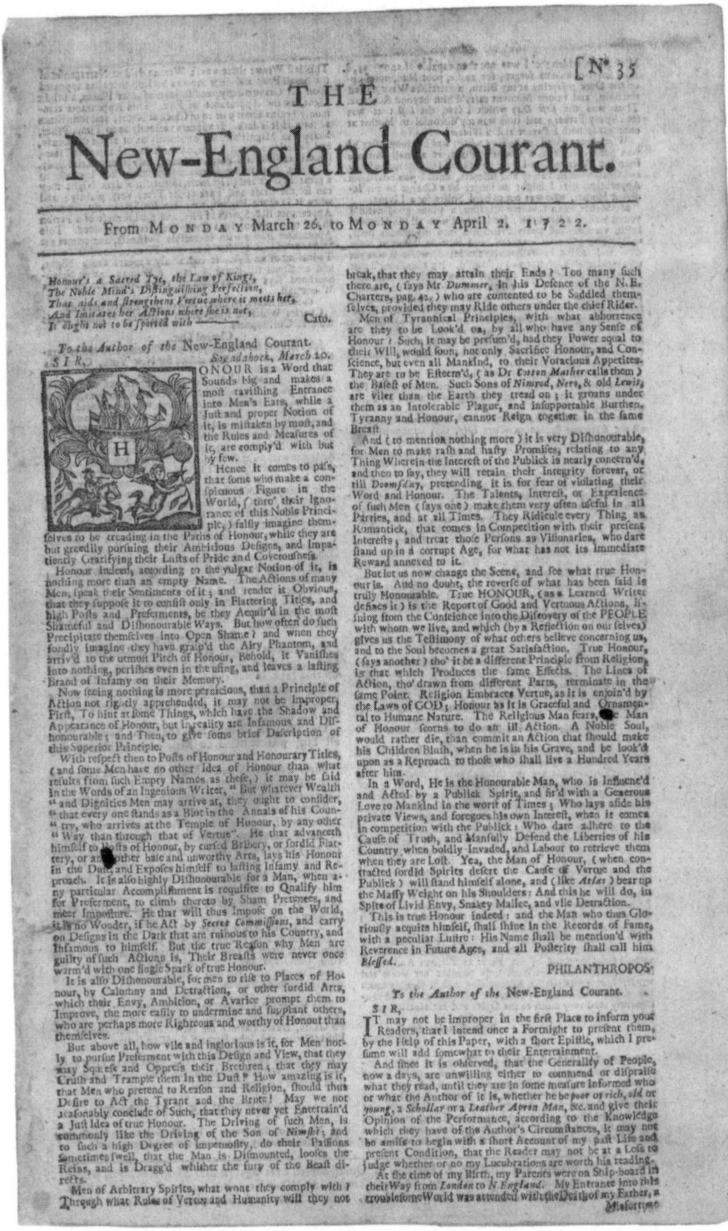

[No 35

THE

New-England Courant.

From MONDAY March 26. to MONDAY April 2. 1722.

Honour's a Sacred Tye, the Law of Kings,
The Noble Mind's Distinguishing Perfection,
That aids and strengthens Vertue where it meets her,
And Imitates her Actions where she is not,
It ought not to be sported with ——— Cato.

To the Author of the New-England Courant.

Sagadahock, March 20.

SIR,

HONOUR is a Word that Sounds big and makes a most ravishing Entrance into Men's Ears, while a Just and proper Notion of it, is mistaken by most, and the Rules and Measures of it, are comply'd with but by few.

Hence it comes to pass, that some who make a conspicious Figure in the World, (thro' their Ignorance of this Noble Principle,) falsly imagine themselves to be treading in the Paths of Honour, while they are but greedily pursuing their Ambitious Designs, and Impatiently Gratifying their Lusts of Pride and Covetousness.

Honour Indeed, according to the vulgar Notion of it, is nothing more than an empty Name. The Actions of many Men, speak their Sentiments of it; and render it Obvious, that they suppose it to consist only in Flattering Titles, and high Posts and Preferments, be they Acquir'd in the most Shameful and Dishonourable Ways. But how often do such Precipitate themselves into Open Shame? and when they fondly imagine they have grasp'd the Airy Phantom, and arriv'd to the utmost Pitch of Honour, Behold, it Vanishes into nothing, perishes even in the using, and leaves a lasting Brand of Infamy on their Memory.

Now seeing nothing is more pernicious, than a Principle of Action not rightly apprehended, it may not be improper, First, To hint at some Things, which have the Shadow and Appearance of Honour, but in reality are Infamous and Dishonourable; and Then, to give some brief Description of this Superior Principle.

With respect then to Posts of Honour and Honourary Titles, (and some Men have no other Idea of Honour than what results from such Empty Names as these,) it may be said in the Words of an Ingenious Writer, " But whatever Wealth " and Dignities Men may arrive at, they ought to consider, " that every one stands as a Blot in the Annals of his Coun- " try, who arrives at the Temple of Honour, by any other " Way than through that of Vertue". He that advanceth himself to Posts of Honour, by cursed Bribery, or sordid Flattery, or any other base and unworthy Arts, lays his Honour in the Dust, and Exposes himself to lasting Infamy and Reproach. It is also highly Dishonourable for a Man, when any particular Accomplishment is requisite to Qualify him for Preferment, to climb thereto by Sham Pretences, and meer Imposture. He that will thus Impose on the World, it is no Wonder, if he Act by *Secret Commissions*, and carry on Designs in the Dark that are ruinous to his Country, and Infamous to himself. But the true Reason why Men are guilty of such Actions is, Their Breasts were never once warm'd with one single Spark of true Honour.

It is also Dishonourable, for men to rise to Places of Honour, by Calumny and Detraction, or other sordid Arts, which their Envy, Ambition, or Avarice prompt them to Improve, the more easily to undermine and supplant others, who are perhaps more Righteous and worthy of Honour than themselves.

But above all, how vile and inglorious is it, for Men hotly to pursue Preferment with this Design and View, that they may Squeese and Oppress their Brethren; that they may Crush and Trample them in the Dust? How amazing is it, that Men who pretend to Reason and Religion, should thus Desire to Act the Tyrant and the Brute! May we not reasonably conclude of Such, that they never yet Entertain'd a Just Idea of true Honour. The Driving of such Men, is commonly like the Driving of the Son of *Nimshi*; and to such a high Degree of impetuosity, do their Passions sometimes swell, that the Man is Dismounted, looses the Reins, and is Dragg'd whither the fury of the Beast directs.

Men of Arbitrary Spirits, what wont they comply with? Through what Rules of Vertue and Humanity will they not break, that they may attain their Ends? Too many such there are, (says Mr *Dummer*, in his Defence of the N. E. Charters, pag. 42.) who are contented to be Saddled themselves, provided they may Ride others under the chief Rider.

Men of Tyrannical Principles, with what abhorrence are they to be Look'd on, by all who have any Sense of Honour? Such, it may be presum'd, had they Power equal to their Will, would soon, not only Sacrifice Honour, and Conscience, but even all Mankind, to their Voracious Appetites. They are to be Esteem'd, (as Dr *Cotton Mather* calls them) the Basest of Men. Such Sons of *Nimrod*, *Nero*, & old *Lewis*, are viler than the Earth they tread on; it groans under them as an Intolerable Plague, and insupportable Burthen. Tyranny and Honour, cannot Reign together in the same Breast.

And (to mention nothing more) it is very Dishonourable, for Men to make rash and hasty Promises, relating to any Thing Wherein the Interest of the Publick is nearly concern'd, and then to say, they will retain their Integrity forever, or till *Doomsday*, pretending it is for fear of violating their Word and Honour. The Talents, Interest, or Experience of such Men (says one) make them very often useful in all Parties, and at all Times. They Ridicule every Thing as Romantick, that comes in Competition with their present Interests; and treat those Persons as Visionaries, who dare stand up in a corrupt Age, for what has not its Immediate Reward annexed to it.

But let us now change the Scene, and see what true Honour is. And no doubt, the reverse of what has been said is truly Honourable. True HONOUR, (as a Learned Writer defines it) is the Report of Good and Vertuous Actions, issuing from the Conscience into the Discovery of the PEOPLE with whom we live, and which (by a Reflection on our selves) gives us the Testimony of what others believe concerning us, and to the Soul becomes a great Satisfaction. True Honour, (says another) tho' it be a different Principle from Religion, is that which Produces the same Effects. The Lines of Action, tho' drawn from different Parts, terminate in the same Point. Religion Embraces Vertue, as it is enjoin'd by the Laws of GOD; Honour as it is Graceful and Ornamental to Humane Nature. The Religious Man fears, the Man of Honour scorns to do an ill Action. A Noble Soul, would rather die, than commit an Action that should make his Children Blush, when he is in his Grave, and be look'd upon as a Reproach to those who shall live a Hundred Years after him.

In a Word, He is the Honourable Man, who is Influenc'd and Acted by a Publick Spirit, and fir'd with a Generous Love to Mankind in the worst of Times; Who lays aside his private Views, and foregoes his own Interest, when it comes in competition with the Publick: Who dare adhere to the Cause of Truth, and Manfully Defend the Liberties of his Country when boldly Invaded, and Labour to retrieve them when they are Lost. Yea, the Man of Honour, (when contracted sordid Spirits desert the Cause of Vertue and the Publick) will stand himself alone, and (like *Atlas*) bear up the Massy Weight on his Shoulders: And this he will do, in Spite of Livid Envy, Snakey Malice, and vile Detraction.

This is true Honour indeed: and the Man who thus Gloriously acquits himself, shall shine in the Records of Fame, with a peculiar Lustre: His Name shall be mention'd with Reverence in Future Ages, and all Posterity shall call him *Blessed*.

PHILANTHROPOS.

To the Author of the New-England Courant.

SIR,

IT may not be improper in the first Place to inform your Readers, that I intend once a Fortnight to present them, by the Help of this Paper, with a short Epistle, which I presume will add somewhat to their Entertainment.

And since it is observed, that the Generality of People, now a days, are unwilling either to commend or dispraise what they read, until they are in some measure informed who or what the Author of it is, whether he be *poor* or *rich*, *old* or *young*, a *Schollar* or a *Leather Apron Man*, &c. and give their Opinion of the Performance, according to the Knowledge which they have of the Author's Circumstances, it may not be amiss to begin with a short Account of my past Life and present Condition, that the Reader may not be at a Loss to judge whether or no my Lucubrations are worth his reading.

At the time of my Birth, my Parents were on Ship-board in their Way from *London* to *N. England*. My Entrance into this troublesome World was attended with the Death of my Father, a

Misfortune

New-England Courant, 26 March–2 April 1722.

once nascent and connected to the British metropolis. Some settlers had left to escape the Old World, while others were seeking new opportunities without turning their backs on Britain. Commercial, familial and cultural links continued to tie the American colonies to Britain, even as a distinct sense of American identity was forged, particularly in the latter half of the eighteenth century, when the bonds that linked Britain to her colonies were tested and torn. It was also a process that went two ways, and informed British identity, too. Indeed, as Daniel O'Quinn argues, the American War of Independence led to a 'reconstitution of British subjectivities', or awareness of self. In particular, he neatly links the real and imagined spaces of the newspaper and theatrical performances that reflected a thirst for 'news', which gave voice to how Britons thought about themselves during the loss of Empire. In the relative dark of the theatre, whose productions often included allusion to or direct discussion of the latest events in the American War, or in reading or discussing that day's papers, questions about nation and the empire were played out. Such events also sold. O'Quinn highlights the commercial impetus behind the press and stage, noting that in John Wilkes's innovative – and illegal – 1771 publication of parliamentary debates in the *Middlesex Journal*, *The Gazetteer* and the *London Evening Post*, while he and 'his supporters pushed on the limits of the law for political reasons . . . the printers wanted to print parliamentary debates because they sold papers. Readers wanted access to parliamentary debate because of the intense interest in the furore surrounding events in America.'[7]

Wilkes provides a particularly lively example of how news operated on both sides of the Atlantic in the mid-eighteenth century. Wilkes was not just news in London or Glasgow, but was of concern to Englishwomen and men living in the North American colonies. In 1763 reports of Wilkes's earlier incarceration for the publication of issue 45 of the *North Briton*, which criticized George III and the terms of the Treaty of Paris, could be read in American papers not long after it was reported in Britain. The *New-York Gazette*, which often received some of the first ships out of Falmouth, reported an 'extract of a Letter from London', dated 30 April, in its 20 June issue. The letter – something we now predominantly think of as private, but which was rarely the case in the eighteenth century – suggested that Wilkes's imprisonment for compromising parliamentary privilege would 'no doubt make a terrible Noise, and no doubt the City will be all on Fire upon the Occasion . . . It is probable that Mr Wilkes will remain in the Tower until Parliament meets.' The next sentence on the page read – and arguably this is the important bit in the newspaper's column for New York readers – 'Capt. — of the Charlestown, is to leave London for New York, in 3 or 4 days'. More reports, it seems, were on the way across the Atlantic, along, of course, with more physical cargo.

On the same page as the *New-York Gazette*'s reprinting of the London letter, the reader of the paper – or, rather, readers, given the nature of how a newspaper was read together or passed around a coffeehouse, tavern or club (American statesman and Founding Father John Adams, for example, noted in his diary that he visited a New York coffeehouse 'full of Gentlemen' to read the papers) – could read a full account of much more grizzly 'Noise', as the paper phrased it.[8] Letters had arrived at Philadelphia from Fort Pitt and Fort Bedford, detailing clashes between the Delaware, Shawnee, Mingo and Wyandot Native American and British settlers and military. The letter from Fort Bedford prefaces its remarks in this fashion: 'As the news current must have reached you, with various Circumstances, e'er now, the following is the most authentic that I can as yet depend on.' The report then details the scalping of two soldiers, two women and a child during Pontiac's War, along with a fight between a soldier, who carried off a piece of an ear of a Native American, whom he left for dead 'under the water'. By August 1763, half a year after the conclusion of the Treaty of Paris that had been attacked by Wilkes in the *North Briton* in April, the French and Indian War came to what seemed to be an end. Colonel Bouquet and five hundred soldiers were victors at the Battle of Bushy Run Creek and relieved the Siege of Fort Pitt. Newspapers were quickly marshalled to celebrate this victory (a temporary one, it transpired), bells rang all night in Philadelphia, and George III added his voice to the triumph.

The report, which we can suspect to have been at least partly propagandistic in intent, is also couched in the language of objectivity

– a key feature of a newspaper's claim to truth. The letter-writer understands the value of information and the special value placed upon its veracity. This, no doubt, was also something valued by the editor who put the newspaper together. News reporting, it was also recognized, was imperfect, and it followed that inferences had to be made by pulling together evidence. Another entry on the same page carried a couple of 'Intelligences' from Albany, below sections copied from letters which suggested that there was reason to fear an attack on Fort Augusta. Each snippet of news, which ran without much discernible order in three or four columns across the page, is prefaced by a line or two that explain the source: again and again, the printer laid out over time the phrases 'we hear', 'A recent letter from London reports', and so forth. This was in part a rhetorical habit that reminds the reader that this is 'news', in part a claim to truth and authenticity, and, no doubt, in part a sleight of hand by the printer. The mid- to late eighteenth-century newspaper was filled with forms of language that placed the reader and printer firmly and explicitly within a network of correspondents, newspaper 'clubs', ships' captains and, of course, other newspapers.

As well as attesting to the interest in veracity (and, arguably, its commercial benefits), this example – taken somewhat at random – speaks of the networks present in the production and consumption of newspapers.[9] Far more than a folded broadsheet carrying advertisements and recycled news, the paper is carrying on a conversation in terms understood by its producer and consumer, the printer and the reader, which link them to their community and the wider world. It tied the local credit networks on which printers so desperately relied for their business with local elites and, as the historian Joseph M. Adelman notes, 'long-distance information suppliers'.[10] The Atlantic world was made conceivable on the physical black-and-white pages of the printed newspaper, held between two hands. Our imagined reader, perhaps sitting in a tavern near the Battery in New York or at Spring Garden by King's College (advertised in the paper as under new ownership), was placed neatly between east and west a narrow gutter on the page balancing and connecting news from London and from the Ohio Valley. Here, the local, the national and the transatlantic all sit in some measure of comfort on the same physical page.

It was, of course, a view of the world that both presented and reinforced white, European dominance, in which their hierarchy of power – London, the colonies, the enslaved – were reflected in the language and content of newspapers. News of the enslaved workers' rebellion near the Stono river in 1739, for example, which took eight weeks to arrive in London via manuscript letter, presented events in a certain way. At least four of the London papers, the *London Evening Post*, the *Daily Gazetteer*, the *Daily Post* and the *London and Country Journal*, immediately ran with the news, which it knew would be of concern to its readers, many of whom depended on the fruits of the Atlantic slave economy. The time-delay no doubt only exacerbated concerns for their human property. The report in the *Daily Gazetteer* reassured such readers that the colonists had been able to kill 'about 30 and drove the rest into the swamps where they must either surrender or be put to the sword'. Slave revolts and insurrections were a common concern in the colonial, and British, press. As the print historian Catherine Armstrong notes, the language used in the press depicted the 'slaves as skulking in the swampland', whereas the South Carolina General Assembly reported these people as 'moving confidently around the built environment: "they bent their course to the southward burning all the houses on the road."'[11] The press reinforced racial differences and the inequalities of colonialism, while presenting the settler society of colonial America as normal, rational and as part of the proven order of things.

Cutting Up the Press

The editorial labour in creating newspapers drew on this shared web of information and dissemination of news via the press. Anyone reading eighteenth-century papers today will be struck by the prevalence of what is termed 'scissors and paste-pot' journalism; that is, the snipping of stories from other papers and sticking them onto their own pages, usually, but not always, without attribution. Such borrowings took many forms. Benjamin Franklin recalled, 'I consider'd my Newspaper also as another Means of Communicating Instruction, and in that View frequently reprinted in it Extracts from the Spectator and other moral Writers.'[12] John Adams offers us a sense of how newspapers were prepared, taking materials from wherever one could, noting one evening in 1769 spent 'preparing for the Next Days Newspaper – a curious Employment. Cooking up Paragraphs, Articles, Occurences, &c. – working the political Engine!'[13] The *Philadelphia Journal*, to take just one example of many, reprinted William Livingston's conservative 'Sentinel' column from the *New York Gazette* in 1765, a political choice as well as a means of making up the paper. Livingston later wrote under the pseudonym 'The American Whig' on the subject of the Stamp Act and its related riots, 'I could not look on the late tumults and commotions occasioned by the unhappy Stamp Act, without the most tender concern, knowing the consequences ever to be dreaded, of a rupture between the mother country and these plantations, which is an event never to be desired by those who are true friends to either.'[14] Franklin and William Hunter of Virginia were appointed deputy postmasters in 1758 and soon established the postage-free exchange of newspapers, sharing information across the colonies, in order 'not to discourage the Spreading the News-papers, which are on many Occasions useful to Government, and advantageous to commerce, and to the Publick'.[15] Snippets of news regularly passed also between the print shops via the post, often battling with the weather and geography. In March 1766, for example, the *Boston Gazette* noted that a snowstorm at 10 p.m. on Thursday had prevented the eastern post making the crossing with the Charlestown Ferry. It informed its readers that the storm 'we imagine has hindered the Southern and Western Mails, as they are not arrived at this Publication'. This said, readers could be reassured that 'the OBSERVATIONS on Mr J's Criticism, we have receiv'd,' and the editor 'shall give them a Place in our next'.[16]

As a way of creating papers, this practice of postal exchange came into its own in the new American Republic following the passing of the 1793 Act that secured the right for editors to exchange newspapers freely via the U.S. Post Office, and enforced low postal rates for subscribers, ensuring that during the nineteenth century printers 'put out-of-town news into local hot lead as soon as a pony rider and his bag arrived'.[17] This practice was also true for the hand-press era, when type was still cold and laid out as the news arrived, usually from ship at the ports of Boston, New York and Philadelphia. There could even be news about the arrival – or non-arrival – of news from Britain, as the *Boston Evening-Post* in January 1766 shows: 'We hear that there is an English Print of 14th of Nov. at Marblehead, which is not yet come to hand.' The demand for news of British political responses to the Stamp Act crisis is palpable here, as it was a year earlier: '*There are reports*,' inserted the editor in italics after details of the arrival of two ships in late 1765, '*of another ship with the English Prints*.' The *Boston Gazette*'s editor also had disappointing news for his readers: 'Yesterday arrived the Lord Hyde Packet boat, Capt. Goddard, from Falmouth, but brings no papers so late as have been brought by other vessels.'[18] There could also be news about more news to come, such as the detail of debates in London: 'It is reported that Sir GEORGE SAVILE, Sir WILLIAM BAKER, and some other, Members of Parliament, spoke in favor of the Colonies as well as Gen. CONWAY and Mr BARRE, but the Speeches of the two last mentioned Gentlemen only have as yet been seen in Print.' The efforts of Boyer, Wilkes and others to enable reporting on Parliament reverberated across the oceans.[19]

Such activities also drew on the parasitic relationship between newspapers and newsletters and other forms of handwritten information dissemination. The explicit acknowledgement of the use of letters fulfilled two functions. It nodded to the earlier privileging of letter-writing over print, an activity that continued well into the eighteenth century as a systematic form of exchanging news. This represented access to information that only the rich and powerful could afford, even forming, in the historian Andrew Pettegree's phrase, 'a central attribute of power', although these circles of access expanded over time in the form of merchants' letters and corresponding societies.[20] Such networks existed in the colonies: the Boston postmasters Duncan and his son John Campbell, like their predecessors in the post, made use of their position to collate and disseminate information. From around 1702 John Campbell produced a weekly newsletter on European affairs derived from the *London Gazette* and other papers, which he sent to Governor Fitz-John Winthrop of Connecticut and, it is suspected, other leading New England figures. It is likely that other postmasters did much the same.[21] From the earliest days of printed newspapers they were cast as an economical and notably less sophisticated alternative to manuscript newsletters, in which news was shared widely and hence lost something of its scarcity value as a commodity formerly limited to diplomats, merchants, ministers of the king – and the king himself. Second, including information about the epistolary origins of information helped to place the newspaper within its transatlantic context, an acknowledgement of the existence of that wider world, and, in paper and ink form, a way of representing it. By the 1760s, though, there was also a recognition that the small typefaces and several columns of the newspapers enabled a greater density of news, some of it possibly fresher, than could be glossed, analysed and sent on in letter form.[22] In 1762 a William Burns wrote to the publisher Thomas Bradford in Trenton, sharing a concern for the culture of the newspaper and a recognition of the role of the letter, asking him to 'Please to send me the News papers and direct them to me near Penington.'[23] Campbell also took the step into newspaper production, founding the *News-letter*, which was modelled in format and content on the *London Gazette*, and was also, it was claimed on the masthead, 'printed by authority'.[24]

As well helping to tie together the Atlantic world, at least for literate free men and women, the press helped to form American connections and an American identity. If the colonial press relied on the supply of papers and letters from Europe, it also relied on good connections between the newspaper printers along the Eastern seaboard. The surviving letters and papers of printers are full of attempts to gather news, maintain and grow networks of subscribers, drum up advertisements and chase payments for earlier advertisements or subscriptions. Some simply subscribed to English papers such as the *London Gazette*, but others, such as the Philadelphia printer David Hall, hired agents in London to gather and send collections of cuttings and other bits and pieces of information in each monthly packet ship. Hall's connection with his agent, William Strahan, dated from his apprenticeship in Edinburgh before he emigrated. Strahan established a successful London printing office with excellent government connections, and he was able to provide Hall with a stream of British political news for the *Pennsylvania Gazette*.[25]

The finances of newspaper production and sales also underpinned the creation of colonial networks. For example, a document in the Library Company in Philadelphia – the library founded by Benjamin Franklin and others – offers a record of the often-precarious economics of newspaper production in the New World. In the hierarchy of printing success, newspapers can be placed somewhere in the middle. Most newspapers failed, but then most books also lost money – and much more than newspapers. Successful papers, like Benjamin Franklin's *Pennsylvania Gazette,* could provide the bedrock for a printer's future commercial success, and as an item of exchange could be used to build networks with other printers around the colonies. Real money could come with government or other official contract work, notably printing posters or official records. For most printers, their finances were based on successful jobbing work, the day-to-day publication of flyers, calling cards, advertisements, blank legal and commercial forms, and other ephemeral materials, along with the annual sale of almanacs. A clear notion of where one's readers were, who owed money and who might be looking to place some advertisements were all things that an effective newspaper publisher had to keep a prudent eye upon.

A selection of advertisements from newspapers in New York and Philadelphia in early 1765 give a sense of how many aspects of colonial society, however mundane, could be found within the pages of a newspaper. They include a notice promoting Milligan's Women's Shoe Store in New York; a notice from a Robert Smith who found a lost watch in Philadelphia, and who also took the opportunity to announce that also 'continues his hatters trade as usual, and gives the highest price for furs'; and a call for a 'person capable of building and working a saw mill, about 20 miles above Winchester in Virginia'. The parents of schoolchildren in Philadelphia were advised that a Mr Tioli 'takes this method of acquainting the parents of those children whom he hath had the honour to teach, that he intends to leave this province the ensuing April'.[26] In contrast, successful squirrel hunters were in luck: 'WANTED: A Number of Ground-squirrel skins: Whoever will bring any quantity to the London Coffee-house before the twentieth of next month, shall receive Three pence for each.'[27] These local announcements reveal a mixture of commerce and everyday social life, helping to animate a local community. As well as readers consuming such advertisements, their authors would have had to visit or write to the printer and correspond with those replying to their notices.

Newspaper printers also had to master the complex infrastructure required to put the paper into the hands of its reader. Once the copy had been prepared (at least in its first state), the type had to be set at a print shop before it was printed by hand and sent to booksellers or wholesellers and passed along a dense network of street sellers and hawkers, whereby the paper would reach its purchaser or subscriber. The Library Company document mentioned above lists the subscribers to Mathew Carey's *Philadelphia Herald*, and reveals the way that the city was dotted with deliveries. These 'newspaper lads', 'printers' boys' or 'devils' responsible for these were celebrated on New Year's Day, long an occasion for gift-giving, and celebrated in broadsides. In a tradition begun in England and imported to the colonies, newspaper lads carried a specially composed poem, often reflecting on national events and the nature of news.

Printers had to invest a lot of time in maintaining these contacts to ensure that they could make a profit and find copy for their papers. Managing a network of newspaper subscribers was not a straightforward matter; nor was maintaining a group of like-minded printers, shopkeepers or riders in other towns who could be persuaded to distribute copies of the paper locally. William Bradford, the publisher of the *Pennsylvania Journal,* maintained an extensive set of subscribers, resellers and exchanges for his paper, which became a standard-bearer for the independence movement. James Askey in Lancaster wrote to Bradford in March 1766, revealing difficulties with cash flow in such an arrangement: 'I desire you insert in your next a smart advertisement in my behalf as I cannot yet pay any either for carriage of papers for last year nor the Entire money for this New Year.'[28] The *Boston Gazette* had similar issues, even with the honest folk of Massachusetts, printing in 1765 an oft-seen plea at the foot of newspapers of the age: 'All persons indebted for this Paper, whose Accounts have been above 12 Months standing, are requested to make immediate Payment.'[29] William Rind, the printer of the *Virginia Gazette*, complained, 'I hardly receive enough from my Gazette to pay the riders I am obliged to employ to dispense it; so that all my paper, the maintenance and pay of workmen, &c. &c. are hitherto sunk,' and called on his readers to pay their accounts 'to save myself and family from utter ruin'.[30] It is no wonder, as Adelman remarks, that printers 'constantly hounded, hectored, and cajoled [their subscribers] into settling their accounts'.[31] Newspapers spoke of real, physical networks and connections, as well as the ones constituted by their text. Behind the scenes, in the laying out of type and the dissemination of the printed product, a community was forged, one that might be marshalled in a period of crisis and which led to revolution and independence.

4
News and the American Revolution

On 30 November 1774 the *Pennsylvania Gazette* carried the news that the vessel *Captain Cooke* had arrived from London with the usual 'Advices'. Deeply unwell from the voyage across the Atlantic and unable to move, a 37-year-old man had to be carried off the typhoid-ridden ship after it docked on the Delaware at Philadelphia.[1] Despite his illness, the sick man could perhaps be considered fortunate: five others had died of the disease during the crossing. The invalid had also managed to secure a letter of introduction from the eminent man of science and prominent Philadelphian living in London Benjamin Franklin, furnishing him with a vital entrée into society in the eighteenth century. As luck would have it, Franklin's physician was also on the ship and arranged for the man to be carried ashore, where he recovered after six weeks.

This traveller was Thomas Paine, who, like tens of thousands before him and millions after, was seeking a fresh beginning in the New World. Recently separated from his wife Elizabeth, having been fired from his job as excise officer, failed as a tobacconist and narrowly avoided debtors' gaol by selling most of his possessions, Pennsylvania was suggested to him by friends as perhaps the only way to avoid destitution. Now remembered as the pamphleteer of two revolutions (the American and French), and a central figure in British radical history, Paine was then little known and badly connected. Yet despite these disadvantages, he had managed to obtain a letter of introduction from Philadelphia's most influential adopted son. The two men had met in London, during Franklin's long sojourn by the banks of the Thames at 36 Craven Street, and Paine's reformist zeal (he had at that point written a few pamphlets demanding an increase in pay for the excise) had impressed Franklin. Bringing news of Franklin's work in London, Paine also carried letters relating to the political crisis for Richard Bache, Franklin's son-in-law, who introduced Paine to the editor of the *Pennsylvania Magazine*. By January 1775 the Englishman had become a citizen of the city by oath and began to edit the paper.

Paine had arrived in America at the moment when a political crisis erupted into a revolution. Fuelled by inept British governance and a growing conviction of the virtue of their cause, long-simmering tensions between the American colonists and the British government could no longer be calmed. Since at least the mid-1760s, British rule in the colonies had increasingly been seen as heavy-handed by the ruled – 'tyrannical' in the language of the day. Seeking streamlined colonial administration and some financial contribution from the American colonists following the French and Indian War, the British government imposed a series of taxes and the requirement to provide housing and food for their troops. Many in the Thirteen Colonies found these measures unacceptable. Their opposition was intensified by ill-judged attempts to impose the new rules, particularly when it came to garrisoning troops. Protests and boycotts led to displays of British military might and, via pronouncements from London, a series of statements that the British had a right to govern in such a fashion. Laws were passed in the British Parliament, which was elected by British constituencies alone. Colonies were subject to this authority and colonists did not have a vote. At best, they could petition Parliament, but otherwise their cry was: 'No taxation without representation.' What might have remained economic and logistical disputes, or matters of administrative tact and style, quickly became matters of high political principle, with each side raising the stakes after every incident.

The Stamp Act Crisis

Before the Revolution, British North America was a collection of separate colonies running from the wealthy plantation economies of the British West Indies and up the eastern seaboard of America from the former Spanish colony of Florida, through the wealthy southern colonies of Virginia and Georgia, dominated by slave plantation economies, up through the Commonwealth of Massachusetts, with its strong tradition of religious and political freedoms, and to the territories of what is now Canada: Newfoundland, Nova Scotia, Rupert's Land, St John's Island and Quebec. While local power existed, usually through governors, it was based on the authority of the Crown and Parliament. Decisions could be made locally, but sovereignty resided in Britain, not in Boston, New York, Georgia or Jamestown, a fact underscored by the military might of the British Army and Navy.

Politically, culturally and economically tied to the British Empire, newspapers played a crucial role in maintaining the links between these far-flung colonists and the metropole. While many of the American colonies were well-established, life was still precarious and, for many, isolated. Although the European population was growing at the continued expense of the indigenous peoples, towns and villages were often sparsely populated. There was undoubtedly a growing American self-consciousness, but cultural, familial and economic ties with Europe remained strong, and maintaining these ties provided an important sense of security, familiarity and financial advantage. When the very existence and nature of the empire was threatened, it is perhaps not surprising that its most obvious repercussions were felt in the pages of the press.[2]

Although relatively numerous, American newspapers could suffer in comparison to the diversity of the London and British provincial press. Colonial papers were poorly funded, often irregular in production and limited in their content and size. Yet, as the last chapter showed, they fulfilled vital economic functions and were an important part of many colonists' daily lives. Any increase to the costs or viability of newspapers would be keenly felt. The four folio pages that typically constituted a colonial paper contained news, of course, but were also packed with advertisements of various kinds. These short texts, sometimes with generic illustrations of a man, a ship or an agricultural implement, provide us with a window into the world of the eighteenth century, one that is at once charming and shocking. Alongside adverts for servants, and women and men advertising their trades, one could read, for example, adverts for 'Quilting of All Kind' offered by Sara Munro in Annapolis, together with news of newly arrived ships bearing pots, pans, tools, cloth, ribbons, books, crockery, furniture, medicine and all the other items that made for a pleasant domestic environment or the smooth-running of a farm. Mixed among these are found an inescapable series of notices offering a reward for a runaway slave or a sale of enslaved people.[3] The American colonies were tied closely into the Atlantic economy, deeply embedded in a system based on the violent enslavement of millions. The sale of commodities and information about the likely price of wheat or other cash crops underpinned the economic viability of newspapers. Slavery underpinned nearly all of this, either providing much of the labour for the crops sold and hence the advertisements or desire for commercial information, or more directly funding printers and their papers through the placing of advertisements for buying, selling or hunting down enslaved men, women and children.[4] Eighteenth-century newspapers are imprinted with the reality of slavery, most visibly in the shockingly matter-of-fact fugitive and other slave advertisements, but each page is also a witness to the system of colonial capitalism in which newspapers could thrive, and which relied on the millions of hours of enslaved toil that underpinned that system.[5]

In a structural, economic fashion, newspapers were bound up in the society in which they were produced. They also fulfilled a particular function within colonial society, reliant as it was on news from the metropole, be it political, legal, military or simply catching up with royal or other gossip, as well as news of the latest book or play. Newspapers also formed the link between the local, the regional and the wider trade routes that crossed the Americas. Within such far-flung contexts, newspapers had a special meaning, providing contact with the recent (or ancestral) homeland – be it Scotland, England, Ireland, Germany or elsewhere in Europe – and a practical purpose in terms of consumption or commerce, which was important in a community without a traditional network of markets, trading routes or partners, and with a steady influx of new settlers, farmers and merchants. Newspapers helped to bind colonial society together and to bring into being a new, American one. In the often precarious environment of the New World, the information contained in newspapers could be vital. As the historian Jean B. Russo notes, where local newspapers were uncommon or non-existent, such as in Talbot County, Maryland, communities relied on local knowledge: 'anyone looking to purchase barrels, get a tool ended, or order a suit of clothes would have to rely on word-of-mouth referrals from kin or neighbours if he did not personally know the appropriate workman.'[6]

The British government made an undoubted error in allowing itself to be seen to be attacking this institution. Within the New World, the press could also stand for an ideal that was linked to the promised freedoms that led many Europeans to start a new life across the Atlantic. Freedom of thought and expression, and, for many, a Protestant view of religion that emphasized the importance of the written word in general as well as scripture in particular, ensured that the press was given a special place within the scheme of things. An attack on press freedom was potentially an attack on the reason why the colonies existed in the first place. In their attempt to secure extra finance to support the defence of the colonies, the British Parliament passed a series of Acts raising revenue through taxation on the sale of a range of products. In Britain itself, newspapers were subject to a small tax from 1757 (with most papers avoiding the Stamp Act of 1724 through various loopholes), but the notion that paper – and newspapers – could be taxed was incendiary in the colonies. The Stamp Act of 1765 was universally unpopular among the colonists, already aggrieved by the previous year's Sugar Act, and particularly affected lawyers, printers, merchants and tavern keepers, all of whom could form a nexus for organized protest. The tax extended beyond newspapers, covering all forms of printed papers. As the historian John C. Miller notes,

> Americans could not engage in commerce, exchange property with each other, recover debts, buy a newspaper, institute lawsuits or make wills, without paying for a stamp. Every diploma awarded by a college or academy required a stamp of two points, and – what was more important to the

> common man – every tavern owner who retailed spirituous liquor was obliged to pay twenty shillings for his licence.[7]

The costs of the Act combined with the symbolism of taxation of knowledge in the form of newspapers and the legal and constitutional claims made by the Crown. While the British authorities had no doubt about their right to impose such taxes, in the Americas the issue became one of freedom and the belief in local rights. These arguments flourished in the pages of the press before they spilled over into the streets, docks and fields. To take one example, on the night of 10 August 1766, Redcoats cut down the Liberty Pole that had been erected in New York. The newspaper reported that this had been done 'by Way of Insult to the Town', and 2,000 citizens marched to the Commons to demand an apology from the soldiers who were training there. Fighting soon broke out, and the newspapers reported that 'the Soldiers were intirely the Aggressors'.[8] As well as routinely presenting the patriotic side of the story, newspapers were able to present the argument that the Americans were standing for their freedoms. Letters purporting to be from London fuelled fears: one such missive suggested that the British government had kept the duty on Tea as a 'Test of American Liberty' and that its response would determine 'its future fate'. The information that newspapers carried was also vital to the course of the protests. On 31 May the *New York Journal* carried fresh intelligence from London that the tax on tea would not be removed, feeding directly into the heated debate between the colonies and their varied groups of citizens about the continuation of the boycott on British manufactures.[9]

Soon after his arrival in Philadelphia, a city of some 6,000 enslaved people and many thousands of slave-holders, it was long assumed that it was Paine who composed an essay denouncing 'African Slavery in America'. The text was published in the *Pennsylvania Journal and the Weekly Advertiser* (8 March 1775). The newspaper also carried an advertisement for a 'stout healthy young negro man'; those interested could 'enquire at the printers'.[10] Addressed to 'Americans', the article began with a striking contention: '[that] some desperate wretches should be willing to steal and enslave men by violence and murder for gain, is rather lamentable than strange. But that many civilized, nay, christianised people should approve, and be concerned in the savage practice, is surprising.' The article, it seems, begins with a display of his ability to get to the moral heart of the issue. Soon after its publication, a small group of Philadelphians founded the Society for the Relief of Free Negroes Unlawfully Held in Bondage, the first American abolition society.

Paine has since been associated with protests against slavery, even being dubbed by his early biographer, Moncure Conway, as America's first abolitionist. Eager to restore Paine's personal reputation in nineteenth-century America, Conway alighted on Paine's Quaker upbringing and sought to closely associate him with abolitionist activity wherever possible, even suggesting that he proposed a clause on slavery in the Declaration of Independence that was struck out from the final Declaration by Congress. In reality, this article followed in the footsteps of many other American critics of slavery, including Benjamin Franklin and Benjamin Rush, Paine's future colleague, who produced an abolitionist pamphlet in 1773. No friend to slavers, Paine was not the abolitionist that he was later depicted as by biographers.[11]

The text, according to the most recent linguistic and content analysis, should no longer be counted as part of the Paine canon. We are reminded of the complicated relationship that newspapers had to authorship: the newspaper imposed its own voice on its contributors, who were often disguised, anonymized or invented. We remain uncertain about the authorship or origins of much of the content of eighteenth-century papers. The by-line, if it existed, was one of the great works of eighteenth-century fiction, as can be seen from Benjamin Franklin's 'Silence Dogood' and 'Alice Addertongue' and Arthur Lee's 'Junicus Americanus'.[12] Textual play such as this made newspapers work on several levels of readership: those in the know who could decode the cipher, and those outside the circle who could read newspapers and only sense a hidden, publishing machine, which somehow had access to secrets, better information and a network of informants. All this made the papers seem much more powerful than the product of a busy printer, desperate to find copy to fill the four or so pages he or she ushered out once or twice a week in order to sell advertisements and fulfil their obligations to subscribers. It created the sense of a community, even if, as the authorship to Paine's article suggests, it was uncertain. A multiplicity of writers might instead be the creations of a single, imaginative pen.

We are, though, certain of Paine's first article, published in 24 January 1774 in the *Pennsylvania Magazine; or, American Monthly Museum*, a miscellany of literary selections, anecdotes, materials from British publications, and a summary of monthly events from London and the American colonies. It later included news of the war and military maps. Published by Robert Aitken from his shop on Front-Street and Market Streets, 'opposite the London Coffee-house', it was sited at the heart of commercial Philadelphia, right by the bustling docks of the Delaware river, which carried trade from the Caribbean along the eastern seaboard and across the Atlantic to Europe. The London Coffee House had been opened in 1754 by the printer William Bradford, who drew on funds from more than two hundred Philadelphia merchants who were seeking a meeting place in which to socialize and do business. Merchants, ships' captains and slave traders – since it was but a short distance from Philadelphia's slave market – all met here to make deals, exchange news and drink coffee, while private booths were often taken by the governor and other officials to undertake business.

Born in Dalkeith, Scotland, Aitken had emigrated to the colonies with his wife and daughters in 1769 and began as a Philadelphian bookseller shortly after. The *Magazine* was a new venture for 1775. Paine's first article made the case for its importance. Aitken later became the printer of the first Bible in America: known to historians and bibliophiles as the Aitken Bible, it was approved by Congress in 1782. Before this point, all Bibles had to be imported from England, where the Crown jealously guarded the privilege of printing editions of the King James Bible. Supplies of the text were limited during the Revolutionary War, bringing 'a famine of the word of God' (Amos 8:11) to the new nation. Prompted by a petition by Philadelphian Presbyterians, Congress offered its approval to the project, believing that an American-printed Bible would help aid morale, and Aitken cannily included this commendation to the binding of his Bibles.[13] Despite this, Aitken lost money in the venture, and other printers soon began to publish American editions of the King James Bible.

We might imagine the *Magazine* as a means of connecting Britain with America, with the corner of Front and High Street the nexus of this interchange of ideas, stories and, in Paine's case, careers. Paine's first article was titled 'The Magazine in America', and he began it by noting the 'narrow and limited' channels of communication offered by America, writing that the 'weekly papers are at present the only vehicles of public information'. The piece argues that America was outgrowing its 'infancy' and improvements in science, commerce and the arts, as well as its rising population, demanded a richer literary experience. Journals such as the *Pennsylvania Magazine*, he argues, did not just offer an additional forum for literature and science, but helped to nurture America society as it matured. As well as puffing up the importance of the *Magazine*, Paine's piece also provided a lens through which to view the relationship between Britain and America. For Paine, America was a land of opportunity and even represented a form of virtue; in contrast, the British magazines were 'the retailers of tale and nonsense' and, with a few exceptions such as the *Gentleman's Magazine*, which held on to some of the qualities of its youth, were 'no better than incentives to profligacy and dissipation'. Journalism, Paine argues, reflected the moral state of the two countries. Britain suffered from a 'dissolution of manners', while in contrast, 'degeneracy is here almost a useful word . . . there is a happy something in the climate of America.' Paine identifies the press as the main source of 'influence over the manners and moral of a People'; the press, like a fountain, pours a stream of either 'vice or virtue' over country, and nothing was 'more calculated to improve or infect than a periodical'. Through repetition and a constant search for an audience, newspapers and journals exerted a powerful hold over the public, for good or, in the case of Britain, ill. Drawing perhaps on the experience of typhoid during his Atlantic crossing, Paine notes that 'foreign vices, if they survive the voyage . . . either expire on their arrival, or linger away in incurable consumption.' They also had the advantage of their limited size: by being short, they avoided wearing the reader's patience and through concision could be more persuasive by retaining the reader's focus on the argument.

Paine continued to work for Aitken, publishing articles and poetry, such as 'The Snowdrop', which compared the *Magazine* to the shoot that 'comes forth in a barren season, and contents itself with foretelling that choicer flowers are preparing to appear', lessons drawn from nature following a stroll across the Schuylkill river, and in an article attributed to Paine an exploration of how people might fight for independence in 'Reflections on the Life and Death of Lord Clive' in India: 'I see his arrival pompously announced in every newspaper,' he noted about the general who arrived to impose British control on the subcontinent. By the summer of 1775 he was offering explicit support for the American Revolution with the publication of 'A Song, Written Early in the American Revolution' in the *Pennsylvania Magazine*. Calling for a military defence of 'our Liberty Tree' in the face of the tyrannical powers of British 'Kings, Commons, Lords', the verses were republished in the *Pennsylvania Evening Post* on 16 September 1775.

Common Sense

Around the same time, Paine had become editor of the *Pennsylvania Magazine*, and, perhaps feeling more secure in his situation, felt able to confront the towering issue of the day directly. While the troubles of the Revolution had been smouldering, and often broke into outright rebellion, the nexus of local grievances and political rights lacked a formula to bring them into sharp focus. As if in answer, Paine provided clarity with his incendiary pamphlet *Common Sense: addressed to the inhabitants of America*. Published on 9/10 January 1776 by the printer Robert Bell at his shop on Third Street, Philadelphia, this revolutionary text took the form of a short pamphlet that attacked both the idea of the monarchy and the behaviour of the British government.[14] Paine had originally intended it as a series of newspaper articles, but became convinced that it stood on its own as a pamphlet. The plain but effective title was given to him by his friend Benjamin Rush, and in it Paine set out in clear prose the case that a 'government of our own is our natural right', as well as concluding his case with rhetoric set to kindle patriotic fervour:

> O ye that love mankind! Ye that dare oppose, not only the tyranny, but the tyrant, stand forth! Every spot of the old world is overrun with oppression. Freedom hath been hunted round the globe. Asia, and Africa, have long expelled her– Europe regards her like a stranger, and England hath given her warning to depart. O! receive the fugitive, and prepare in time an asylum for mankind.

It is a powerful statement with undoubted influence, but it is possible to overstate the importance of Paine's text. There were numerous other texts making the same or a similar case; revolutionary ideology was already being developed, along with outright revolt against British forces and representatives. Paine's arguments reinforced or re-stated passions and sentiments that had already been shaped and expressed. But the numbers sold help to reveal the galvanizing effects of his prose on the revolutionary process. Bell printed 1,000 copies at first, with a second print run soon afterwards. The printer argued that he had been unable to cover his costs, and the pair fell out (Paine had planned to use any profits to buy mittens for the Continental Army in chilly Quebec), so in February, Paine published a third, augmented edition through the printers Thomas and William Bradford. This 'new edition' contained 'large and interesting additions by the author' and attempted to assuage pacifist Quaker objections to a military rebellion. It undercut Bell's in terms of price as well, selling for one shilling. Bell responded with a 'third edition', incorporating 'Large Additions to Common Sense' culled from other authors, including 'The American Patriot's Prayer' and 'The Propriety of Independency' by 'Demophilus'. The dispute was continued in the pages of the press, with both Bell and Paine denouncing each other. This did nothing to harm sales, which continued to be brisk in Philadelphia. Perhaps 150,000 copies were sold in the first three months, if Paine is to be taken at his word (and we would be cautious of so doing – a more reasonable, if still very generous, estimate suggests a total print run of 75,000 in a population of 3 million). It soon took on the mantle of having 'proselytized an entire continent' and was labelled by later historians as an eighteenth-century 'best seller'.[15] We should be suspicious of this claim, but also aware that it went through 25 editions, almost twice as many as any other pamphlet of its time. John Dickinson's *Letters from a Farmer in Pennsylvania* (1767) ran to seven editions, and Jonathan Shipley's now forgotten *Speech . . . on the Bill for Altering the Charters of the Colony of Massachusetts Bay* (1774) managed an impressive twelve American editions. No editions, however, were published in what we now call Canada, Maine, Vermont or Florida, or in the western hinterlands of territories of the other colonies. Its influence was felt most strongly in the north, in Massachusetts and Pennsylvania, and it was only printed once in the south (in Charleston). Rather than appearing like mushrooms all across America almost overnight, reprints of *Common Sense* form a trail along the northeastern seaboard, tracing the 'King's Road' that linked the cities and towns along its route from Philadelphia to Cambridge in Massachusetts.

Looking afresh at the dissemination of the pamphlet, and the problems posed by the lack of viable distribution networks, we need to turn, as Paine had originally planned, to newspapers, which carried snippets and sections of the pamphlet further and wider than the myth of the best-seller ever did. In Virginia, Thomas Jefferson noted that 'copies of the pamphlet itself had got in a few hands', although an extract 'had appeared in the Virginia papers'. Jefferson did little to help its dissemination there, despite being a supporter of Paine: he received two dozen copies from the publisher Thomas Nelson in February 1776, but appears to have done nothing further with them. It was down to entrepreneurial newspaper editors, such as John Pinkney, who spotted a single pamphlet in the Williamsburg post office waiting to be collected by the planter John Page, from which he copied out several passages before printing them over the next few days in the *Virginia Gazette*. And if the southern colonies failed to find much of interest in the pamphlet, in the north, editions suffered from disruptions to the presses by fighting and lack of resources: for example, the printer of the Salem edition apologized 'for the poor quality of the paper, owing to the scarcity of rags'.[16] The dissemination of

Common Sense seems to have been largely the result of snippets in newspapers. After all, the newspaper industry in colonial America was based on this system of exchange and reuse of texts.

Common Sense's publication and dissemination also provoked a reaction, and fuelled the divisions between those who were loyal to the British Crown and those demanding liberty. Such conflicts could be complicated, as the case of publisher Samuel Loudon demonstrates. Born in Scotland in about 1727, Loudon migrated to America in around 1760. After first working as a ship's chandler, he became a bookseller in New York from 1773, and began a printing press with Frederick Schober and Samuel Loudon in 1775. From the summer of 1776 he established the *New-York Packet*. In March he advertised that he would be selling copies of *The Deceiver Unmasked; or, Loyalty and the Interest United: In Answer to a Pamphlet Entitled Common Sense,* which was critical of Paine's *Common Sense*. As a result, the patriotic group known as the Mechanics Committee stormed his print shop, nailed shut a box containing the printed sheets and locked the door to the room where the other sheets were drying. Loudon agreed to cease its printing, but that night, around forty of the Mechanics returned and burned the 1,500 copies of *The Deceiver Unmasked* that had already been printed.[17] Each printer in the city received a notice that they could fear 'death and destruction, ruin and perdition' if they published materials opposed to Americans' 'rights and liberties'. Loudon remained a patriot, and as hostilities broke out, he fled upstate to Fishkills, returning to New York with his paper after the defeat of the British.[18]

While printers and newspapermen and -women were setting their type, events continued to gather apace. In March 1776, the Battle of Nassau saw the first actions of the Continental Navy and Marines, who captured 162 barrels of gunpowder from the Bahamas and carried them back to Connecticut in April. That month the siege of Boston ended, with the British evacuating by sea, marking General George Washington's first major victory of the war. The city that began the rebellion – Boston – was at last liberated. In early July the Second Continental Congress, gathered in Philadelphia, issued a resolution declaring independence from the British Empire, and approved the Declaration of Independence on 4 July. Fighting continued around New York over the summer, with the British gaining control of New York at the end of August in the first major battle of the Revolutionary War.

The battle between Britain and what became the United States was fought in the woods, fields and seas of America (and sometimes beyond, as the naval exploits of John Paul Jones brought the fighting to the waters off Leith in Scotland), but it also exploded on the pages of the press. Newspapers carried information about the course of the war and the political battles that surrounded it, ensuring that they played an important role in the trajectory of the war, but perhaps even more influential was their use as propaganda, in the sense that they were used to shape and firm up public opinion both in support of independence and on the British and loyalist side. Printers of newspapers had always relied on networks of exchange and communication to populate and sell their pages; during the Revolutionary era, these contacts were vital in helping to mobilize people politically, ensuring that news of British atrocities or defeats spread quickly from town to town and from one colony to another.

At the outbreak of the Revolution, there were 37 regularly published newspapers in the colonies. The war presented a series of practical and financial difficulties for printers, including the lack of paper and ink, and only twenty of the titles published at the outbreak of the war managed to last until the British defeat in 1781. New newspapers were born, but the total number only reached 35. Following the engagement at Lexington and Concord in April 1775, three patriot papers had to cease publication as they fled the city. One, Isaiah Thomas's *Massachusetts Spy*, was able to start publishing from Worcester, 65 kilometres (40 mi.) west of Boston. Benjamin Edes managed to restart publication of the *Boston Gazette* at Watertown, 16 kilometres (10 mi.) west of the city, returning to Boston in 1776. On 16 September 1777 John Adams failed to receive his usual paper, since 'Mr Dunlap has moved or packed up his Types.' The British were close on two sides and the city 'seems to be asleep, Dead, and the whole State scarce alive'; the prospect for the Americans was 'chilling, on every side. Gloomy, dark, melancholy and dispiriting'.

Adams hoped for light to 'spring up'; if it was to come it would be in the form of hopeful intelligence: 'Shall we have good News from Europe?'[19]

In 1789 the early historian of the Revolution David Ramsay argued that 'in establishing American independence, the pen and the press had merit equal to that of the sword.'[20] This view of the centrality of print and printers to the patriotic cause was solidified by the writings of those printers themselves, notably Isaiah Thomas, who would later write an influential history of American printers, *The History of Printing in America* (1810). This cast printers of the period in a historic mould, emphasizing their importance for the patriots' cause. Ever since, historians have tended to agree with this assessment of the importance of the press in mobilizing patriotic opinion and shaping the ideology of the early Republic. Some self-interest can also be detected; it paid for publishers of newspapers to follow public opinion as well as lead it.

Patriotic papers were not the only newspapers in the colonies, of course. Many in the colonies did not seek independence and instead remained loyal to the British crown. And although most newspaper

Modern-day reconstruction of a colonial printing office, Franklin Court, Philadelphia.

publishers supported the cause of Independence there were a handful of influential royalist and loyalist publications, notably in New York and some of the Southern colonies. Twelve loyalist newspapers were published in cities occupied by the British: three in New York (1776–83), one in Newport (1777–9), three in Charleston (1780–82), one in Savannah (1779–82) and one in St Augustine, Florida (1783–4).[21] Newspapers were also shipped over from Britain and other European countries, and news continued to circulate in manuscript and verbal form. Some printers attempted to maintain a form of independence, and presented the news from both sides, but soon found it impossible not to follow a partisan line.

How did news of events in the colonies spread? The distance imposed by the Atlantic Ocean imposed a time-delay, but also provided a nautical link between Britain and the Americas, with a regular supply of ships carrying the latest news. The post packet continued to dock at Falmouth, along with other ships to ports on the south coast as well as Liverpool and Dublin. From these towns, news could be sent via mail coach to London, where it reached the main papers, and was then distributed and copied back across Britain in local papers and newsletters and, of course, by word of mouth.

While the fighting took place in America (with rare nautical interventions by the American Navy under the command of Jones and the threat of French naval intervention in the Atlantic and Caribbean), the American War stamped itself into the British cultural consciousness. Military camps were established across the south coast, society concerned itself with military matters, and the politics of the day were dominated by the American crisis. News formed a continuum with a whole range of other cultural activities, from jokes shared in public houses to caricatures and painting, all of which dealt with the issues of the day, attempted to place them in their context and drew out relevant, local meanings. Nowhere was this more acute than the London stage. Here, the leading actors of the day gave voice to current concerns and spread awareness of the course of the war.[22] News of victory – or, more often towards the end of the war, defeat – was announced on stage as part of a series of plays that were malleable and adapted to the most current information. Here we find news acting as part of a wider culture that helped to create a sense of Britain's place within the world and its relationship with the colonies.

Perhaps the most striking piece of news to arrive from America during the conflict was the Declaration of Independence. Congress's 'olive branch petition' had already been rejected by the king and his ministers when it arrived in Britain, and the Declaration also overlapped with events. Agreed on 4 July, it was quickly printed by John Dunlap before a formal parchment was prepared and signed. American newspapers quickly reported the news, with the *Pennsylvania Evening Post* being the first paper to print the whole text of the Declaration on 6 July. News of Independence arrived in August on London on the *Mercury* packet ship in letters between General William Howe and Lord George Germain. The *London Gazette* included a snippet from this letter on 10 August: 'I am informed that the Continental Congress have declared the United Colonies free and independent States.' The *London Evening Post* reported later that day, 'Advice is received that the Congress resolved upon independence the 4th of July; and have declared war against Great Britain in form.' Three days later the *London Chronicle* carried the same advice, and the following day, the *Morning Chronicle and London Advertiser* alerted its readers that 'Copies of the Declarations of War by the Provincials are now in Town and are said to be couched in the strongest terms.' *The Crisis*, a patriotic paper whose early issues were burned outside the Houses of Parliament, was the first to print the document, prefacing publication in its entirety in issue 84 with the words: 'The following is the Declaration of Independence of the brave, free, and virtuous Americans, against the most dastardly, slavish, and vicious tyrant, that ever disgraced a nation, whose savage cruelties are covered under a mask of religion, Horrid impiety! Execrable hypocrisy!' The *London Chronicle* and *Lloyd's Evening Post and British Chronicle* published the text in full on 16 August, with the text reprinted in Edinburgh on 20 August and Dublin on 22 August.[23]

The Declaration was printed in Frankfurt on 23 August, and it was then disseminated throughout the Continent. The French could read the text of the Declaration through the *Gazette de Leyde*, since the dispatch from the Committee of Secret Correspondence of 7 August to Silas Deane, the American agent in Paris, never arrived, along with the instructions to translate the text into French and disseminate it through the French gazettes. The Continental newspapers continued to follow the war and its leading figures with interest. In 1780, after his ship was damaged and forced to land in Galicia, John Adams travelled through northern Spain and the Basque country on his way to Paris. At one point his trunk was held up to be searched by a government official, who was sent his passport. This 'produced a polite Message by his Clerk, that he had seen my Name in the Gazette, that he was very glad I was arrived, wished me Success and Prosperity, and desired to know if I wanted any Thing, or if he could be any Way usefull to me'.[24]

Both parties seized on the importance of the flows of information, both to plan military strategy and for propaganda purposes. In England, Franklin, who had become the colonist's representative, was desperate to dispatch up-to-date information, and placed numerous pieces in the British press in an attempt to argue the colonists' case. Eventually he was forced to leave after supplying the rebels with information stolen from General Hutchinson, revealing the plans of the British Army as it encircled Boston.

The importance of influencing British public opinion was known in America. John Adams noted in his diary that John Witherspoon, the president of the College of New Jersey (the precursor to Princeton University), believed that 'it is necessary that the Congress should raise Money and employ a Number of Writers in the Newspapers in England, to explain to the Public the American Plea, and remove the Prejudices of Britons.'[25] Such 'grey' propaganda was attempted by the revolutionaries, with Franklin placing many hundreds of pieces in British papers attempting to explain their complaints in a sympathetic light, but he also deployed more underhand propaganda methods, including in 1777 a fake letter supposedly from a German prince fighting for the British, which he composed with the – effective – aim of stirring up European opposition over Britain's use of mercenaries. The prince claimed that he was letting men die in order to increase the amounts he could charge for mercenaries. In 1782, while on a mission in Paris, he printed a fake supplement to the *Boston Independent Chronicle* (March 1782, number 705). This single sheet of paper contained two articles and a number of advertisements, making it indistinguishable from a real paper. Into this verbiage, Franklin smuggled two false letters, forming the meat of the articles. The second was a report from the American naval commander John Paul Jones that denounced the treatment of American prisoners-of-war in British jails. Few readers paid much attention to this report, but were instead taken by the gruesome content of the first letter, purportedly from Captain Samuel Gerrish, an American militia officer. He reported on a collection of captured packages that had been intercepted on route to the Governor of Canada. He was

> struck with Horror to find among the Packages, 8 large ones containing scalps of our unhappy County-folks, taken in the three last Years by the Senneka Indians from the Inhabitants of the Frontiers of New York, New Jersey, Pennsylvania, and Virginia, and sent by them as a Present to Col. Haldimand, Governor of Canada, in order to be by him transmitted to England.

The package was reported to contain a letter from a British agent, explaining the scalps:

> At the Request of the Senneka Chiefs I sent herewith to your Excellency, under the Care of James Boyd, eight Packs of Scalps, cured, dried, hooped and painted, with all the Indian triumphal Marks, of which the following is Invoice and Explanation.
>
> No. 1. 43 Scalps of Congress Soldiers killed in different Skirmishes; these are stretched on black Hoops, 4 Inches diameter; the inside of the Skin painted red, with a small black Spot to note their being killed with Bullets. Also 62 of Farmers, killed in their houses; the Hoops red; the Skin

> painted brown, and marked with a Hoe; a black Circle all round, to denote their being surprised in the Night; and a black hatchet in the Middle, signifying their being killed with that Weapon.

The agent listed the numbers of settlers who had been scalped in this way: 98 farmers killed in their houses and 97 in their fields, numerous farmers with their 'Nails pulled out by the roots', 193 boys of 'various ages' and '88 scalps of Women; hair long, braided in the Indian Fashion, to shew they were Mothers; . . . 17 others, hair very grey . . . no other Mark but the short Club . . . to shew they were knocked down dead, or had their Brains beat out.' Also included along with the account of these atrocities was a letter from a Native American king, writing to the British: 'we are poor, and you have Plenty of every Thing. We know you will send us Powder and Guns, and Knives and Hatchets: but we also want Shirts and Blankets.' Native American allies had been used many times by various sides in the North American colonies, but Franklin's purpose here was to portray the British in a cruel light, as rulers who would employ and exploit the native peoples to inflict terrible punishments on the families of honest American settlers.

The gruesome accounts fitted easily into existing methods of portraying conflict between white settlers and the native population in the British newspapers, and the letter in Franklin's fake supplement was reprinted in the *London General Advertiser and Morning Intelligencer* (29 June 1782), and John Almon's annual register, *The Remembrancer; or, Impartial Repository of Public Events*. To help shape opinion in the Continent, Franklin sent copies to Adams and the American diplomats Charles Dumas in Amsterdam and John Jay in Madrid, as well as a contact in England. The scalping letter was also picked up in America, after the *New Jersey Gazette* printed an account copied, it reported, from the *London General Advertiser* and *Boston Independent Chronicle*.[26]

News continued to have its value, as Franklin's later correspondence underscores:

> I have received your kind Letter of May 24 . . . and I wrote immediately to Mr. Childs, Printer at New York, who prints the Proceedings of Congress, that he should send them with the Newspapers to Mr. Sansom, by every Ship from that Port to London for you, promising him that some of the freshest Newspapers wish [with?] now and then a good Pamphlet should be sent him by every Ship from London to New York. This, as he prints a Newspaper will be more agreable to him than Payment in Money, and will make Accompts unnecessary.[27]

Newspapers were of use to those concerned with directing the course of the war. Although both sides used a range of intelligence-gathering methods, including deploying men and women as spies to pass on information about the location and movements of troops, grand strategy and the political picture could be informed by reports in the foreign press. While serving abroad, John Adams speculated about intercepting an English vessel, with all the possibilities for understanding the plans of the enemy that that might enable:

> Oh that We might make Prize to day of an English Vessell, lately from London, with all the Newspapers, and Magazines on board, that We might obtain the latest Intelligence, and discover the Plan of Operations for the ensuing Campaign.
>
> Whenever I arrive at any Port in Europe, whether in Spain or France, my first Enquiry should be concerning the Designs of the Enemy.[28]

Access to information before the newspapers obtained it could also be useful for political or diplomatic purposes. Those with access to reliable news could use it to their personal advantage. Writing in 1782, while in Europe, Adams noted this exchange in his diary, in which Van Asp sought to maintain his position in court:

> This Day Mr Van Asp made me a Visit. This Gentleman is Charg d'Affairs of Sweeden [sic] since the Departure of The

> Baron D'Ehrensword for Prussia. He is a solid prudent Man. He very much admired my House, and its Situation. I said smiling it was very well for a Beginning, and that I hoped We should have an House at Stockholm e'er long. He smiled in return, but said nothing. His Visit was not long. There is not a more sensible, manly, happy, or prudent Countenance in the whole Diplomatick Body. He has desired Mr. Dumas to inform him as soon as the Treaty is signed, that he may write itt to his Court before it arrives in the News papers.[29]

While the war was brought to an end for all practical purposes in North America in 1781 following the British surrender at Yorktown, Virginia, the state of war continued while all parties discussed peace. Information was power in such diplomacy, as the great powers of Britain, France, Spain and the Netherlands sought to reassemble their overseas empires to their own advantage. Where knowledge was asynchronous, one side could gain an advantage. In 1783 John Adams noted that 'Soon after the February Packet arrived, at New York, from whence English News Papers were sent out and the Provisional and Preliminary Treaties all published in the Philadelphia Papers.'[30]

From the formation of the American republic, the Founding Fathers recognized that the widespread dissemination of information was central to national unity. They realized that to succeed, a democratic government required an informed electorate, which in turn depended upon a healthy exchange of news, ideas and opinions. George Washington and Thomas Jefferson disagreed on several issues, but never on the importance of a robust free press. In 1788 Washington wrote:

> I entertain an high idea of the utility of periodical Publications: insomuch that I could heartily desire, copies of . . . Magazines, as well as common Gazettes, might spread through every city, town and village in America. I consider such easy vehicles of knowledge, more happily calculated than any other, to preserve the liberty, stimulate the industry and meliorate the morals of an enlightened and free People.

In a similar vein, Jefferson argued in 1804:

> No experiment can be more interesting than that we are now trying . . . that man may be governed by reason and truth. Our first object should therefore be, to leave open to him all the avenues to truth. The most effectual hitherto found, is the freedom of the press.

Despite the realities of the press's complicated relationship to power and objective truth, the fourth estate had become integral to the story the new nation told about itself. Printers and journalists were now seen as agents of change, and even of revolution.[31]

5
The French Revolution

At first glance, the press in pre-revolutionary France was strictly controlled. With the exception of the sole authorized newspaper, the *Gazette de France*, which by 1749 was reprinted by authority in 28 cities and paid an annual sum for the privilege, domestic newspapers were banned in the kingdom.[1] The royal censor played a central role in marking the terrain of what could and could not be discussed in the *Gazette* itself, such as any hint of criticism of the government and its policies. Printers or journalists who broke these rules risked imprisonment, the burning of their work and the seizure of their presses. There was, as many lamented, no such thing as freedom of the press in the *ancien régime*.

There were, though, always exceptions and attempts to circumvent the authorities. Newspapers were imported from overseas, and the periodical press smuggled political comment alongside cultural news or literary and advertising materials. The existence of the Royal Censor had its benefits for printers, too, since it operated as a mark of approval, giving them some protection against pirated works. Other sources of information were prevalent. Rumours, gossip, intrigue and political libel also circulated relatively widely in French society, forming a key space for political news to circulate: in the heart of Paris, specialist gossipmongers known as *nouvellistes* gathered under the infamous 'Tree of Cracow', a large chestnut tree in the Palais Royale, to tell the latest tales.[2] Political news circulated in manuscript and oral forms, such as songs and crude ballads.[3] The international, 'cosmopolitan' press, based in the papal enclave of Avignon, London or the Dutch cities (The Hague, Amsterdam, Leiden and Utrecht) and Germany and written in French, carried high-quality information of foreign affairs, and reported on insiders' views of French domestic affairs.

Other printed formats provided a medium for the transmission of news and current affairs. Almost by accident they helped to build the networks and modes of thinking that helped to support the conditions that allowed a form of public politics to take place. *Affiches*, or advertising sheets, were produced in nearly every town across France. Their function was ostensibly to provide a forum to offer goods for sale, accompanied by official announcements alongside such classified advertisements. While by no means newspapers with regular news, and certainly not carriers of opinion pieces, regularly produced texts such as these certainly contributed to the creation of what might be termed a public sphere, in that their very existence suggested the existence of a broader society. Their regularity and periodicity even helped to create a form of an 'imagined community' of the French, to use historian Benedict Anderson's phrase. Since such *affiches* were about consumption, they also helped to create what Colin Jones, their historian, has dubbed the 'great chain of buying'. A form of community, of nation, even a public sphere can be seen to be created within the minds of the network of readers of these advertiser-newspapers.

Underpinning this world of print were the writers, journalists, printers and publishers of Grub Street, men and women whose schemes, careers, hopes and fears helped to create the environment that shaped the course of the French Revolution. Many of the leading figures of the Revolution, both in its early days and at the height of the Terror, rose to prominence through their pens, and many of them had at least something of a career as a journalist or writer. For some, this exposed them to the repressive nature of the state and wider society's inability to create a space that would value their talent. Their experiences of the *ancien régime*, as it became known, and their access to the ideas and then the thoughts of other reformers, helped to shape what they wanted the new world to be like. Rumour and information also played a crucial role during the spring and summer of 1789 as the indebted French state collapsed in the face of ministerial opposition to the king and a reluctance among the aristocracy to pay taxes without a greater political say. A series of political crises were intensified by the way information and misinformation circulated, and the idea of 'revolution' itself was in part forged in the pages of the press, as it sought to describe the enormity of the political transformation that engulfed France in the late 1780s and '90s and in the process found a public eager for its product.

Revolution

The Revolution that broke out in the early summer of 1789 was a complex event, but arguments about finance were at its core. Like most European states, France was technically bankrupt in the 1780s. A series of wars culminating in France's support for the hugely expensive American War of Independence had consumed vast amounts in terms of military expenditure, in particular, a race with Britain to build the most powerful navy. The royal court and its long list of subsidized posts and positions was also a drain on finances, but perhaps it was more a signifier of corruption or excess than a genuine threat to the finances of the state itself – and, like most states, it depended on its assets and future revenues to fund itself. In this way, private money could be counted on to refill the national coffers. By comparison, Britain's national balance sheet was similar in terms of debts, but Parliament retained the confidence of the markets and a sustainable means of raising taxes.

This system relied on trust and a political framework that could resolve the difficult issues when major refinancing was required. An absolutist state was not necessarily equipped to do this. Even though the French monarchy was more absolutist in appearance than reality, since it relied on the goodwill and skilful management of the aristocracy for its survival, it demonstrated over the course of the eighteenth century an increasing inability to retool the French state. With a monarch lacking the necessary skills of court management and statesmanship, the tensions between the various factions and estates of France easily became a stalemate, revisiting long-fought battles over influence, prestige, patronage and ancient rights. Usually the king and his ministers found a path through, but the late 1780s proved to be a political crisis too far. A series of schemes of sacked or resigning finance and First Ministers, notably Charles-Alexandre de Calonne and Jacques Necker, failed to raise enough funds on the international financial markets, and their schemes also undermined public confidence in the finances of the French state. The public could read all about these affairs, notably Necker's *Compte-rendu au roi* (Report to the King, 1781), in the pages of the international press.[4] In 1788 Louis XVI called the Assembly of Notables in an attempt to find a political accommodation that the nobility would accept in order to be taxed. While generating great controversy, it failed to bring about a solution.

Given the gravity of the situation, the only option appeared to be summoning the Estates General, something that had not taken place since the early seventeenth century. It brought together the three 'estates' of France: the clergy, nobility and the 'common people' (the 'third estate'). These groupings, while based on long tradition, failed to represent the different interest groups or sociological make-up of French society in the 1780s. The clergy, for example, ranged from poor rural priests to wealthy abbots or bishops, who were rarely seen celebrating mass in a church but accepted the role almost as their inheritance, along with the tithes that it brought. The third estate included wealthy merchants and subsistence farmers, while the nobility were divided between the 'sword' and the 'robe', which served as a rough and not particularly accurate distinction between the older and grander nobles, whose families gained their title through military service, and those whose privileges came from a background in trade or the law. Across these social divides could be patterned religious differences, such as in the long-rumbling Jansenist controversy, a theological and churchmanship dispute that was in part a method for coding political divisions in an absolutist state with no official public political culture and splits between town and country, north and south, east and west. Long-standing opposition to the king and his ministers could also be found in the various 'parliaments' or law courts, which had ancient privileges in a number of French provinces

– their relationship with the king had been a long-running fissure in royal politics. With a few exceptions only the third estate paid taxes; one of the privileges of nobility was to be largely excluded from taxation, although, like the Church, the nobility could from time to time be convinced to make a 'free gift' to the monarch. Revenue could be raised through the sale of such privileges, creating a forest of fiercely guarded (and sometimes fungible) local rights.

Out of this delicately balanced and somewhat dysfunctional web of obligations, privileges, grievances, hopes and fears a solution was intended to be found that, if not garnering the support of all, or even most, could at least be accepted as workable. As part of the process, the various estates were required to list their concerns or 'grievances' before a great meeting of the three estates at Versailles in May 1789. Representatives of the estates recorded their concerns in physical notebooks, *cahiers de doléances*, which were then to be presented to the king and his ministers as a means of judging the opinion of the country as a whole. *Cahiers* were created for a large number of bodies, such as guilds, lawyers, religious orders and so on. Every village and town across France also created their own books of grievances, with the villagers gathered around the mayor or clergyman with the authority and literacy to write down their concerns. Many of hundreds of thousands of these *cahiers* survive, and a set of patterns emerge. The population still regarded the king in a paternal light, believing that he would ultimately look after them and provide them with bread, even if he was surrounded by ill-judged advisors. The books of the third estate had a common set of themes, which argued that landowners had overstepped their ancient rights by curtailing access to common lands, forbidding the capture of pests, such as rabbits or pigeons, that the nobility kept for their own kitchens. Taxation was often an issue of particular concern.

Such gatherings did more than collate lists of problems, but they generated a febrile atmosphere of expectations. Many believed that the king would now right these wrongs. The selection of representatives to head to Versailles similarly contributed to the expectation of change and the sense of a national discussion. It was into this atmosphere that the press helped to shape the debate. The authority of the censor collapsed, and the political moment gave birth to a vast number of pamphlets and what we might consider to be newspapers. The process of royal censorship began to break down. Many of these were subsidized by the nobility, provincial magistrates and, in particular, the king's cousin the Duke d'Orléans, who was opposed to the direction the king and his ministers were taking. A more profound statement was also made in the pages of the press. The democratic will of the nation was being expressed. Unlike the city-states of Athenian democracy, the only vehicle that might effectively express something approximating this will was the press. Its was the only means of enlightening the voters, too. As Jacques Pierre Brissot, the future politician, expressed it in a 1789 pamphlet, 'One can teach the same truth at the same moment to millions of men; through the Press, they can discuss it without tumult, decide calmly and give their opinion.'[5]

Tumult was to come. For millions of French women and men, dearth and hunger created by the poor harvest of the preceding year could not be ignored. Although the weather during the spring of 1789 promised a good crop, the summer of 1788 had been cold and damp; crops never came into harvest or rotted in the fields. The wider economy was troubled, with many industries yet to adjust to the removal of many tariffs negotiated by Calonne, the French controller-general of finances. For many in France, the winter of 1788 and early 1789 had been terrible. Such a mixture of hope and despair proved to be a tinderbox.

In May 1789, the Estates General began to meet at Versailles, the first gathering of this institution since 1614. It did not take long for a crisis to emerge. The meeting was supposed to vote by estate, meaning that the much-larger-in-number third estate would be beholden to the combined vote of the nobility and the clergy. The third estate, and a not insignificant number of clergy and nobility, decamped to the king's indoor tennis court, taking an oath that there they would remain until there was voting by head and a constitution. Across swathes of the French countryside, which was being drip-fed with news of the latest events in Versailles, heresay of brigands began to spread, creating what became known as the Great Fear. Following weeks of rural unrest, bands of peasantry armed themselves, sounded the village bells in warning and sought out invaders. Soon these actions turned against the lords and the symbols of the feudal regime. The hated dovecotes, rabbit warrens and strongrooms containing the papers recording feudal dues were burned by the hundred. Rumours also circulated. Troop movements were believed to herald the king's deployment of foreign mercenaries to suppress the National Assembly and to attack Paris, where the Assembly could count on much of its support. On 14 July the Bastille and other buildings were stormed in search of gunpowder and arms to defend the city. The Paris streets were filled with cries demanding liberty and rights. A political crisis had become a social revolution.

A Public Sphere?

From where else than the fears on the street and the anger of the countryside might a desire for change come? It is possible that Grub Street, the inky world of journalists, writers and blackmailers that survived from week to week by the fortunes of patronage and sale of work, provided a well of discontent, feeding the political turmoil unleashed by revolution. France provided a rich if precarious habitat for those seeking to live by their pen. Journalism as a profession was closely tied to networks of patronage and was possessed of a close and often contentious relationship to those holding power. Because of the power of censorship and the close links between the printing centres of the Low Countries, Switzerland and Britain, it created a cadre of writers who ventured close to the legal line, sometimes falling foul of it, and often continuing their work from these other centres of – sometimes illicit – publishing. Young writers were attracted to the world of the salon and the pamphlet, drawn by the career and writing of men such as Voltaire. But rather than finding fame and fortune, they were instead exposed to the corrupt machinations of the state, with its summary arrests, police spies and regular use of the press to blackmail or libel its enemies.

As the crisis of May–July 1789 demonstrated, part of the reason for the collapse of political authority was the inability for a broader political debate to take place. While the royal, courtly and traditional rules and codes of conduct failed to provide answers, another legitimate source of political authority was establishing itself: a 'bourgeoise public sphere', to use the language of the political theorist Jürgen Habermas. In the pages of thousands of pamphlets, the meeting rooms, lecture halls and salons of Paris and provincial society, and the correspondence of men and women of letters, an alternative identity to that of traditional adherence to the king and the court was developed. By participating in this world, the educated and relatively wealthy members of the third (and the other) estates helped to create a forum that could critique the status quo, and created the idea of a public whose voice should be heard. By denying it, most crucially in the way the third estate was treated at the opening of the Estates General, the monarchy risked losing its claim to authority, which had been eroded in any case over the years by clandestine publishing ridiculing the monarchy and, in particular, casting slurs on his Austrian queen, Marie Antoinette. Unlike their predecessors, the royals largely remained at Versailles and neglected to tour their kingdom, with the exception of a royal visit to Le Havre.

The uniqueness of royal authority was also eroded by the most unlikely of publications. While newspapers as we understand them today were rare in *ancien régime* France, there were numerous alternative types of publication that offered news on a regular basis. Perhaps the most widespread of these were classified news sheets, best known as *affiches*. As previously mentioned, these had begun as adverts posted to walls – hence their name – in the late seventeenth century but had by the mid-eighteenth century become four or eight pages crammed with small advertisements. They were sold to subscribers for six or seven *livres* annually, roughly equivalent to a week's wages for an artisan. While news, letters and editorials were initially restricted to the *Gazette* and the *affiches* were meant to be devoted solely to advertisements, the commercial content was soon augmented by literary and cultural material, such as poems and even references to current events. By 1789, along with two widely disseminated Paris publications, 44 towns could boast their own *affiche*, making them, in the words of Colin Jones, 'the French provincial press prior to 1789'.

This number places France roughly on a par with England, which had perhaps fifty provincial titles at this time. Circulation is difficult to determine with any accuracy, but most of the papers had between 200 and 750 subscribers, making a total of between 8,000 and 30,000. Papers were, of course, more widely read than subscribed to, with copies shared in cafés and reading rooms or among friends and colleagues. One contemporary *affiche*, the *Journal de Champagne*, suggested it had four readers for every copy; historians speculated that the figure might be as high as ten during the revolutionary decade, suggesting a total readership of between 50,000–200,000 (out of a population of some 20 million, perhaps 4 million of whom lived in towns and cities, one in twenty had access to the *affiches*).[6] By 1789, 14 per cent of the *Affiches de Toulouse* was devoted to political reports, a percentage that increased rapidly as the year progressed.

While they were not quite newspapers as we would define them today, these *affiches* reveal the existence of a broader constituency, one that was increasingly informed of political events and able to imagine itself as a wider public. Publications such as this emphasized the fact that they were produced within a community, and also helped to shape that community. Letters from readers underscored this sense, creating an eighteenth-century information network. Many thousands of these were written to the *Affiche* and similar journals during the 1770s and '80s. As one correspondent, François de Neufchâteau, wrote in 1778, 'I like to imagine your Journal as a faithful image of our rapid conversations, which touches on everything, without writing extensively on any; where frivolous quips cross profound discussions; where philosophical reflections intersect the neighbourhood news; where imperceptible transitions link the most disparate matters.'[7] Within this network of readers, correspondents, vendors and consumers, another source of legitimacy began to take hold: the notion of a critical public sphere.

Cosmopolitan Press

This home-grown form of news was complemented by the international press, particularly for the elite. Over the eighteenth century, a francophone cosmopolitan press increasingly catered to an elite audience across Europe. Largely based in the Low Countries and Germany, such 'international gazettes' had a growing readership and were increasingly influential. Over sixty papers were published from 1760 until the outbreak of revolution, bringing a diet of international affairs, domestic reporting, cultural commentary and more political essays, many of which were broadly supportive of the ideas of the Enlightenment. Before 1759 such papers were few in number, and, because of the high costs in postage, prohibitively expensive, limiting their influence and reducing the concern that the authorities might have had about them. But in that year, the French government introduced what became known as a 'postal revolution', cutting the rates for licensed papers. The cost fell by as much as 70 per cent. By 1781 the international press had a combined circulation of around 14,000. This was at a time when domestic papers had a circulation of perhaps 31,000.[8]

Their circulations tended to expand at moments of international crisis, such as during the Seven Years War, when interest in news naturally increased. The *Gazette de Cologne* in particular did have some influence in French public affairs, provoking in the 1780s a denial, no doubt deriving from the court, in a rival paper rebutting the involvement in a dubious financial scandal involving a favourite of Marie Antoinette. In contrast, the *Courrier d'Avignon*, based in the papal enclave within France, was by the 1780s almost totally under the control of the French government, which selected its editor and controlled its access to its market. In exchange for this oversight, the paper had a virtual and lucrative monopoly over southern France, northern Italy and the Iberian Peninsula. The disturbances of the late 1780s were mentioned, but only in a very guarded way: for example, reports on the disturbances in Grenoble in June 1788 do not mention the bloodshed or that the royal troops had lost control of the city.[9]

Both of these papers were overshadowed by the Dutch international press in the form of the *Courier du Bas-Rhin* and the *Gazette de Leyde* (the shorter name for the *Nouvelles extraordinaires de divers endroits* (Extraordinary News from Various Places)). Perhaps the most successful of these was the *Gazette*, described by its historian Jeremy

Popkin as 'the *New York Times* of its day', with its editor Jean Luzac regularly 'receiving mail from Voltaire, from George Washington, and from the ministers of all the crowned heads of Europe'.[10] Its competitor, the *Courier du Bas-Rhin,* proffered a Prussian view of the world from its offices in Cleves, a Prussian enclave within the Dutch Republic, and as a result was nicknamed the 'oracle of Berlin'.[11] But the patronage of the Prussian Crown did not prevent its editor, Jean Manzon, from exploiting his position and involving himself in numerous blackmailing schemes. London – whose papers also typically operated along the same lines as Manzon's – also provided a base for the *Courier de L'Europe*, which was funded surreptitiously to the tune of 4,800 subscriptions by the French government. Readers would learn much about the American Revolution and accounts of parliamentary affairs, but little French news. No mention was made, for example, of Necker's dismissal in 1781 or the arrest of the Cardinal de Rohan as a result of the Affair of the Diamond Necklace in 1785. A blind eye was turned to the publication on the British side, since they paid the publisher to spy on his French masters.

From these cosmopolitan papers, and from the eight-page *Gazette de Leyde* in particular, French readers could learn more about happenings in their own country than they would otherwise have gleaned from reading the authorized press. The *Gazette de Leyde* 'firmly eschewed spicy anecdotes', and instead reported more fully on French domestic issues in measured, calm tones.[12] During the affair of 1757, when Louis XV was stabbed by the would-be assassin Damiens, the paper alone explored the unhappiness Louis had provoked and the broader detail of the religious controversy that Damiens claimed to be his motive. It maintained its support for the French *parlements* over the century, recording the attempted limits placed on the king's, and his ministers', authority.

The French government did from time to time suppress such papers. Over thirty accounts of attempts to suppress reports can be found in the archives, many of them raised by important government officials, testifying to the level of concern such papers could generate. At other times, the government would ban a particular title, demonstrating its displeasure at their reporting.

The cosmopolitan press directly contributed to the pre-revolutionary debate. The journalist, blackmailer and spy Charles Théveneau de Morande made use of his London-based *Lettres d'un voyageur* to expound on his view of patriotic reform, attempting to lead opinion as much as report or comment on events. His style was soon copied by the news sheets and journals that were springing up in Paris, creating a kind of journalist decried by their enemies as a 'new type of demagogue'.[13]

With such heterodox and often radical voices now in print, the revolutionary era posed challenges to elite journals such as the *Gazette de Leyde*. With the relaxation of censorship within France, the paper lost its near-monopoly on independently reported domestic news. Its coverage of the outbreak of the Revolution soon became critical of radicals, deemed by the paper to be opponents of the form of Enlightenment absolutism it supported. Even worse, as a foreign paper at a time of intense nationalist paranoia it was no longer seen as an independent and respected source of information, but instead could be suspected of conspiring with émigrés, foreign powers and counter-revolutionaries. Its traditional links to the elite, who provided it with trustworthy information and a well-heeled audience, also tarnished its reputation at a time of democratic revolution: in 1792 one of its competitors, the *Chronique de Paris,* condemned the *Gazette* for having an 'aristocrat' as its editor. More practically, the news it contained was now potentially stale compared to the many domestically produced newspapers that emerged following the collapse of the royal control of the press.[14] Despite these blows to its reputation, with real consequences for the paper's bottom line, its access to reputable information ensured it still retained a readership, one which now sought it out for its extensive coverage of foreign news rather than revelations about French domestic affairs. Several Jacobin Clubs maintained a subscription to the paper along with other Paris reading rooms – spaces where citizens could find the latest paper or pamphlet for a small fee.[15] With France facing real and prospective military invasion, the machinations of European chancelleries held a real and immediate interest. And, from 1793, as the Terror began and internal censorship returned, the *Gazette* supplemented this information with reports and letters revealing splits with the Committee of Public Safety that barely any domestic paper dared to publish. Censorship under the Jacobins again provided the *paper* with a market for those who had a hunger for information.

Printers and the Demand for News

Clearly neither the *affiches* nor the international press could meet the demand for information unleashed in 1789. Every day brought new revelations, fears and rumours about which a fascinated public wanted to hear more. The printed page offered a certain amount of authority compared to oral rumour and second- or third-hand reports. Dozens of newspapers, ranging in size and format, were founded to take financial advantage of this demand. Many also existed as mouthpieces for certain political views. There was an explosion in the number of newspapers sold in Paris and the main provincial cities of France: at one point, perhaps more than a hundred papers or journals were published. In the last six months of 1789, 250 newspapers circulated, and 350 or more were published in 1790.[16] Of these, perhaps 25 or 30 were successful, and were taken by the majority of reading rooms or clubs. August 1789 confirmed the liberty of the press and expression in article XI of the Declaration of the Rights of Man and of the Citizen, and named it 'one of the most precious rights of man', but also, it should be noted, specified that it was subject to the law.

Reading the news became a common event among the people of Paris, even among the more modest citizenry; illiteracy was not necessarily a bar, since newspapers were often read out loud in company. Searches undertaken by commissioners following arrests typically revealed the presence of a couple of newspapers, such as in the case of *citoyenne* ('female citizen') Lafrête, a second-hand clothes dealer and wife of a day-labourer, who in the Year III (1794/5) had in her home copies of the *Journal universel*, sixteen issues of Lebois' *L'Ami du peuple*, two issues of another paper by that name and *L'Orateur du Peuple*. This, the historian Dominique Godineau reveals, was typical: in 1791 a cook, Constance Evrard, subscribed to the *Révolutions de Paris* and 'very often' read *L'Orateur*. A *sans-culotte* (person of lower-class rank) household, such as a Gaspard Charvet and his wife, might take 'almost all the newspapers of Audoin and some others of Marat'. Poorer workers, such as the water-sellers and others residing at 255 rue des Fossés-l'Auxerrois, might gather each evening in the porter's lodge to hear the paper being read. Others might pull down the copies of papers posted on walls around Paris, keeping cuttings that seemed interesting and using the remains to fuel lanterns. Others still might meet to eat and drink, in the popular republican fashion, sharing wine and discussing loudly the latest news from the Convention or Assembly.[17] Regular consumption of news, the communal sharing of newspapers and discussion of the latest events became woven into the pattern of the day. When the weather and light was good enough, occupants of rented flats brought chairs out into the streets or courtyard to read the papers and discuss the latest events. Typical of this was the Maurier family who, on 5 July 1793, were recorded in the police archives as enjoying the cool of the evening in the company of their neighbours, discussing 'whether the section would accept the constitutional act', referring to the Constitution of 1793.[18] We can imagine how the consumption and discussion of news fed into the emotional intensity of the revolutionary period. The presence of such large numbers of newspapers, journals and reports created a desire for more and more rapid information. As the revolution became increasingly violent and divisive in the early 1790s, newspapers both fed off this tumult of events and added to its intensity.

Such a revolution in newsprint also had practical implications for the production of papers. Paris could boast only one daily newspaper before 1789: the *Journal de Paris*, an organ concerned with cultural reporting rather than political news. As we have seen, events in Versailles and Paris created an enormous demand for news, and news sheets of various kinds filled the gap in the market. Meeting this greatly increased demand was no mean feat for printers, with the most successful papers printing 10,000 copies or more. In order to satisfy demand and to keep up with the appetite for news, printers' workshops ran their presses overnight, setting several sets of copy so multiple presses could run at once. This created a demand for typesetters and printers, who ignored guild regulations, deserting their existing jobs for the more profitable newspaper publishers. Capital investment was also required. Multiple presses required a large amount of expensive type in a range of sizes and cases (as well as large quantities of candles or oil to light overnight printing). The successful publishers of newspapers ran very large workshops, the largest of which was that of the *Moniteur*, which established itself as the most successful, and eventually official, record of the government. It was printed in a huge atelier containing 27 wooden hand-presses and employed 91 workers, including typesetters, printers, clerks and women employed to fold the sheets. There were also several proposals in the early 1790s to train women in typography to meet the demand, as well as provide employment for women.[19] In common with printing elsewhere in Europe and Britain over the eighteenth century, there were few technological developments in the process, which still relied on forms made of moveable type, pressed by hand on a stationary press. Quantity and speed instead were a product of investment in machines and the increase on the amount of human labour that could be drawn upon.[20] Other papers, such as the *Chronique de Paris* or the *Gazette universelle*, deployed seven to ten presses, printing around 11,000 copies per day – an extraordinary number. The expansion of print not only added to the cacophony of debate in the streets, clubs and homes of Paris, but ensured that print shops were the sites of intense activity and labour.

These workers then passed the product to teams of street sellers, with perhaps two hundred Parisian Mercury Women required to distribute a print run the size of the *Chronique de Paris*.[21] In some ways, these women became a political force of their own, with their street cries, such as 'The people are weary, the people are hungry and dying of cold', or 'Robespierre has been arrested!', which were, in Godineau's words, 'capable of moving public opinion'.[22] Newspaper publishers faced an ongoing struggle to keep hold of their workers during a period of such competition, as well as obtaining paper and ink. Perhaps inevitably, the papers that survive from the era reveal a range of formats, numbers of pages and quality of paper and production over the years. If they found a successful formula, there was nothing to stop a competitor publishing a paper with the same or

GAZETTE NATIONALE, OU LE MONITEUR UNIVERSEL.

N° 312 *Duodi, 12 Thermidor, l'an de la République française une et indivisible. (m. 30 Juillet 1794 vieux style.)*

CONVENTION NATIONALE.

Présidence de Collot d'Herbois.

SUITE DE LA SÉANCE PERMANENTE DU 9 THERMIDOR.

Collot d'Herbois. Il est une mesure que je crois essentielle, c'est de demander que Saint-Just dépose sur le bureau le discours qu'il devait prononcer pour contribuer aussi à amener la contre-révolution.

Cette proposition est adoptée.

Collot. Citoyens, il est vrai de le dire, vous venez de sauver la Patrie. La Patrie soupirante, et le sein presque déchiré, ne vous a pas parlé en vain. Vos ennemis disaient qu'il fallait encore une insurrection du 31 mai.

Robespierre l'aîné. Il en a menti...

(L'assemblée fait éclater la plus vive indignation.)

Clausel. Je demande que les huissiers exécutent le décret d'arrestation.

Le président. J'en ai déjà donné l'ordre; et lorsque les huissiers se sont présentés, on a refusé d'obéir.

(A la barre, à la barre, crie-t-on de toutes parts.)

Louseau. Je rappelle à la Convention que lorsqu'elle mit en arrestation plusieurs de ses membres, elle les fit passer à la barre. Je demande qu'il n'y ait pas plus de privilège pour ceux-ci, et qu'ils y descendent.

Plusieurs voix. Oui, oui, à la barre.

La Convention décrete cette proposition.

Les individus décrétés d'arrestation descendent à la barre. (On applaudit à plusieurs reprises.)

Collot-d'Herbois. La Patrie sourit à votre énergie; ses ennemis disaient qu'il fallait une insurrection du 31 mai. Non, ce n'était pas une insurrection qu'il fallait, car 100,000 contre-révolutionnaires étaient prêts à saisir le premier mouvement pour égorger la Liberté. Ils étaient déjà tout radieux, les partisans de la contre-révolution; mais la journée sera funeste pour eux. (On applaudit.) Ce n'était pas une insurrection à leur maniere qu'il fallait, c'était une insurrection contre la tyrannie, et c'est vous qui l'avez faite. (Vifs applaudissemens.) Elle aura sa place aussi dans l'histoire, cette insurrection qui a sauvé la Patrie. (Nouveaux applaudissemens.) Voyez, Citoyens, les hordes fugitives de vos ennemis, voyez leurs armées consternées se répandre au loin; leur derniere ressource était la guerre civile au sein de la Convention, afin de nous forcer d'accepter un tyran. Mais tous les Français périront avant de transiger avec la tyrannie. Jamais, non, jamais le Peuple Français n'aura de tyran. (*Non, non* s'écrie-t-on de toutes parts. — Les membres de l'Assemblée et les spectateurs se levent simultanément en criant: *Vive la République*.)

Il fallait tenter la dissolution de la représentation nationale, rompre le gouvernement, amener la guerre civile. Eh bien! un instrument se préparait dans l'ombre. Savez-vous quel était cet instrument? C'est le discours de Robespierre. (On applaudit.)

Un secrétaire avertit les membres du Comité de sûreté générale qu'ils sont attendus au lieu ordinaire de leur séance.

Ils traversent la salle au bruit des applaudissemens plusieurs fois répétés.

Collot. Citoyens, vous qui l'avez entendu, ce discours, je vous le demande; était-il rien de plus propre à briser les liens de la confiance, de plus habil pour dissoudre la Convention nationale? Était-il enfin quelque chose de plus enflammé pour allumer la guerre civile?

Ce n'était point assez; il fallait encore corrompre l'esprit public, déterminer la morale, égarer l'opinion. Eh bien! tout cela s'est fait; car dans une société célebre qui résista jusqu'à présent à l'aristocratie, qui fut égarée un instant, mais qui va sans doute bientôt reprendre son lustre et son énergie; dans cette société qui manifesta toujours la vénération la plus profonde pour la représentation nationale, qui reconnut toujours la bonté de ses décrets, où toujours le frere allait au-devant de son frere, j'y parlais hier des inquiétudes de la Patrie; des murmures repoussans me firent taire.

Je parlais des doux épanchemens de l'amitié, et l'on ne me répondait que par des menaces. Je disais que j'avais échappé aux deux coups de feu de l'Admiral, et l'on souriait ironiquement. (Mouvement d'indignation.) Certes je n'étais pas là avec des Jacobins. (On applaudit.) Mais j'y suis aujourd'hui. (On applaudit de nouveau.) Quand les vrais Jacobins qui étaient absens hier y reparaîtront, quand ils verront le grand œuvre que vous avez consommé, quels grands coupables vous avez punis, ces bons citoyens qui n'osaient y prendre place, se réjouiront; ils étaient tristes hier, ils prévoyaient les dangers qui menaçaient la Patrie; leur ame, l'ame de ces athletes de la liberté, était palpitante, leur cœur était oppressé; mais maintenant il n'y a plus d'oppression. (Vifs applaudissemens. — Oui, oui, s'écrie-t-on, il n'y a plus d'oppression.) Cependant on craignait même pour aujourd'hui le retour de ces fideles athletes; on craignait ce sentiment énergique, qui devait dans tous les coins de Paris réveiller les amis de la Patrie; oui, on le craignait, c'est-à-dire les traîtres que vous avez frappés; c'est pour cela que le discours de Saint-Just devait être prononcé aujourd'hui; la motion que Couthon fit hier aux Jacobins devait précipiter le mouvement; Couthon avait demandé qu'il fût fait un nouveau scrutin épuratoire dans la société; il ne déguisait pas qu'il fallait exclure les membres des deux Comités que ce conspirateur osait appeler des traîtres. C'est pour cela que Saint-Just est venu, contre sa parole donnée aux deux Comités, lire le discours que vous avez interrompu. Il est bon à cet égard de faire connaître quelques détails: Saint-Just était au Comité; j'y arrive en sortant de dessous les couteaux, car plusieurs de ceux qui m'accompagnaient dans le trajet, entendirent répéter plusieurs fois à mes oreilles, *dans deux jours tu ne parleras pas tant, tu y passeras*, on disait à Dubarran, *il faut lui couper le caquet*; ces propos étaient tenus par les acolytes ordinaires, par les gardes du corps de Robespierre.

J'arrive donc au Comité: mes regards se portent sur Saint-Just; j'exprimai énergiquement ce qui venait de se passer; il vit combien j'étais ému, il était de marbre. Il annonçait froidement au Comité ce rapport, dans lequel il ne cachait pas que plusieurs membres étaient accusés, sans pourtant oser proposer contre eux le décret d'accusation, car il faisait cette réticence. Savez-vous sur quoi ce rapport était basé? Sur tous les récits des espions de Robespierre. Il y en avait un notable à mon égard. Il prétendait que j'avais tenu tels et tels propos dans un café, et tout le monde sait que je ne mets le pied dans aucun café; un autre rapportait que j'avais dit à Fouché de préparer le décret d'accusation contre Robespierre; que Fouché avait dit à quelqu'un que si Robespierre consentait à changer de conduite à son égard, il dévoilerait toute l'intrigue: or, je n'avais pas vu Fouché depuis deux mois, depuis que l'opinion publique était suspendue sur son compte. Nous dîmes à Saint-Just qu'il fallait déclarer à la Convention les faits, s'ils étaient vrais; mais qu'auparavant il fallait les examiner, afin de ne pas jeter le trouble. Nous décidâmes, avec lui, que nous enverrions chercher Fouché pour qu'il s'expliquât en sa présence.

Nous quittâmes Saint-Just à 5 heures du matin; il devait revenir à 11 heures. Il n'a pas tenu sa parole. Les deux Comités se sont assemblés. Fouché y a été appelé; Ruhl l'a questionné: il a déclaré qu'il ne m'avait pas vu depuis deux mois, et qu'il me trouvait sévere à son égard. Il y a bien d'autres infamies dans ce rapport. C'est pourquoi j'ai demandé qu'il fût déposé sur le bureau. Ce second volume du discours de Robespierre aurait été lu ce soir aux Jacobins, et nous ne savons pas ce qui serait arrivé à la fête de demain. C'eût été peut-être un jour de deuil; ce sera, au contraire, un jour de triomphe. (On applaudit.)

Vos Comités vous feront un rapport circonstancié sur cette conspiration, et il ne sera pas difficile de vous convaincre qu'il se préparait ici quelque chose de favorable à la cause des despotes terrassés. Il ne sera pas difficile de prouver qu'ils se réunissaient pour comploter.

Remarquez, Citoyens, que ceux qui viennent réclamer la loi, sont ceux qui la violent impunément. Remarquez que le frere de Robespierre, au mépris de l'arrêté qui lui enjoignait de partir pour l'armée d'Italie, est resté ici malgré les dispositions de cette campagne.

Saint-Just a été rappelé deux fois de l'armée du Nord, par Robespierre, pour dresser un acte d'accusation contre les hommes courageux qui s'opposaient au despotisme de ces nouveaux tyrans.

Je le dirai, c'étaient les véritables proscriptions de Sylla; car il ne s'agissait pas ici d'amis ou d'ennemis du Peuple; il s'agissait de proscrire ceux qui ne voulaient pas obéir à tel ou tel individu. Je vais citer un fait qui prouvera que Robespierre qui, depuis quelque tems ne parlait que de Marat, a toujours détesté cet ami constant du Peuple. A la fête funebre de Marat, Robespierre parla long-tems à la tribune qu'on avait dressée devant le Luxembourg, et le nom de Marat ne sortit pas une seule fois de sa bouche. Le Peuple peut-il croire qu'on aime Marat, lorsqu'on déclare avec humeur qu'on ne veut pas lui être assimilé. Non, ils avaient beau, ces hypocrites, parler sans cesse de Marat, de Chalier, ils n'aimaient ni Marat, ni Chalier. Chalier dont j'ai vu la conduite, dont j'ai chéri, admiré et respecté les vertus: Le Peuple le sait bien; c'est dans les vertus de la vie privée qu'on reconnaît les vertus publiques. (On applaudit.)

Fayau. Je demande la parole pour un fait. Un des commissaires d'une Section a fait demander au directeur d'un atelier des fusils pour en armer les jeunes gens de cette Section demain à la fête. Les fusils ont été refusés. (On applaudit.)

La séance est suspendue.

Du 9 thermidor, à 7 heures du soir.

Bourdon, de l'Oise. Citoyens, ce matin la Convention a pris des mesures de sûreté nécessitées par les circonstances; tous les bons citoyens y ont applaudi. Cependant il se répand ce soir un bruit sur lequel j'appelle toute votre attention. On prétend que la Commune de Paris s'est liguée avec les Jacobins pour opérer une insurrection. (Mouvemens d'indignation.) Une telle résolution serait dangereuse sans doute pour tout autre que le Peuple de Paris: avec lui elle ne doit point vous inquiéter. Je rappelle à la Convention que dans une pareille circonstance elle fraternisa avec le Peuple, et calma par sa présence l'effervescence du Peuple. Non que je croye cette démarche nécessaire; cependant il est utile de s'assurer de la vérité; je demande donc que la Commune soit mandée à la barre pour vous rendre compte du fait.

Cette proposition est appuyée.

Merlin, de Thionville. N'ayant pris la parole ni pour ni contre dans la discussion qui a eu lieu ce matin, je ne suis pas suspect dans ce jour. Je vais vous dire, (Léger murmure.) je vais vous rendre compte d'un fait. S'il était quelque bon citoyen qui pût douter encore de l'existence de la conspiration qui s'ourdissait et du danger éminent qu'ont couru la liberté et la représentation nationale, ce fait l'en convaincrait facilement.

Je sortais de chez moi pour me rendre à mon poste, quand Hanriot, à la tête de 40 forcenés, le sabre à la main, se présenta à ma vue. M'apercevoir, fondre sur moi, me poser le pistolet sur la poitrine, et couvrir ma tête de leurs sabres, tout cela fut l'affaire d'un moment.

J'étais sans armes, je ne pouvais me défendre; je leur présentai ma poitrine, en leur disant: *Frappez.* Ils m'enleverent, ils me conduisirent ainsi au corps de garde du poste du Palais de l'Égalité. Là, reprenant mon caractere de représentant du Peuple, je haranguai les citoyens armés qui s'y trouvaient. Fideles aux principes et pénétrés de respect pour la représentation nationale, ils me mirent sur le champ en liberté. (Vifs applaudissemens.)

J'annonce à la Convention que ces citoyens étaient de la Section de la Montagne. On avait dressé procès-verbal de mon arrestation et de ma mise en liberté; il est déposé au Comité de sûreté générale. Cependant Hanriot poursuivait le cours de sa marche furieuse, portait le trouble et la terreur dans les différens quartiers de Paris où la vérité, sur les événemens de cette journée, n'avait point encore pénétré. Cinq gendarmes prennent la résolution généreuse d'arrêter ce scélérat; et d'exécuter votre décret. Ils partent, le rencontrent, fondent le pistolet au poing sur Hanriot et ses satellites, et font prisonniers ces scélérats. (On applaudit. — Tous les citoyens crient: *Vive la République!*)

Tel est, Citoyens, le fait dont j'avais à vous entretenir; après vous en avoir rendu compte, je fais un amendement à la proposition de Bourdon de l'Oise. Il a demandé que la Commune de Paris fût mandée à la barre; je demande que le département y soit appelé aussi, et vienne recevoir les ordres de la Convention.

Ces deux propositions sont décrétées.

Legendre. Qu'importe à la Convention, qu'importe à la République qu'un conseil général de la Commune se déclare en insurrection? Prenez garde de confondre le Peuple de la Commune de Paris avec un conseil nommé peut-être par les conspirateurs. Toutes les fois qu'il émanera de vous un décret, comptez sur le Peuple, comptez sur les montagnards, car la Montagne existe partout où l'on veut la République. (Applaudissemens.) Il n'est pas facile de mettre en insurrection un Peuple instruit; vous ici avez donné aujourd'hui une grande leçon; la liberté est consolidée d'aujourd'hui. (Vifs applaudissemens.) Le Peuple, en conservant l'instinct qu'il avait au commencement de la révolution, pour s'insurger contre les tyrans, ne se rattachera qu'à vous; mais il n'adorera plus personne.

Quand un individu fera son devoir, il lui dira: J'étais aux loges, je t'ai vu sur le théâtre, tu as bien fait, je t'ai applaudi; mais je verrai ce que tu feras demain. (Vifs applaudissemens.) Le Peuple se souviendra qu'on disait: *Point de constitution sans Pétion, Pétion ou la mort; point de patriote sans Robespierre*: il dira aujourd'hui: *Point de patriotes sans les principes.* (On applaudit.) Je demande que le président dise à chaque pétitionnaire qui viendra féliciter la Montagne, que la Convention entiere n'est qu'une montagne; la Convention renferme autant de montagnards qu'il y a d'hommes de bien; et la preuve que la Convention est composée d'hommes de bien, c'est que le décret d'arrestation

Gazette nationale; ou le moniteur universel, 12 Thermidor II/30 July 1794.

similar title. Many papers were short-lived, failing to find a loyal audience of subscribers. Nicolas de Condorcet founded the *Journal de la société de 1789* in 1790. Full of detailed articles about financial reform, the liberty of the press and women's rights, it nonetheless floundered financially. Only 23 out of 450 members of the *Societé de 1789* bought shares in the paper, and it found just 147 subscribers (few of which, as it happened, were in the club). The paper closed in September 1790.[23] The influential *Cercle social* also founded its own newspaper, the *Bouche de fer*, which ran from October 1790 to July 1791.

The demands on the technologies of production perhaps partly explains the aesthetic conservatism of the press during the period, which is at odds with the innovation in other aspects of French cultural life. Despite the important changes to the structure and content of the French press, it is curious to observe the limits the Revolution had on the format and style of French newspapers. These did not follow the English or Dutch style of newsprint before the Revolution, and this remained the case during it.On the whole they resembled books, rather than the multi-column format of newspapers familiar to readers elsewhere. With the exception of the large folio-sized *Moniteur*, which became the paper of record, most papers were small, at first octavo in format and then increasing during the 1790s to quarto; none tended to depend on advertisements. In appearance, papers avoided a revolution in style. Fonts and format resembled publications of the *ancien régime*, and experiments with headlines or illustrations were on the whole avoided. What were the reasons for such conservatism, given that so much of revolutionary culture adopted new forms that signalled the hopes of a new era? Rather than move towards a new newspaper aesthetic, the press already encapsulated much that the new regime stood for, as a pre-existing voice of the public. The tendency of printers to use modern, neoclassical fonts before 1789, and the government printing presses' reuse of similar fonts from the pre-revolutionary era for official proclamations, gave their publications a certain authority. Practical concerns no doubt also played a part, as the demand for printed materials ensured that existing type was very much in demand; we have seen already how much lead alloy type was required to publish large numbers of newspapers. The financial challenges of the times, the disruption to trade and industry and the ephemeral or short-lived nature of many publications meant that few were willing to invest in new type designs to reflect the novel times. Newspapers instead resembled the mass of printed materials, suggesting that news was part of the world of print and a vital component helping to continue debate within the public sphere.

Camille Desmoulins

Camille Desmoulins trained as a lawyer, and had a fine reputation as a student. A stammer interfered with his desire to practise, and instead he took up his pen as a journalist. Unable to take his seat in the Estates General owing to illness, he found employment as a journalist writing for the Comte de Mirabeau, making the case for an alliance between reformist aristocracy and revolutionaries. But by the summer of 1789 Desmoulins' radicalism led to a split. In September he published his inflammatory pamphlet *Discours de la lanterne aux Parisiens*, written about an infamous lamppost on the Place de Grève and the rue de la Vannerie, from the iron bracket of which had been hanged enemies of the people such as those accused of being food profiteers. Written from the perspective of the lamppost, this impromptu gallows gave Desmoulins the nickname the 'lantern prosecutor'. That November, he began his weekly newspaper, the *Histoire des révolutions de France et de Brabant* (Revolutions of France and the Netherlands). Satirical, opinionated and offering reportage on revolutionary events, the paper attacked the monarchy and conservative revolutionaries, and brought Desmoulins wealth along with a political platform. He attacked political opponents with a savage fervour. As a result, Desmoulins was sued and often attacked in the press, notably in the pro-aristocratic paper the *Actes des Apôtres.*

The factionalism of revolutionary politics was reflected in the press. Despite his early radicalism, Desmoulins came to oppose the extremes of the revolution, particularly the Terror. In 1793 he founded the *Vieux cordelier*. Although dedicated to both Danton and

Robespierre, its name, the 'Old Cordelier', evoked the earlier, less extreme incarnation of the Cordeliers Club, and attacked the ultra-radical members of the dominant Committee of Public Safety, such as Saint-Just. The paper compared the implementation of the Terror to the cruel and mad reigns of Roman emperors, and appealed directly to his old school friend, Robespierre: 'Remember the lessons of history and philosophy: love is stronger, more lasting than fear,' he wrote.[24] Like Desmoulins, the *Vieux cordelier* was short-lived: he was executed the following year and the newspaper folded.

Jean-Paul Marat and *L'Ami du peuple*

Journalism was rarely a low-risk career, particularly during a time of revolution. Perhaps no figure demonstrated this more vividly than Jean-Paul Marat. Born in the Prussian-ruled principality of Neufchâtel, he had a nearly two decades of experience as a journalist and radical pamphleteer, alongside attempting to develop a career as a natural scientist. Following his early medical training in Paris, he spent time in England, where he was inspired by the Wilkes affair, writing anti-slavery tracts and medical treatises. In 1788 he threw himself into political pamphleteering, and in the same year started his newspaper, *L'Ami du peuple* (the paper began with the name *Publiciste Parisien*, but swiftly took on the mantle of 'Friend of the People'). He used this organ as a bully pulpit against those he saw as the people's enemies: the merchant and lawyer-dominated Paris Commune, the Constituent Assembly and government ministers, particularly the finance minister, Jacques Necker. The paper quickly found popular success and was soon flattered by piratical copycat printers. Marat also attracted criticism, and was singled out by name in the *Gazette de Leyde* among the 'horde of periodical writers' who were 'so dangerous to France'.[25] Allying himself with the radical Cordeliers Club, which was under the influence of the first president of the Committee of Public Safety Georges Danton, Marat was forced to flee to London for a while as a result of his attacks. On his return he briefly established another newspaper, *Le Junius français*, which took its name from the pseudonymous author of the series of polemical letters published in the British *Public Advertiser* in the late 1760s and early '70s.[26]

Initially a proponent of the constitutional monarchy, the king's flight to Varennes in 1791 finalized Marat's conversion to republicanism, and he denounced the National Assembly for refusing to depose the king. By 1792 Marat was regularly in opposition to the Girondin faction's attacks on those he saw as counter-revolutionaries, which often forced him into hiding, allegedly, in the Paris sewers. Unable to publish *L'Ami*, he issued a series of pamphlets from 10 August, welcoming the overthrow of the monarchy by the people. Elected to the National Assembly and then as a member of the Committee of Public Safety, he fiercely attacked opponents of the Revolution, his prose whipping up support for the violence that erupted on 6 September 1792. He called on supporters of the people to kill imprisoned counter-revolutionaries before they could be freed by royalists and support a military suppression of the Revolution. On 22 September, France was declared a republic, and the newspaper was renamed *Le Journal officiel de la république française*.

It was not just Marat who suffered from the consequences of his writing (in December 1790, for example, he called for a general insurrection and attacks on the enemies of the people). He did not print *L'Ami* himself but relied on established printers, who found themselves under threat of physical attack as well as dragged into legal cases. In 1789 Marat libelled a member of the municipal council, and in his defence claimed the importance of the liberty of the press to hold power to account.[27] Copies of the paper were confiscated.[28] In 1790 his printer, Anne Félicité Colombe, the proprietor of the Henri IV print shop – an ardent militant and in 1793 member of the Society of Revolutionary Women – was included in the libel lawsuit and had copies of the paper seized. She was asked to reveal Marat's whereabouts, but refused to tell the commissioner and declared the search of her premises illegal and against her rights as a citizen (the next year, she was one of the four women arrested after the massacre on the Champ de Mars, a popular protest against the Constitutional Monarchy that was violently suppressed by troops under the authority of General Lafayette, leaving as many as fifty dead).[29] Colombe also published her own paper, *L'Orateur du peuple*, and declared in court that she preferred to print that rather than *L'Ami du peuple*. She ultimately won the court case, distributing the 20,000 (or 25,000 depending on the account) livres she was awarded among the poor of her neighbourhood.[30]

Marat continued to edit the paper, consolidating his attacks on the Girondin faction, and ramping up their ferocity following the execution of the king. He was arrested and brought to the Tribunal, where pieces from his paper was used as evidence against him. On being acquitted, he was met with jubilation from his supporters. His own fame – or infamy – at this point was huge. Soon after, in the summer of 1793, the Girondins were overthrown, with Marat taking much of the credit for his encouragement of their removal in the press.

Marat had long suffered from a skin complaint, which he relieved by bathing in a therapeutic bath, his head wrapped in a vinegar-soaked towel. It was during one of these baths that Charlotte Corday entered his room, claiming to have information concerning escaped Girondins. Removing a dagger hidden in her corset, she stabbed him above the heart, severing an artery. Marat died within seconds. At her subsequent trial, his murderer declared that she had killed one man to save 100,000. She was guillotined on 17 July 1793. For Marat, already famous, his assassination brought him apotheosis. The journalist and politician was mass-memorialized in hundreds of obituaries, speeches, prints and paintings, and his body was transferred to the Pantheon in 1794. In his death, the Revolution had found its own secular saint – a journalist of the people.[31]

Counterrevolution: *L'Ami du Roi*

Newspapers were also important to those opposed to the forces unleashed by the Revolution, particularly in the first two years following the summer of 1789. One such conservative paper was *L'Ami du Roi*. Produced and distributed by the abbé Royou and his sister Mme Fréron, the widow of the journalist Elie-Catherine Fréron, who gained a reputation for his attacks on Voltaire and the *Encyclopédie* (Voltaire created a character based on him in his *L'Ecossaise* of 1760),

L'Ami du Roi was a journal clearly aimed at a conservative or reactionary audience. Like many newspapers, it counted the nobility and clergy among its subscribers, as well as many who can only be identified as members of the third estate. Its content is even more telling, and it soon became known for printing anti-Revolutionary material, to the extent that the journal and its editors were denounced in the Assembly. In July 1791, following the massacre on the Champ de Mars, the journal was temporarily closed. The doors of its offices at 37 Saint-André-des-Arts were sealed, copies of the paper were seized and Mme Fréron was arrested, while Royou went into hiding.

Unusually for publications of this period, subscription records for *L'Ami du Roi* survive, and they support the view that many Revolutionary-era newspapers were remarkably profitable. *L'Ami du Roi* published some 5,700 copies a day at the height of its popularity. Like many other publishers of the era, Royou and Fréron also published numerous one-off pamphlets, such as editions of papal briefs denouncing the Civil Constitution of the Clergy; as for many other newspaper publishers who also produced pamphlets, these proved to be remarkable money-makers – with one estimate putting their profit margin at 1,500 per cent.[32] The newspaper, and its extensive collection of subscribers, enabled Royou, Fréron and their supporters to advertise and circulate anti-Revolutionary tracts, as well as make them available for purchase from their office.[33] When their offices were raided, the police found 'innumerable quantities' of 'aristocratic and incendiary works'. Most of these publications were contracted out to other printers, underscoring the popularity of *L'Ami du Roi* and the demands that it placed on the presses at 37 Saint-André-des-Arts. Creating papers and pamphlets in large quantities with a quick turnaround presented practical issues given the speed with which hand-presses operated. For example, the print run for an April 1791 pamphlet on the right of inheritance was 10,000 copies; others may have been 70,000 or more. Even though printers of the day demonstrated remarkable skill and speed, which is hard for modern-day hand-press printing enthusiasts to recreate, there were limits on the numbers of impressions that could be made in a day, as well as bottlenecks caused by the business of getting paper, laying out the type, drying and folding the printed pages and stitching them (then costed at 5 *livres* per 1,000 items) – a problem not just limited to France but something of a common issue for printers across the Atlantic world. In politically fraught times such as France in the 1790s, it may also have been astute to spread some of the risk of association with controversial texts. At a time of relative dearth, the siblings also provided these printers with papers to enable them to carry on with their mission. As the clash with the papacy intensified during the spring and summer of 1791, *L'Ami du Roi* contained a series of announcements of the publication of 'bulls' and 'briefs' emanating from the Catholic Church which could be purchased from their offices. Some of these were published in runs of as many as 35,000–40,000. In this way, news of the papacy's condemnation of the Civil Constitution of the Clergy, which placed the Church under secular authority, reached the widest possible audience. Many of the pamphlets were purchased in bulk by clerics, who could then disseminate them to their flock or other priests, as did many booksellers from across France – Orléans, Marseille, Saintes, Bordeaux – who also subscribed to the newspaper. Smaller orders from tiny villages in Brittany, such as Auray or Hennebont, reveal the potential reach. Again, the networks provided by a newspaper helped to enable such dissemination.[34]

Jacques-René Hébert and the Street

The press was never far from the street, with the practical politics that entailed. Printers ran the risks of attacks from mobs and wreckers, as well as the police. Their workshops were not hidden away from the life of the city in industrial zones, but shared the same roads, squares and buildings as many of their readers, as well as the events of the revolutionary era. Printers often lived above or close to their press, ensuring that they and their journeymen and apprentices could make the most use of the hours of daylight, as well as labouring long into the night, working to the dim, smoky light of candles or the new technology of Argand lamps, if urgency demanded. More technical work, such as setting type, might give way to the more routine labour of folding, cutting and stitching (although collations could, of course, be complex). Living above or next to the press protected the expensive machinery, stock and raw materials, such as paper, from potential thieves; and a place to sleep and eat might also be an expected part of the apprentices' contract. A known address was also vital for a printer, since they were part of a network of communications. Visits to their office provided them with information, letters, gossip and advertisements to place in their paper. Printing shops also operated as clearing houses, accepting letters or other goods for a small fee or a mark in the ledger of favours and debts of service that made up so much of the early modern economy.

Many of the radical presses of the era were to be found on the Left Bank of the Seine, close to the Sorbonne with its dense population of scholars, students, teachers, lawyers and clerks. This place also provided a home for many Paris artisans, and its cafés, such as the Procope, offered hubs for people to meet, discuss and agitate. All these groups provided fertile ground for the political ferment of 1789 and the years that followed.

While the streets of Paris echoed to the sound of many voices during these years, by 1792 those of the *sans-culottes* became the loudest. Taking their name from their distinctive trousers, as opposed to the fine-cloth (such as silk) culottes worn by the wealthy, these were the groups that took to the streets at the great moments of revolution, marching, shouting, singing and threatening violence to those opposed to revolution. More than just a sociological category, the movement became a self-defining group, using their dress (republican red bonnets, tricolour sashes), language (such as the use of familial *tu* rather than the formal *vous*) and songs to present an image of the common people, united in their republicanism, patriotism and support for the Revolution. While, in truth, their membership may well defy class analysis, with a whole host of social types and representatives from all points in the economic hierarchy of eighteenth-century France to be found among them, the *sans-culottes* dominated Paris streets, meetings and political language from the overthrow of the monarchy in 1792 to the fall of the Jacobins in 1794. The creation of the *sans-culottes* resulted from a mass of people taking their politics to the street at a time of great economic distress, political chaos and the threat of external military invasion, drawing on the tropes, 'clubbability' and social networks that had sustained journeymen, artisans and other workers in the precarious conditions of eighteenth-century France. Workers and guilds had long created shared meetings, charitable and informal insurance schemes, feast days and public processions to protect their trade and its members, as well as offer a place within the broader society of the day. In this way, the *sans-culottes* were also a cultural creation. They were deployed in the speeches of politicians in the National Assembly and could be found in songs, pamphlets and caricatures of the day as well as depicted in ceramics and other forms of material culture. They physically manifested on the streets and squares of Paris, especially in the Jacobin Clubs and communes that effectively governed the city during these years.

Of all the many appearances of the *sans-culottes*, none was more influential or prevalent than that depicted in the *Le Père Duchesne*, a newspaper published by the political journalist Jacques-René Hébert. Appearing in 1790, the newspaper took its name from a fictive character associated with the carnivals and fairs of the *ancien régime* who was used in several pamphlets produced during the Estates General and the debates of 1790. That year, Hébert founded the paper which would bring him influence, fame and ultimately claim his life. Writing in the first person, he took on the persona of 'Father Duchesne', a purportedly honest, plain-speaking man of the people who attacked those oppressing the people or seeking to thwart the Revolution. As such, *Le Père Duchesne* combined news, commentary and opinion, all through the demotic lens and voice of a potential street-fighter. He reported the many imagined conversations he held with the royal family, government officials, politicians and others, offering a man of the people's view of the world. The printing was often slapdash, the paper and language both rough and blue-tinged. Swear words abounded, as did jokes and the threat of violence. The paper spoke of a very particular world, that of the trades and streets of Paris. Regularly sexist, it also presented an image of a type of family man, with physically inflected politics that reflected a very masculine view of the world. Violence is never far away, either against the enemies of the Revolution ('Whenever aristocrats take a swipe at freedom, [the *sans-culotte*] takes his sword and pike and races over to the section') or at times within his household.[35] The newspaper also intersected with the worlds of print and oral dissemination, spreading further than the more staid forms of political commentary. Perhaps a third of adults living in Paris could not read, and so relied on others to read and discuss the papers in bars or section meetings.

Trained as a lawyer in Alençon, Hébert had fled to Paris in 1780 following a failed legal suit. He worked for a while at a theatre, writing unperformed plays in his spare time, before losing his job through an accusation of theft, and finding work assisting a doctor. He continued to write, and in 1789 his pamphlet *La Lanterne magique* found favour with radical readers. He joined the Cordeliers Club, known for its anti-noble views, and published the first issue in 1790. It is possible he took the title from *Le Père Duchesne*, a pamphlet published by Antoine Lemaire at roughly the same time, who was attacked in the right-wing and less radical press – as well as in the cries of newspaper boys on the streets. At his printing shop, Hébert was well located to observe and participate in the intense politics of the clubs and sections of the Left Bank. Its location and the sights and sounds he observed provided the materials out of which he could fashion his paper. Out of its doors emerged thousands of copies of the journal, which ran to 365 issues.

The paper was initially broadly supportive of the monarchy, but in 1791 Hébert was caught up in the massacre on the Champ de Mars, which saw fifty protesters shot by troops. His politics took a more radical turn, and Père Duchesne turned on conservatives such as Lafayette and his political allies, the comte de Mirabeau and Jean-Sylvain Bailly, portraying them as wealthy aristocrats attempting to undermine the Revolution. When the king and his family attempted to escape Paris, Hébert turned on the monarchy. The papacy, with its condemnation of the Oath of the Civil Constitution, also became a subject of attack. The paper became a propaganda tool for the Jacobin authorities, who sent thousands of copies to the army in an attempt to improve morale and Republican sentiment.

> Yes, fuck, we'll triumph over all the enemies within and without; sooner or later all the traitors will be immolated; it's impossible to force things on a people of 24 million people armed for their defence, and where the whole country is covered with pikes, bayonets and cannons.
>
> What a pleasure it was to see in their camp those young buggers who are going to fly to the defence of the frontiers; they wait as if it were a holiday the day when they can finally reach that worthless bastard de Bouillé; let that old shit de Condé come here at the head of his black army and he'll be properly received. Oh how well I was received by these young citizens! I had barely stepped foot in camp before this one took me by the arm, that one by the hand, the other one hugged my neck and 'c'mon along Père Duchesne! Come into our tent drink to the health of the nation.'
>
> It's there, great gods, that by cursing the aristocrats I earned friends where it counts. After having joyously passed the day like that I left our young warriors and made my farewell. Oh fuck, my friends, if I wasn't such an old bugger, I said while leaving them, I would follow you, I'd want to march at your head. Don't worry, Père Duchesne, there are enough of us to fuck up the enemy without; you, go fuck, just watch over the one within.

Unity was imposed only by force. Following the summer of 1793, when the *montagnards* (the grouping known for sitting at the top, or the 'Mountain', of the seats in the Assembly) and the *sans-culotte* movement purged the government and clubs of its enemies, Hébert was able to turn the Duchesne franchise into a government-subsidized monopoly.[36]

This expletive-strewn prose pitches Duchesne's political views to the great mass of the people, creating a democratic, and at times demotic, voice and persona. Here the newspaper is far removed from the *Gazette de France*, both in terms of style and in content. Rather than the appearance of royal approval and government authority, the paper speaks of the power and authority of the people, of the street and of its representative, the revolutionary government. The information it contains is not aimed at the merchant, the lawyer or the royal official, intrigued about the prices of commodities, the arrival and departures of ships and insights into the operations of foreign chancelleries. Instead, the information it contains is at once fantastic and more real for its audience of everyday Frenchmen and women, making use of a recognizable persona to discuss the issues of the day, even if the lens used was one of pure fabrication.

While the enthusiasm of France, and of Paris in particular, for this earthy, heavy-drinking man of the people underscores the tenacity and power of this stereotype, it also reveals the deep divisions within French society. It contributed to discord as much as uncovering truth. When a new issue hit the streets, a competitor journalist wrote, it 'causes murmurs and discord: everyone gives his opinion, preaches, those with evil intentions triumph, error and ignorance assure them of followers'.[37] Furthermore, violence – always present in *ancien régime* society and unleashed by the Revolution – was given centre stage in the language, thinking and feeling of this small-sized but powerful publication. By the autumn of 1793, the journal pitched itself as the voice of the Commune, increasingly opposed to the government. During the queen's trial, whom Père Duchesne had increasingly demonized as the 'Austrian Wolf', he accused Marie Antoinette of incest with her son, an accusation the young Jacobin leader Louis de Robespierre found distasteful. Hébert and many of his followers would fall victim to the furies of the Revolution: increasingly opposed to Robespierre and others on the Committee of Public Safety, he was guillotined on 24 March 1794. In a stunt that would perhaps have amused the fairground Père Duchesne, the executioner adjusted the fall of the blade, so it stopped a centimetre from the screaming Hébert three times before it fell upon his neck.

Paris and the Provinces

These well-known journalists and their influential papers were all based in Paris, close to the centres of power. Here they were able to observe, as well as attempt to shape, the course of political events.

But there was also a provincial press that initially flourished following the relaxation of censorship. Networks of pro-revolutionary clubs sprang up across France, and they quickly began corresponding to one another by letter, desperate to hear and share news and opinion through a network of clubs.[38] These were also often closely linked to newspapers. In late 1789, one of these clubs launched a paper, the *Club des observateurs*, with different members of the club charged with reporting on municipal politics, trials and debates at the National Assembly. Like many newspapers, it was short-lived as a publication, and only seven copies now survive. There were also clubs for women, one of which issued a prospectus for a newspaper, *Les Événements du jour*. Due to be issued from 1 January 1790, no copies are extant.

Clubs in Dijon and Marseille founded their own papers; the Jacobin club at the latter founded no fewer than six papers between 1790 and 1793. In Avignon, the *Courrier d'Avignon*, which had taken advantage of the papal enclave's exemption from the censor during the *ancien régime,* was taken over by the pro-revolution Sabin Tournal as editor, and offered its support to the *Société des amis*. Elsewhere, there were close connections between the clubs and the editorship of the papers, such as in Limoges, Bordeaux and many northern towns and cities. Unsurprisingly, club business played an important role in the content of many of these papers. Not only were they supported financially by the members, and on occasion wholly owned by the club, but members edited or wrote for the journal, providing reports on club debates and informing their readers of the latest news from Paris, as well as the club's line on such matters as the Civil Constitution of the Clergy. Other local and national news was included, as well as regular columns such as readers' questions about new legislation, which could be found in the *Journal du département de Maine-et-Loire*. Were customary river rights, for example, enforceable following the abolition of feudalism?[39] Newspapers here played an important role in developing the civic culture that was built during the revolutionary years, despite the tumult of those times.

This said, many local papers that were founded with enthusiasm for the Revolution, such as the weekly *Citizen surveillant en Riom*, failed to endure. It was published for just two months, its radicalism

N°. II.

LE PUBLICISTE.

Rue des Moineaux, n°. 423.

Je reconnois avoir reçu du citoyen Jean Baptiste

demeurant à Vaucouleurs

la somme de vingt-six francs pour six mois d'abonnement à ladite Feuille, commençant le 16 Prairial

savoir 19 fr. pour la feuille et 7 francs pour les frais de timbre.

A Paris, ce 13

l'an 8e. de la république française une et indivisible.

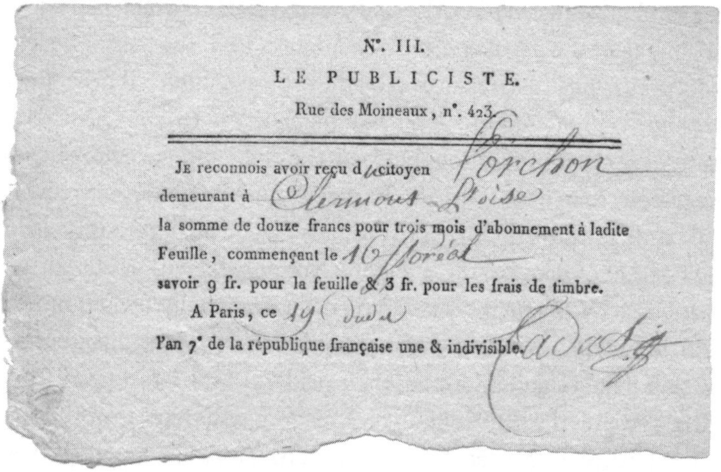
N°. III.

LE PUBLICISTE.

Rue des Moineaux, n°. 423.

Je reconnois avoir reçu du citoyen Porchon

demeurant à Clermont l'Oise

la somme de douze francs pour trois mois d'abonnement à ladite Feuille, commençant le 16 floréal

savoir 9 fr. pour la feuille & 3 fr. pour les frais de timbre.

A Paris, ce 19

l'an 7e de la république française une & indivisible.

Subscription receipts for *Le Publiciste*, Years VII and VIII (1798 and 1799), a reminder that newspaper printers needed to be paid.

and strident anticlericalism not finding a paying local audience in the rural Puy-de-Dôme. Only one of the first flush of club papers, the *Journal des frontières*, survived beyond 1793. New papers were founded in 1794, more closely aligned to the Jacobin party and supportive of the radical revolution. Following the fall of Robespierre and his supporters on 9 Thermidor II (27 July 1794) and afterwards, the papers and clubs that survived were converted into moderate papers, reporting political and other news, or were stripped of their club connection, as was the case for the *Feuille politique, littéraire et commerciale de la Gironde*.[40]

In terms of the numbers sold, the Paris papers retained several crucial advantages. Thanks to economies of scale, Paris papers could be produced more cheaply and sold at a lower cost, with print runs of perhaps 10,000. In contrast, the local market was small, and the political focus of the papers narrowed the audience further, despite their aims to be a tool for propaganda and civic regeneration. Provincial editors needed at least three hundred subscribers for their title to be viable. Only a handful, such as the *Journal du club national de Bordeaux*, reached this figure. Paris papers could also often boast famous editors and journalists, as well as contacts and proximity to the centre of political affairs. The claim of the provincial press to be able to sift the Paris papers for the most current and accurate news, and to supplement it with details of local affairs, was rarely enough to compete.

The Revolution Overseas

Of course, the Revolution had global consequences as well as provincial or local ones. From Goa in India to the Caribbean, France's colonial lands became wrapped up in the wars that erupted between it and Britain, the Netherlands and other European powers. Revolutionary ideas, as well as conflicts, also travelled around the world. The flow of news, detailing events in France and the latest political speeches, as well as the actions of royalists and counter-revolutionaries, was carried across the oceans by merchant and naval fleets, informing those in the New World of events and political currents. The Revolution itself was not restricted to France, and sympathetic movements took to the streets across Europe, notably in the Austrian-governed Italian lands, as well as in the Low Countries and Sweden. Fraternal Jacobin Clubs were formed, unnerving the authorities, as they did in Britain, where such activities were soon suppressed both through government action and the creation of loyalist groups, which required subjects to swear an oath of allegiance to the crown. Revolutionary ideas and actions particularly affected the Caribbean, and Saint-Domingue especially, where the language of the rights of man helped to spark a revolution. For printers of newspapers, the Revolution was a constant source of copy, as well as feeding into the complex relationship newspapers had with political patronage and the expectations of their audience.

In the young nation of the United States of America, the Revolution was observed with avidity and some concern. As the first military ally of the republic, events in Versailles and Paris were closely followed, together with a fascination with French cultural and intellectual life. While there was initial broad sympathy for the outbreak of liberty and constitutionalism in 1789, growing anticlericalism and the force of popular politics became matters for increasing concern. Furthermore, the Revolution's export to the Caribbean sugar islands posed a profound challenge to the heavily slave-based society and economy of the United States. The news from Saint-Domingue had widely been reported as a 'calamitous event' in American newspapers.[41] As well as column inches devoted to reporting on the latest political developments in Paris, the Revolution influenced American politics themselves. Newspapers also used the Revolution as a cipher to discuss, dispute, or warn about American politics and policies.[42] Events in France were naturally also closely followed in Britain. As well as publishing letters and other reports from France and republishing materials from the French press, the British domestic press began to despatch its own reporters at the turn of the century.

The realities of the Revolution also reached the *Gazette de Leyde*. The Low Countries experienced their own revolution, as the French armies consolidated their gains in the Flanders Campaign in the winter of 1794/5. Luzac's response to the creation of the Batavian Republic, essentially a client state of France, was a speech as new rector at the university in February 1795, which he printed and sent to numerous friends. He argued for moderation in the face of radicalism, suspicious of the effects of democracy. The following year, the French authorities attempted to fire him as editor of the paper and removed him as professor of modern history. His brother (and the paper's printer), Etienne, took on more control. Jean Luzac finally lost command of the paper in 1798 and it folded a few years later. While offering reliable information and a range of opinion, it always represented the press of the old regime; the creatures ultimately of governments, rather than a genuine space for public opinion. Created as a tool of the elite, the role of such papers was less certain in the post-revolutionary world. While elite journalism had helped to build the modern world, they also led to the destruction of what might be considered to be a single, unified public opinion, one that reflected the opinions of a cosmopolitan elite, rather than national politics and society.[43]

The press and the course of the Revolution was interlinked, although the relationship can only be described as a complicated one. Did the press, for example, influence events or instead follow its audience and reinforce their assumptions and preoccupations? Many contemporaries, including leading journalists, believed that they could lead the tiger of revolution, rather than just riding it. On hearing of the death sentence passed on twenty-one members of the Girondin faction, Desmoulins is famously said to have exclaimed, 'My God, my God! It is I who kills them!' The journalist and politician believed that his press had led public opinion in Paris to turn fatally against the Girondins, through a stream of attacks in his paper and, in particular, through the publication of misleading accusations that the Girondin leader Brissot was a British spy. It is clear that the press played a role in such events. Arguably they were as much a tool for politicians – a device to disseminate misinformation or scandal – as they were part of a broader plot to unseat opponents, or a cohesive fourth estate with a political status on its own. Desmoulins' power and influence, while it lasted, came from the blurred distinctions between his journalism and his role as a politician and activist. As Popkin notes, the press was more of a barometer of political pressure than it was the main force behind it. This is not to say that it did not amplify popular opinion. Much like the press elsewhere, the economics of newspaper publication gave encouragement to those editors who hitched their vessel to a strongly held view, rather than attempted to forge their own course. While the press may have created the conditions in which revolution could become a possibility, like most other actors during the late 1780s and '90s, it could not control events, only contribute to the general drama.

6
Scandal

Between 1812 and 1814, readers of the London papers were treated to many accounts of the Prince and Princess of Wales's troubled marriage, including items that purported to be genuine copies of letters that passed between the two households. A series of letters begun by what became known as the 'Regent's Valentine', published on 10 February 1813 in the *Morning Chronicle*, revealed Princess Caroline's attempts to visit her daughter, who was under the prince's charge, and to gain an improvement in her living and financial arrangements. Correspondence appeared in the London papers *The Courier*, *The Sun* and *The Star*, as well as in many other provincial papers. As a later trial for perjury revealed, many of these letters were placed by Bridget, Viscountess Perceval (and the future Lady Egmont), in an attempt to gain public support for the princess's plight. Although Lady Perceval composed many of the items, and also made use of materials apparently made available to her through Princess Caroline, she did not place them directly into the hands of the papers' editors, but instead made use of intermediaries. One, John Mitford, was a relation to Lady Perceval, former sailor and hack journalist, and the other, 'Captain' Thomas Ashe, gained some notoriety as a writer, blackmailer and fraudulent traveller. Both men played a role in her downfall and were persuaded by the Prince of Wales's party to turn against Lady Perceval and the princess. The Mitford affair, in particular, became the subject of contemporary gossip and comment, as Lady Perceval had placed him in a madhouse in order, she hoped, to help him escape detection and undermine his credibility as a witness. After Mitford published an account of her involvement in the publication of the letters, she unsuccessfully brought the case to trial. Newspapers were at the heart of this attempt to influence public opinion, and helped to shape the scandal that ensued.

The scandal took place within the context of a society that was thoroughly suffused with newsprint. By the start of the nineteenth century London could boast numerous weekly and daily newspapers, some short-lived, others more durable, and linked into a web of provincial papers that circulated news from the capital. A third of Londoners, if not more, read a paper. Over 17 million copies were produced annually, and by 1821 the number of titles in England increased to 135 (it was fifty in 1782).[1] Subscriptions, street sales, advertisements and government funds helped to finance their growth and support the numerous trades involved in the physical production of newspapers, and provided a medium that could reflect, inform, entertain and scandalize society. In terms of their content, they reflected many of society's concerns, interests and amusements, publishing items that went beyond straightforward news of battles, shipping and politics. This vibrant press also covered a range of social intrigues, religious disputes, literary and artistic developments, and fashions in clothing, as well containing amusing – or terrifying – stories, short verses, poetry and word games such as acrostics. Readers often had their own preference for sections of the paper, as skewered by Thomas Rowlandson in his lightly satirical caricature *The News Paper* (circa 1809), which depicts twelve seated figures, from a well-fed man welcoming the gastronomic news of the arrival of 'several fine lively green turtles', to a lady who will 'perish with cold before I'll submit to their vulgar fashions'. In novels, newspaper reading could also be used as a signifier, whether of gender (men are often depicted with a paper), social class or as a plot or characterization device – in Jane Austen's *Mansfield Park* (1814), for example, Mr Price avoids interaction with Fanny through this means: 'there were soon only her father and herself remaining; and he taking out a newspaper – the accustomary loan of a neighbour, applied himself to studying it, without seeming to recollect her existence.' Later Austen counterposes private and public information, when Fanny reads a cryptic letter about Henry and her cousin's elopement as her father arrives with the newspaper, which contains another version of this news. Austen's irony cleverly heightens the trivial and the profound nature of news, the self-important and sometimes allusive language of the press, and the ways in which public affairs introduce themselves into the domestic space of the home.[2]

The Prince and Princess of Wales

There is perhaps no better case of such dramas, which pricked public concern and prurient interest, than that of the Prince of Wales and his wife, Caroline. The saga of the royal marriage of the royal heirs is well known. In 1796 George, the Prince of Wales, had been induced to marry his German cousin Caroline of Brunswick in order to settle his vast debts. He was also obliged to put aside Maria Fitzherbert, his mistress whom he had married in secret (a union declared void by the Royal Marriages Act of 1772, since the act required the prince to obtain the permission of the monarch). For the prince, the marriage with Caroline was one of convenience rather than of love or friendship: according to Lord Malmesbury, who had escorted Caroline to Britain before her fateful marriage to Prince George, the prince notoriously demanded a glass of brandy after his first meeting with his future bride, whom he considered plain, and spent the wedding night drunk. Caroline, several years his junior, quickly realized that her initial expectations of a fairy-tale match with the future king of Great Britain were to be disappointed. The marriage was consummated, but following the birth of Princess Charlotte Augusta in 1797, the Prince and Princess of Wales lived increasingly separate and mutually antagonistic lives. Charlotte was taken away from her mother, and Caroline went to live at Shooter's Hill and then at Montague House, in Charlton near Blackheath; a fashionable enough address but well removed from Windsor and Carlton House. The Prince of Wales again took up Maria Fitzherbert, and Caroline found some consolation in

overleaf: Thomas Rowlandson, after George Moutard Woodward, *The News Paper*, 1800, etching.

"Yesterday arrived at the Hotel
" several fine lively green Turtle
Ah – this is News indeed – I must send John, down with the cart immediately.
" It is said the Ladies intend to
" put on some kind of Cloathing,
" now the Winter approaches
I'll perish with cold before I'll submit to their vulgar Fashions
" It is reported that in complimen
" to a certain Countess, Dutch Botto
" will be all the rage amongst the
" leaders of the Ton
Ay that's a hit at me – Grace and elegance always creates Envy!
" Yesterday died – Mrs. Jenkins,
" wife of Mr. Jenkins, Coal Merchant.
What a happy Man! but some people are born to be fortunate!
" Crim Con –
Oh – fie for shame! I wonder they put such things in the public papers!
" Poets Corner.
Now for it – ay heres
little production
" To Delia.
" Cherries red – and plu

Woodward Delin.

THE NE

Author receivd
nds, for the Copy
last Novels and —
vels.
l six guineas for
nslation of Virgil.'
" A few days since was married Jeremy
" Starch Esq.r — to Miss Prim —
Ha! Ha! Ha! — well said Jeremy
it will now be my turn to laugh
at you.
A Case of Real Distress!
" An elderly Gentleman between eighty and ninety years
" of age, possessed of a considerable property, wishes to have an
" heir to his estates, he is therefore desirous of entering into the
" connubial state, with a healthy young Woman of unblemished
" character (already with child) The utmost secrecy may be
" relied on — &c Please to address to X Y Z under cover
" to the publisher.
Bless me what do I see, — the very advertisement I
wanted — well the Fortune teller was right — she said though
Johnny had deserted me — I should be made an honest
Woman of!!
dents &c during the week
w we shall come to
ething entertaining!
" It is reported that Lord Limp
" has had a relapse —
Very good that — always
a sure patient.
" We are assured from good Authority that
" the First Consul of France — has been
" swallowed by a Whale!
Has he so! — I thought we should have
my Gentleman at last!
Etch'd by Rowlandson
Pub.d Oct.r 7. 1800 by R. Ackermann N.o 101 Strand
PAPER.

a life of glittering parties, travel and, her enemies charged, amorous flirtation. Her residence was later described, with allusion to the ribald activities to which it played host, as 'an incongruous piece of patch-work . . . all glitter, and glare, and trick; everything is tinsel and trumpery about it; it is altogether a bad dream'.[3]

The gaiety of the public appearance masked private sadness. Caroline found the separation from her daughter to be particularly hard to bear and, perhaps in an attempt to stem the sadness, adopted a baby boy. The child, probably the son of a Deptford shipwright and his wife, was known as William Austin; rumours soon spread that he was the product of an adulterous liaison of the princess.[4] In 1806 her behaviour led the prince's party to anticipate what became known as the 'Delicate Investigation'. The princess's private – and not so private – amorous indiscretions became subject to a secret report, which attempted to prove her guilty of adultery and demonstrate that William Austin was in reality her illegitimate son. The prince would then be free to sue for divorce.[5] Although the investigation concluded that she had 'romped familiarly' with several naval officers and that her behaviour was open to 'very unfavourable interpretations', there was no evidence of criminal wrongdoing. The investigation was, in the radical politician Henry 'Orator' Hunt's opinion, 'very much to the injury of the princess, because, amongst the Prince of Wales's friends, there were not wanting friends, aspersers of character, to whisper away her fair fame'. Unwilling to settle for the constricted life planned for her by the prince, Caroline and her supporters sought redress, both through increased access to her daughter and in an appropriate financial settlement.

The main weapon proved to be epistolary revelations in the press such as those in the 'Regent's Valentine'. Letters published in the newspapers could portray Caroline as the victim of the prince and his allies, showing how they had failed to respond appropriately to her reasonable motherly concerns for her child.[6] While scholars and critics have examined other female writing, particularly the novel, newspapers have received less critical attention.[7] The affair also took place during a period of transition for the press, which was beginning to escape from the editorial influence of patrons and the government.

As the historian Hannah Barker has shown, although papers often still depended on their political masters, who dispensed cash and information as they saw fit (and threatening legal action if necessary), the profitability of titles such as the *Morning Chronicle* (which could make an annual profit of £12,000) permitted a growing measure of editorial independence. As Barker notes, the 'assumption that newspapers in the eighteenth and early nineteenth centuries had been rendered impotent by political corruption and manipulation is in need of extensive revision'.[8] The press did indeed have a certain amount of freedom, but those who populated Grub Street were also open, as will be seen, to underhand methods of persuasion.[9] The use of such methods may indeed point to the growing freedoms of the press, which could not be controlled by the usual financial methods, but needed more oblique pressures to be placed on opposition.

Lady Perceval

Bridget Perceval, described by Queen Caroline's lady-in-waiting Lady Charlotte Lindsay as a 'spirited Amazon', was the only daughter of Lieutenant-Colonel Glynne Wynn MP, brother of Thomas Wynn, 1st Lord Newborough.[10] On 10 March 1792 she married John, 4th Viscount Perceval, heir to the earldom of Egmont, and the marriage would bring Perceval into a closer political orbit to the princess. The Perceval family had wealth and longstanding political connections, tracing its lineage to Ascelin Gouel de Perceval, who, *Burke's Peerage* suggests, 'accompanied William the Conqueror to England'. The family's wealth originated from their Somerset and Irish estates, which they had acquired through royal service. In the late sixteenth century Richard Perceval's services to Queen Elizabeth included deciphering secret letters giving the first intelligence of the Spanish Armada. This gained him the queen's favour and he rose to the registrar of the Court of Wards in Ireland, where he obtained 'considerable landed property'.[11] His descendant John Perceval succeeded to these Irish estates in 1691 and began a parliamentary career. Attracted to the less brutal world of letters and sciences, he became a fellow of the Royal Society and undertook his Grand Tour in 1707.

He became president of the American colony of Georgia in 1732 and, after a succession of Irish peerages, achieved the rank of Earl of Egmont in 1733. The second Earl became the most prominent leader of the opposition party in the Lords in 1748–9 and was appointed first lord of the admiralty in 1763. His fourth son, Spencer Perceval (and Lady Perceval's uncle by marriage), attained the unenviable position of being the only British prime minister to have succumbed to an assassination. Perceval also had close connections with the princess. In 1809 Perceval, then Chancellor of the Exchequer, helped to settle Caroline's financial claims. The prince agreed to pay £49,000 to cover her debts and £5,000 annually as maintenance (around £2 million and £232,000 in today's money). Perceval had also arranged for suppression of 'The Book', a full account of the depositions to the Delicate Investigation, burning the five hundred copies that he had locked in his house and placing an advertisement in *The Times* for other copies to be sent to him.[12] Lady Perceval had clearly joined a family of some distinction with a reputation for political intrigue.

These skills were deployed when Lady Perceval become one of the key members in the group surrounding the princess, involving herself in the princess's attempts to gain a more secure financial footing. Her husband, Lord Perceval, was a Whig, and their home in Blackheath was close to the princess's household at Montague House. They called at each other's houses and, the Egmont Papers reveal, Lady Perceval regularly corresponded with Lady Anne Hamilton, the princess's lady-in-waiting. She soon took up the princess's cause with the two weapons she knew best: social intrigue and her pen.

Caroline may have 'remained in retirement, without noticing the insects who threatened her with their petty malignity', if her 'maternal feelings had not been deeply wounded' by the prince's attempts to deny her contact with her daughter. In 1812 she attempted to seek a second residence in London and greater access to her daughter.[13] Advised by his supporters that Caroline would become regent in the event of his death, the prince had become more determined to seek a divorce, opening up the question of a new 'Delicate Investigation'. The battle now moved to the pages of the press, which were becoming braver in their attacks on the Establishment. An anonymous pamphlet noted in September 1812 that newspapers 'have been spreading their dangerous doctrines far and wide, [but] they have met with but little resistance from any quarter.' Indeed, they were 'even daring to revile their *sovereign himself*.'[14] According to the diaries of another of Caroline's ladies-in-waiting, Charlotte, Lady Campbell, the prince threatened to publish a correspondence between Lady Anne Hamilton and the princess in the winter of 1812. Perhaps in response, in December the princess published an 'advertisement' for letters that she wished to be published in the *Morning Chronicle*. Lady Campbell dreaded the publication of such epistles, since it would 'give colour to a charge of breach of trust in making letters public that were never written to meet the public eye'.[15]

On 14 January 1813 Caroline sent a letter to the prime minister, Lord Liverpool, and the High Chancellor, Lord Eldon, for the Regent's attention, asking for an improvement in her circumstances. Lady Campbell (who felt that the letter bore the mark of several hands) predicted that no good would come from such methods:

> Oh dear! Oh dear! I wish they would let things go on in their old bad way! I fear that we are playing a deep game at which we may lose much more than we are likely to win – and by [pushing quit]. We had a fine card in our hands that would have played of itself.[16]

The prince refused to read the letter. She sent it again, but Carlton House refused reception. On 26 January the princess wrote expressing 'her surprise that no answer had been given for a whole week'. Carlton House replied that the prince had read the letter on 23 January, but had not wished to answer.[17] The princess responded with further complaints of her treatment and the pain caused by the separation from her daughter. The publication induced Lord Liverpool to deny a visit between Princess Charlotte and Caroline on 11 February, and despite Caroline's appeals, on 25 February the Privy Council concluded that the restrictions on the princess and her daughter should remain in place.[18]

The 14 January letter, which became known as the 'Regent's Valentine', appeared in the Whig-supporting *Morning Chronicle* on 10 February through some 'unknown channel', sparking the production of numerous pro-Caroline prints, plates and jugs decorated with lines from the letter. By January 1813 newspapers contained 'long histories written, with the intention to inflame the public with an idea of the princess's wrongs [against her], and, above all, to make it clear that Princess Charlotte could reign to-morrow'.[19] The affair had entered the public sphere, consumed by her supporters, and becoming, as Lady Campbell feared, a matter of party politics and public opinion, subject to 'warm and repeated discussion' in the press. She worried that the princess had become the 'tool of a party' at a time when the government was under considerable attack.[20]

The instigator of the publication plan is uncertain. Lady Campbell took the view that 'the probability of the story is that, Lady [Perceval] was the contriver and plotter of the whole manoeuvre.' Elsewhere, however, she suggested that Perceval was a 'weak intriguing woman, who seems to me a mere convenience', suggesting that the princess or a third party began the plot.[21] For her part, the princess attempted to deny involvement. Lady Anne Hamilton wrote to Lord Liverpool that 'the Insidious Insinuation, respecting the publication of the letter addressed by the princess of Wales, on the 14 January to the prince Regent . . . is as void of foundation, and as false, as all the former accusations, of the Traducers of Her Royal Highness's Honour in the year 1806.' Lady Anne also suggested that 'dignified silence would have been the line of conduct the princess would have preserved', if the prime minister had not deprived 'Her Royal Highness of the only real Happiness of seeing her only child'.[22]

There is, however, some evidence that implicates Lady Perceval. Some months before this she had taken an interest in the school to which the editor of the *Pilot* newspaper sent his two daughters, and as a result of this connection, the princess 'became acquainted' with the two girls. She then recommended a successful cure when they fell ill with whooping cough, winning 'the *Pilot*'s heart', and the editor devoted the paper to her service, writing to Lady Perceval to inform her that the '*Pilot* is, in what is termed "opposition", now, having so styled since February 1812'. According to this letter, the proprietor of the newspaper, Edward Fitzgerald, had defended the princess from her attackers when he wrote for the *Morning Post* in 1806. The editor now offered the 'steady and warmest support of their paper in the laudable and natural struggle, which engages the princess of Wales'.[23] Lady Perceval was soon placing her letters in the paper, as she believed, on Caroline's behalf; however, these items do not include the 'Regent's Valentine'.[24]

Middlemen

Like much Regency politicking, such journalistic interference required the service of middlemen, forming a link between Grub Street and the Drawing Room. Lady Perceval was able to provide these services to the princess through a distant relative, John Mitford. He had served as a sailor in the navy, claiming to have been a midshipman on the *Victory* and to have been present at the Battles of Toulon and the Nile. According to his account in the *Description of the Crimes and Horrors in the Interior of Warburton's Private Madhouse at Hoxton* (1825), in 1811 Mitford was in the Mediterranean as acting master of the brig *Philomel* when he received a letter from his wife with the news that Lady Perceval would be pleased to find him a civil service post. Attracted by the offer, he took a passage to England, suffering 'a relapse of illness which appeared to affect the brain' on the journey. When he arrived in Blackheath, Mitford discovered that the viscountess was 'engaged in writing letters for the public journals, levelled at the prince Regent and Ministers of State'.[25] It was decided that Mitford could provide a useful service for the princess's party. Thomas Warburton, the notorious proprietor of Whitmore House, a madhouse for rich patients in Hoxton, provided a medical certificate, releasing Mitford from the Navy. Mitford was installed in the Warburton's establishment from May 1812 until February 1813, in order, Mitford recalled, to 'remove suspicion from the parties at Blackheath, where they were watched' (it is also possible that he was suffering from his earlier illness). Mitford was not constrained to stay in the asylum, where he had his own apartment, and he 'went and came as he pleased, being always engaged in writing when within'.[26] He received a sum from the navy as a result of his attested illness and loss of his commission, and the viscountess promised his family financial support; Mitford also claimed to have received financial support from Lord Redesdale. According to the court record, Lady Perceval also offered him £2,000 for acting as an intermediary.[27]

The arrangement might have been relatively unusual but took advantage of the lax rules governing madhouses. Mitford's *Description of the Crimes and Horrors* suggests that families often used such institutions for various extra-sanitary needs, providing a dumping-ground for troublesome wives, husbands or relatives in the shocking manner of many a melodramatic novel. The terms of the 1744 Madhouse Act stipulated that the insane could be placed in a madhouse under the written and sealed 'orders' of 'some physician, surgeon or apothecary'. Poor regulation of these professions ensured that such documents were easy to obtain, and madhouses could often provide a convenient place to put awkward relations or those who wished to be at a remove from society (pauper or criminal lunatics began to be placed in public asylums following the 1808 County Asylums Act). Warburton, who signed Mitford's certificate of lunacy, did so as an 'apothecary', although he was not a member of the Society of Apothecaries. From here, Mitford wrote letters to newspapers and journalistic pieces, and Lady Perceval provided him with pro-Caroline items for the press, such as a column entitled 'Nelson as a Boy', which he then arranged to be published in *The Star*, edited by John Mayne. Lady Perceval also ordered him to write to John Walter of *The Times*, corroborating items placed in *The News* (although she was aware that *The Times* was 'written almost under the dictating of the [Tory] Marquis of W[ellesley]'.[28] On 15 March 1813 Thomas Phipps, the editor of *The News*, wrote to Lady Anne Hamilton offering his paper for the cause, and on 28 March the paper published the news of the new Delicate Investigation by the Privy Council and revealed that Captain Manby had been offered a bribe of £20,000 in the original investigation.[29] Mitford had been used to supply the information.

Mitford was not the only agent in the service of the Blackheath propaganda apparatus. In the spring of 1814 the traveller and journalist

Captain Thomas Ashe called on Lady Perceval, at her home in Blackheath, east of the City of London. Ashe had been summoned to discuss an item that he intended to place in the popular press on her behalf, attacking the Regent's treatment of the princess and her daughter. As Ashe recorded in his scandalous *Memoirs and Confessions* (London, 1815), his visit took place the day after Lady Perceval had been reprimanded in court and publicly humiliated for placing forged letters supporting the Princess of Wales in the press. He recorded that:

> I was announced by name; yet, as I entered the apartment, it seemed that I was entirely unobserved. [Lady Perceval's] eye was sunk, contracted, and dark; it rather operated to make me utter an exorcism, than bless my condition. Her brow seemed more figurative of the love of authority, than the love of her kind; and when a smile stole upon her cheek, at what she valiantly read, it neither mantled nor reddened with delight[:] It was anomalous, portentous, and freezing.[30]

Ashe was a noted forger and blackmailer who had begun his trade under Spencer Perceval's tutelage.[31] In his *Memoirs* he claimed to be employed by Lady Perceval, initially to 'hire vagabonds to hoot the Regent whenever he appeared in any place of public amusements' and 'thereby convince him that the people were decidedly against his conduct' towards the princess and then to write pieces for the public papers.

Ashe's memoir records that he worked for 'a hydra party, among whose heads they counted that of the Princess of Wales'. He claimed Lady Perceval wrote that he 'must attack the prince with a weapon more cold and deadly, with an instrument that murders without the mark of blood, that palls its victim in the covering of public sacrifice, and will make him, in the eye of the ignorant, like Brutus, who stabbed the mighty Caesar for his country's good'.[32] Ashe's melodramatic prose was soon put to use. In February 1813, as outlined earlier, another secret investigation into the princess's fidelity was underway in response to the princess's claims on Charlotte (the princess is recorded as having dropped her pen in shock at the news), and she was 'left without any society whatever – except the opposition'. Her party needed to attack.[33] Ashe 'took up his pen', and was engaged by Lady Perceval to 'to compose parliamentary orations against the prince', and for 'squibs and flights to be put into the newspapers, in order to excite the attention, and exasperate the mind of the public'. The public mind must be made to see how the princess had been wronged, and particularly 'as a woman'.[34] On 15 March 1813, Samuel Whitbread denounced the Tory *Morning Post* and *Morning Herald*, which carried anti-Caroline pieces, 'as teeming with calumnious evidence against her Royal Highness, the falsehood of which had been proved', and defended the princess in Parliament, bringing 'most of his auditors . . . [to] *tears*'.[35] In April 1813 the princess received a sympathetic address from the mayor and aldermen of the City of London.

Ashe's publication in 1815 of his version of the suppressed account of the Delicate Investigation, *Spirit of the Book*, further excited the situation and revealed the political dimensions of the attacks as the Whigs revelled in Tory discomfort. The princess's party deemed the findings highly injurious to the prince, since they might reveal details of his affair with Mrs Fitzherbert. Recognizing the limits of public support, politician and chief advisor to the princess Henry Brougham feared that 'she will be called that compleat letterwriter and become generally despised.'[36] For the princess's part, Caroline wrote, any hurts would be 'less than those which I should be exposed to from my silence'.[37] Booksellers and newspapermen continued to benefit from the scandal and popular support for the princess: For example, *The News*'s circulation, which had published the Regent's Valentine and began to support the princess, rose from 7,000 to 8,900.[38]

Carlton House now needed to rely on underhand methods: Caroline appeared to be winning the campaign for public support. The regent considered publishing the Law Officer's Report on 1807, which would have damned the princess. He also revealed that he had attempted to divorce the princess, but was advised not to take such drastic and public action.[39] More circumspect and secretive methods had to be employed, and Carlton House began to increase the pressure on members of the princess's party. The Supplementary Egmont Papers include several letters received in the spring of 1813, when Lady Perceval was using Mitford to publish her letters, threatening an intermediary (a 'Mr John Smith') who was providing stories for the press. Could this intermediary have been Mitford or Ashe, or perhaps an unknown third party? Mitford later claimed that 'he was watched and pursued, and his house beset by inquiries by those with whom he pretended to have had communications.'[40] Lady Perceval attributed these messages to John McMahon, the prince's long-suffering personal secretary; she also claimed some notes came from 'two gentlemen high in the confidence of his Royal Highness', suggesting that the prime minister, Lord Liverpool, was one; the government certainly devoted a great deal of attention to the marriage and possible divorce.[41] The notes mixed bribes ('We know your embarrassment and connexions and will relieve you under the strict understanding that you tell us the whole you know concerning the business – you may then be independent'; 'your professional career shall be forwarded') with threats ('pray consider how painful it would be to see yourself compelled to full disclosure'; 'we can do you a great deal of good and a great deal of harm . . . you were seen at the Admiralty on Tuesday last, so mark me, we can find you when we please'). These are endorsed in another hand with notes on the appearance of the bearers of the letters: 'Delivered by an orderly Dragoon. A gentleman & Lady waited in a gig & to whom the Dragoon referred before he delivered the letter.'[42]

The Supplementary Egmont Papers also include a copy of an annotated anonymous letter to Lady Perceval, written after the 'publication of the forged state letters', which she believed to be in Mitford's disguised hand. The watermark included the royal crown and three fleur-de-lys, suggesting a connection with the prince. The letter advised her to 'turn off your Butler and his wife, footman also – they are not sincere. She is a —.' The aim was to encourage her to dismiss them, so that they would bear a grudge and swear 'to any falsehood'.[43]

Threats could also be combined with the financial muscle that the regent could now employ; an approach that the historian Iain

McCalman notes was 'if not respectable, then at least a tacitly accepted and widely practised political mode'. In 1812 Carlton House's allies had considered 'the possibility of *buying over The News*' as a mouthpiece for his party. At first, the prince baulked at this course of action (perhaps for financial reasons), and the paper remained faithful to the princess, but in the spring of 1813, the prince's party finally purchased the paper (or at least bribed Phipps) and published 'a correspondence, which [the prince] declares to have passed between the princess herself, and Lady Anne Hamilton, and Lord Perceval' on 4 April 1813.[44] Bills announcing the publication were posted across London. It proved to be an effective investment. The pro-regent *Courier* copied the piece on the next day. The publication shook the princess's court at Montague House. Caroline wrote that Phipps 'has behaved quite scandalously: – he has been corrupted and bribed from Carlton House since a week.' Caroline called on her friends to no 'longer take the *News*, as he must know that people of respectability do not like to be imposed on, and that every body many some day or other be liable to see forged letters of theirs in [*The News*]' and noted that 'Poor Lady Anne and Lady P[erceva]l are in the greatest alarm possible'.[45] Their intrigues had been revealed and their character and 'feminine honour' undermined. Eager to resurrect the prince's reputation, Carlton House lost no time in taking advantage of the situation and McMahon placed fresh 'scurrilous' pieces concerning the princess and attempted to bribe an editor to publish the prince's account.[46]

The interest in the matter caused Phipps to approach Lady Perceval to check the veracity of his story. She denied any involvement and suggested that Mitford had succumbed to a fit of insanity and placed the letters on his own account. She then attempted to persuade Mrs Mitford to hire two men from Warburton's establishment to constrain her husband since, Mrs Mitford claimed, he had beat her and thrown a writing desk at her, and threatened to cut his own throat with a razor.[47] (Warburton often hired his attendants in such a fashion, at one point loaning keepers to Dr Francis Ellis for the care of George III, and often tending lunatics in private homes in order to expand his business and avoid obtaining fresh certification.)[48] As a result, Mitford could not be produced. Despite his confinement, on 13 April he either escaped from his attendants or may simply have been dismissed by them and provided Phipps with what he claimed were letters from Lady Perceval.[49] On 6 June 1813, under the direction of the Regent's party, Phipps revealed in *The News* that he had 'received the letters in question from J. Mitford, who said they were delivered to him by Lady Percival [*sic*]'.[50]

The affair now took a legal turn. On 21 June Lord and Lady Perceval sued Phipps for libel, receiving a ruling from the Lord Chief Justice, Edward Law, 1st Baron Ellenborough.[51] Robert Castlereagh, leader of the House of Commons, raised the matter in the Commons, asserting that the princess was implicated in the scheme to undermine the prince's popularity.[52] In response to these claims, Lady Perceval sued Mitford for perjury at the Court of King's Bench, with the case presented again before Lord Ellenborough on 24 February 1814. The court would not look kindly on her case. Lord Ellenborough had acted as one of the commissioners in the 1806 Delicate Investigation, and had refused to 'concur in any declaration importing the princess's innocence'. At one point, he argued that the princess's 'lascivious kissing' equated with incitement to high treason.[53] Other members of the legal profession, including Henry Brougham, admired Ellenborough's sharp wit and recognized his judicial stature, but like other judges in his profession, his political allegiances were plain. Ellenborough was clearly the prince's man, despite Lady Campbell noting that 'even the reigning monarch is merely a chief magistrate, under the authority of laws which he cannot overpass.'[54] From the late 1780s Ellenborough had represented the state, acting as prosecutor for the libel trial of Lord George Gordon in 1787, the trial of Thomas Walker for conspiracy to overthrow the constitution in 1794, and several other cases. As a judge, the *Oxford Dictionary of National Biography* notes, Ellenborough 'proved himself often to be irascible and impatient with everyone', abusing inadequate barristers and unreliable witnesses alike. Presiding on the King's Bench, he reduced the importance of the jury to trials, preferring to view questions of fact as questions of law, requiring a legal, rather than a jury's, opinion. Although sometimes lending his support to more liberal causes, such as the defence of free speech (for example, during the prosecution of the *Morning Chronicle* in 1810), his prosecution of Jean Peltier for a libel against Napoleon Bonaparte in 1803 underscored his reliability as tool of the state at a time when the court's independence could be limited at best.

Lady Perceval's decision to contest the affair in court was considered very poor judgement on her behalf. She underestimated the prince's party's determination and ability to influence Phipps and Mitford, whom they could promise more patronage than either Perceval or Caroline could arrange. The judicial system cannot be understood without an awareness of the webs of patronage within which it operated; links between Westminster and the courts were also close, with over half of judges formerly elected Members of Parliament. Furthermore, as the historian Vic Gatrell points out, judges 'worked within a criminal justice system which quite purposefully upheld propertied hierarchy first and delivered justice second, in which respectable patronage, perceived character, and local tensions were *meant* to affect sentences and appeals, in which judges and home secretaries *had* to placate great men even if not to capitulate to them, in which juries were often timid'.[55] Ellenborough could be counted to be very dubious of the princess's morality and in favour of supporting the prince, and the court system more generally could be counted upon to defend the status quo and the establishment from such perceived outsiders as Lady Perceval and Princess Caroline, despite their aristocratic and royal marriages. The backdrop of the war in Europe and the king's continued ill health provided further reasons to undermine public dissent, even if the princess's situation lacked widespread popular political charge. Finally, Perceval's case was weak: after all, she had been placing letters in the press and using Mitford's services.

The Supplementary Egmont Papers contain a flurry of notes and documents related to the trial, attempting to prove Mitford's guilt and that Lady Perceval was otherwise engaged when she was in reality meeting Mitford or Phipps.[56] She had counted on Warburton's certificate ensuring that Mitford could not be used a witness, but her confidence was misplaced and the court disregarded the document.

Lady Perceval summoned Mitford's wife to Blackheath and persuaded her to commit him to custody as a lunatic on the advice of Mr Holt, Lady Perceval's attorney. Although Warburton refused to give testimony, other evidence was found and Mitford was acceptable to the court. The defence produced a series of letters from Perceval and her friend Lady Anne Hamilton, together with a letter from the princess that proved to be in Caroline's handwriting. The court found in Mitford's favour, although Lady Anne Hamilton maintained that a 'copy of a copy is not evidence' and that Lord Ellenborough should have disallowed the use of her letters.[57] Ashe noted that Ellenborough 'hinted that he was not ignorant of the mean, mischievous, and ruinous confederacy' of which Lady Perceval was a part.[58]

The specifics of the case are difficult to assess at this remove. Historians have accepted Ellenborough's judgements on Lady Perceval and Lady Campbell's dislike of her, casting Perceval as stupid, intriguing or criminal. The printed evidence was produced by Mitford and Phipps alone.[59] The trial incontrovertibly proved that she had been placing 'paragraphs' in the press and addresses in Parliament using Mitford's intermediary services: Lady Perceval admitted as much. However, the provenance of the 4 April letters remains unclear, as both Lady Anne Hamilton and Lady Perceval argued that they were forged; furthermore, the prince's party had begun to influence Phipps and *The News*. Holt argued that the princess's supporters 'attribute, perhaps, more to your ladyship than you have actually done'.[60]

Yet despite the opacity of the case, it retains a wider interest. First, it underlines the opportunities and limits open to aristocratic women and their engagement with the public press. Lady Campbell and Lady Perceval make for an interesting comparison. Like many figures of the day, Lady Campbell took a keen, if cynical, interest in the affair, but did not involve herself directly. In contrast, she found an outlet for her talents of observation in a series of popular novels, such as *Self-indulgence* (1812) and, partly out of financial necessity, later produced a series of mostly anonymous novels following *Conduct Is Fate* (1822). She also published her diary anonymously, creating something of a scandal in 1838.[61] Lady Perceval's choices were more dangerous. We can only speculate on her motives for intervening in the press, but such actions were not undertaken lightly. She knew that this was more than social intriguing, and engaged semi-directly with the wider public through the medium of the press. On 21 February 1813 Perceval wrote to Mitford, alluding to the Mary Anne Clarke affair (the recent mistress of the Duke of York), that

> John Bull's heart is her's and his eyes are opened, and we must hope that if Englishmen would championize Mrs. Clarke the p— against the king's son, very unjustly and to their discredit I ever thought, those same Englishmen will at heart defend and protect their old king's niece, and their young queen's elect mother.

For the prince's part, the Privy Council similarly concerned itself with the Regent's popularity and his ability to marshal public opinion to his cause. As Lady Campbell noted in her diary, 'Every station has its price – its penalty. Princes and Princesses must live for the public.'[62] It was admitted in the trial that 'the public mind was agitated respecting the affairs of an illustrious personage' (meaning the Princess of Wales).[63] The participants consistently deployed the language of the 'public mind' (Mitford, for example, recalled that 'The public mind was highly inflamed,' and Ashe wrote of 'daily poison' that 'was to be conveyed to the public mind'), and the high sales of London newspapers reflected a wider dissemination of the scandal throughout the provincial journals.[64] Interest in the affair was not limited to the upper and middle-classes. Radical excitement coalesced around pamphlets, prints and copies of 'The Book', and the London mob could be encouraged to boo or cheer as required. For example, Ashe claimed to have been required to orchestrate claques at the opera who cheered the princess and hired a mob to boo the Regent.[65]

As Phipps noted, news could be posted along the main streets of London, and the trial revealed the ways that female engagement with the public sphere took place within gendered terms. Women were able to operate with the official and journalistic worlds, but there were certain restrictions that had to be respected. For example, the perjury case brought against Mitford was done so in Lord Perceval's name, but, Lady Perceval's counsel noted, 'the name of Lord Perceval is added merely as matter of form.'[66] The case became a matter of character, in which Lady Perceval was defended by her counsel as a woman of 'eminent rank and or irreproachable character . . . she has been driven to the necessity of vindicating her honour and character', and who took a maternal interest in Mitford and his family's welfare. The Lord Chief Justice also weighed in on the matter, directing the jury's attention to some lines in 'when Nelson was a Child' ('Rush upon your enemy – surprise, astound him, – terror unhorses him'), lines which 'gave me more pain than I ever recollect to have felt from the reading of any document. It breathes a spirit so bitter and so unchristian . . . Gentlemen, this is a very *masculine* sentence . . . thank God we have very few instances of such conduct, either in men or women.'[67]

By allowing women's interference, the prosecution counsel feared, the order of the nation could be undermined:

> If this sort of *consilium in consilio* (to use one of her ladyship's phrases), if this sort of petticoat government, in directing the affairs of the public, is for one moment to be endured, there is an end to the respectability of the country in the eyes of all foreign nations – there is an end of the good order of society.[68]

Such gendered terms and assumptions appear elsewhere in the affair: Lady Campbell dismissed Lady Perceval as a 'weak intriguing woman' and dismissed the affair as a 'fine kettle of fish' cooked up by Perceval and Lady Anne Hamilton.[69] The prince's party's depiction of the 'hydra' based at Blackheath drew upon a repertoire of gendered political symbolism. Ashe, he claims, was tasked with composing pieces 'defending a highly injured female' (he was also subjected to 'flattering looks' from Lady Perceval).[70] He was alert to the public response to the princess as a 'wronged woman', and commentated on the presentation of the princess's 'female claims' by the Blackheath faction:

> The indefatigable hydra employed me in labouring hard and incessantly to do that for the Princess of Wales, through the medium of public sympathy, which they could not through the medium of justice; – they wanted me to make her claims, as a woman, supersede that influence which should be wholly dependent on veracity.[71]

Lady Perceval could easily be depicted as a 'petticoat politician', 'cooking up' trouble for her mistress, as her confidants recorded.

Finally, class and social station played a role. The jury consisted of one 'gentleman' and eleven working men, such as warehousemen, victuallers, a turner and a barber. The prosecution emphasized Lady Perceval's aristocratic status, which he believed she did not deserve, stating that 'I have more than once, from something in my mind, forgot the rank of Lady Perceval, and have been induced to call her Mrs instead of Viscountess Perceval.' He reminded the jury that 'it is not the powerful influence of a powerful accuser' that should gain justice. Lady Perceval had transgressed all these boundaries.[72]

It was now difficult for Caroline to associate with Lady Perceval, and she was, as the blackmailer and writer Ashe comments, 'dropped'. Such 'martyrdom', Lady Perceval contended, was the Regent's party's aim and she was the victim of a conspiracy; indeed, she even suggested that the Regent had placed the letters in an attempt to slur the princess. The affair underlines how the prince and his government allies were not afraid of acting menacingly: Her agent had been threatened, Caroline had long known that McMahon and others were spying upon her, and Lady Perceval's lawyer wrote that their current object was 'to confine her Royal Highness's friend to as small a circle as possible.'[73]

In this aim they were largely successful, and Lady Perceval was ridiculed in the press: for example, the caricature *Lady P Aragraph CHAMPIONIZING – Vide Letters* showed her penning letters, while volumes such as 'Machiavelli' were strewn on the floor and Mitford put up diabolical pictures. The defence counsel and the judge had repeatedly belittled her 'squibs or crackers' as 'paragraphs'.[74] Mitford himself attacked Lady Egmont in print, describing her and the princess in his *Descriptions of the Crimes and Horrors* as 'petticoat politicians'. All those who hated Spencer Perceval could be counted upon to 'vent some of their ancient malignity on this present situation'.[75]

Yet Lady Perceval still considered pursuing the matter following Phipp's publication of the trial and various letters. Her lawyer urged that she should be careful and avoid engaging with the press, since 'every fresh publication in the papers on either side is a faggot thrown upon the fire, to feed the malice of those who crave for fresh supplies. The thing seems to . . . have reached its natural course, & to be effectively burnt out. Do not shake the ashes into fresh flames.'[76] More widely, the affair damaged the princess's reputation among some reformers, including Sir Francis Burdett, who blamed Princess Charlotte 'for the friendship for Lady Perceval & for all the last publications & declares he will have nothing to do with the business'.[77] Ashe found that publishers returned his pamphlets from Lady Perceval and 'shrunk from a hydra manuscript as they would from a snake in the grass'; he also claimed that the princess's party attempted to buy him with the offer of a £600 editorship. More

Charles Williams, *Lady P aragraph Championizing. – Vide Letters*, 1814, satirical print.

importantly, the affair damaged the princess's popularity and may well have contributed to her decision to leave the country.[78]

Lady Perceval also fell victim to Ashe, who wrote to her with his plans to publish his autobiography, informing her that he was looking for a patron. Rejecting this coded request for money, she unsuccessfully attempted to suppress its publication.[79] Henry Colburn's public library duly published *Memoirs of Captain Ashe* in 1815 in three volumes. Writing from the relative safety of France, Ashe claimed to 'have retired from the world, and with the full determination of employing my utmost ability, and the most sacred regard to truth, in writing the memoirs of my own life'.[80]

Although the historian Arthur Aspinall suggests that Caroline 'dropped' Lady Perceval, the connection had not wholly been broken.[81] According to Lady Perceval's diary notes, they dined together on 9 December 1814, and while many thought that Perceval had acted on her own initiative, it seems clear that the princess had good knowledge of her actions and may even have encouraged them.[82] The relationship was certainly resurrected following the death of George III in 1820, when Caroline had reason to draw on every connection she could to press her case now that she might become queen. Efforts were also made to prevent her return from France; her passport was to be revoked. Caroline went undercover, signing herself the Comtesse d'Oldi, with whom she had stayed during her sojourn in Italy, and wrote to Lady Perceval under this name. Lady Perceval and Caroline's son William Austin also wrote to one another.[83] Yet the connection between Caroline and Lady Perceval had to remain discreet for fear of undermining Caroline's popular support. As a correspondent of Lord Colchester noted,

> Her Majesty will leave no stone unturned to gain popularity. This night she goes to Drury Lane; to-morrow, it is supposed to Covent Garden; and doubtless the Opera, &c., will not lose the like honours. She has visited Mrs Damer, Lady Elizabeth Whitbread, and Lady Perceval; but the latter on foot, whilst her carriage was waiting on the heath at some distance.[84]

Finally, it was not only Lady Perceval who retained an involvement in the queen's melodrama; John Mitford remained an important, if subterranean, player. While Lord Redesdale provided for his wife and children, Mitford found some income from journalism and poetry, writing for the scandalous radical papers, *The Scourge* and *Bon Ton Magazine*. In 1818 he also published *The Adventures of Johnny Newcome in the Navy, a Poem in Four Cantos* under the pseudonym of Alfred Burton (which went into several editions) and *Poems of a British Sailor*. He claimed to have co-authored 'The Vampyre', which appeared in the *New Monthly Magazine* of April 1819, with John William Polidori and Lord Byron. Mitford descended further into alcoholism, working for a time in a gravel pit at Battersea Fields and sleeping on a bed of nettles and grass.[85]

After the princess's departure in 1814, to which the letter-publishing strategy inadvertently contributed, numerous ballad sheets and chapbooks that portrayed Caroline as a wronged mother, forced to leave her child and enter into exile, found a ready market and reinforced the sexualized nature of the affair. Ironically, in 1820 J. L. Marks hired Mitford to produce pro-Caroline propaganda, including the squib *A Peep into W-r Castle, after the Lost Mutton: A Poem*. Initially suppressed by the Palace at the cost of £35 (equivalent to around £2,000 in today's terms) and then published as a shilling pamphlet by William Benbow, the radical reformer, *A Peep into W-r Castle* depicted George as a be-whiskered goat hunting for 'mutton', satirizing his many sexual intrigues as Regent. The sexual allusions would not have been lost on his readers; after all, the agitations of 1820–21 were popularly cast in gendered terms, as they had been during the second Delicate Investigation and Mitford Affair. Mitford's ballads ridiculing the Regent were soon being sung all across London, and pirate editions proliferated (many of which were produced in search of hush money from the palace). Other caricatures and chapbooks from 1814 were recycled for the later agitations.[86]

Many of the political techniques deployed during the Princess Caroline affair were thus developed and tested in her battles of 1813 and 1814. It was in the pages of newspapers such as *The Sun*, *The Pilot* or even the *Morning Chronicle* that aristocratic women could, if they

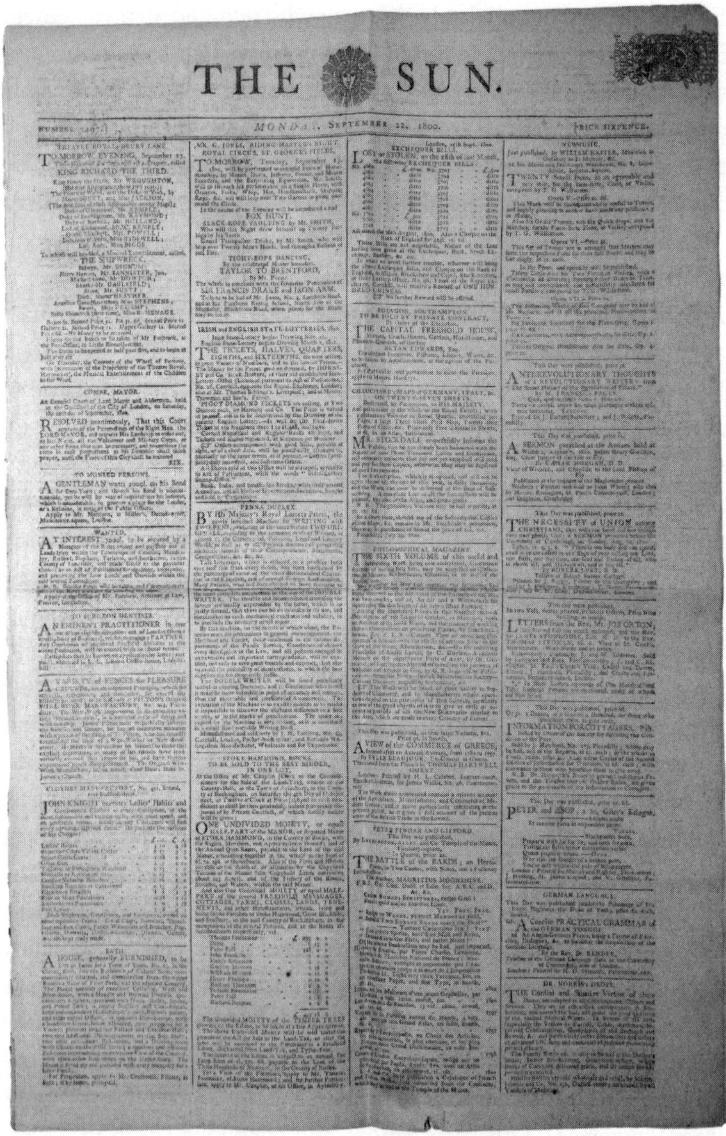

THE SUN.

MONDAY, SEPTEMBER 22, 1800.

The Sun, 22 September 1800.

THE NEWS.

No. 678 SUNDAY, AUGUST 9, 1818. PRICE 8½d.

This Paper is Published at an early hour every SUNDAY Morning, at "THE NEWS" Office, No. 28, Brydges-street, and distributed throughout the Metropolis and within the Two-penny Post District, by Nine o'Clock.—☞ *No Advertisements of any description are ever inserted in this Paper.*

THE WARS OF THE REIGN OF GEORGE THE THIRD.

"It is a war of all principles against all prejudices."
FRENCH CONVENTIONALIST.

"Already have our quarrels fill'd the world
With widows and with orphans; —— mourns
Our guilty wars, and earth's remotest regions,
Lie half unpeopled by the feuds of ——."
ADDISON.

The reign of GEORGE [illegible] consists, with slight [illegible] cipied contest against the liberty of nations, as founded upon the advanced positions of general knowledge, and the extended influence of intellectual improvement. The gross and barbarous contrast, between the maxims of Government, and the opinion of the People, as regarded more or less through the whole of Europe, cannot be denied nor disguised. We may cover over the crater of the Volcano with flowers—but the principle of combustion that slumbers beneath, proceeds uninterruptedly in its generic process. War teaches the art of war; the defeat of to-day, carries with it the attainments of to-morrow's revenge. Cast a reflecting eye, for a moment, over the gigantic Colonial Power of Great Britain! Our dominion in North America, and the West Indies, is destined hourly to melt and merge in the growing strength and influence of America. One generation of men, [illegible] this England of the West, have attained a power [illegible] had never been consolidated by centuries in [illegible] times. At one period of the present KING's [illegible] North America is his Colony, subject to his [illegible] filling his dominion, pouring its riches into [illegible] This very Colony is now the exam- [illegible] more impracticable; and we are, in every contest, beating the natives into the skill and science of European tactics. Every battle gives depth, solidity, and vigour to the blacken[ing] [illegible] of deadly revenge, which slumbers like a thunder-cloud over our heads, in that devoted country. A Day of Retribution will come: the English, [illegible] will have to disclaim the cruelty and [illegible] which was practised against an [illegible] portion of the human race, by a [illegible] of things, over [illegible] politician may [illegible] and the riches of dominion; but the philosopher, and the historian of other times, will call things by their right names, and will not shrink from tracing the "Decline and Fall of Britain," to the absurd and monstrous thirst of gain, which equally lost her the *East* and the *West*—"the wings," as they were termed by a celebrated Statesman, which bore her high above all other nations, to fame, riches, and prosperity. Look at Spain! What have her mountains of gold, and her mines of diamonds, done for her? They have been transformed into the very instruments of her Fall. England at this moment comprehends within herself, the extremes of magnificence and misery. Luxury is debasing one portion of society; and poverty and oppression the other. Their influences meet.—Their reaction must either be through *Reform* or *Revolution*. Our sapient Rulers seem to make a merit of holding public opinion in high contempt; and the Reign which commenced with the activity of every false principle of human policy—which in its progress has desolated all corners of the earth—and waged a ceaseless war against Liberty, under every artifice that can [illegible] the purposes of men

[illegible] hear the writ read. Parliament of course stands prorogued to Friday the 2d day of October next.

Among the improvements in the House of Commons, is a second stair-case to the Gallery, by which no strangers are to be admitted. But, upon orders for clearing the gallery, this stair-case is to serve for egress, while the old one is for ingress. By this arrangement, it is calculated that the delay and difficulty which have heretofore occurred in clearing the gallery, will be obviated, those who [illegible] the one door being sure of the first [illegible] [illegible]

THE AMERICAN papers [illegible] of the removal of General Montgomery's remains, from their obscure grave in Canada, to receive monumental honours from his adopted country. General Montgomery was a native of Ireland, born near Lifford, county of Donegal, in the year 1736, of one of the most respectable families in that country. His elder brother, Alexander Montgomery, enjoyed the paternal estate, and was representative in Parliament for the county of Donegal for many years. The late General entered early in life in the British service as Captain of infantry, and served with distinguished credit during the war which ended in 1763. He then resigned his commission, and devoted all the energies of his mind and person to the service of his adopted country—America.

QUEBEC, JUNE 23.—After resting in peace for 43 years within the walls and under the sod of this garrison, the skeleton of General Montgomery, who fell in an assault on the Lower Town, on the 31st of December, 1775, was, on Saturday last, raised from the place of its deposit and took its departure for New York, where it is destined to a more distinguished place of interment, in the church of St. Paul of that city.

NEW YORK, JULY 8.—The remains of General Montgomery were yesterday morning received at Fort-Ganzevoort, and conducted to the City Hall by a military escort.

The age-stricken widow of our hero yet lives to see [illegible]

The News, 9 August 1818.

wished, engage with a form of politics that combined the attempted manipulation of public opinion with drawing-room calculations. Furthermore, the gendered nature of the debate was already apparent: the editor of the *Pilot* newspaper wrote to Lady Perceval that 'I am induced to express a hope & wish that a very short period of time may see the Princess of Wales cease to require an expression of the strong and manly feelings of Englishmen (for I feel assured they will never be withheld in her cause).'[87] It was a matter of masculine chivalrous duty to support the princess (and hence display one's understanding of the contemporary nature of what it meant to be British: Lady Campbell decried the opposition's action for their lack of 'true knight errantry').[88] Such a view also had political implications, since *The Pilot*'s letter also made it clear that the rift between the Regent and his wife unsettled the happiness and harmony of the royal family and, by extension, the political harmony of the nation. While Lady Perceval never explicitly made connections between wider political questions and the feminine and just cause of the princess, her letters show a keen awareness and interest in politics; after all, she claimed that her son would become Chancellor of the Exchequer within a few years.[89]

The methods used by the princess and her party failed to win them the popular support that they needed. In part, this resulted from the efficiency of the prince's machine and ability to influence Grub Street and the underworld of middlemen that Lady Perceval had attempted to construct. Such methods were also associated with Old Corruption and were unlikely to attract the support of the increasingly influential middling classes. Aristocratic women were denied from entering the underworld, and had to work through intermediaries, inviting men such as Ashe into their salon only at great risk to themselves. During 1820–21, when the protests really did alarm the Establishment, it is telling that they took place in public spaces, such as the streets or meeting halls, not in the privacy of the drawing room. Newspapers provided the sometimes treacherous link between these spaces. The semi-private world of letters was being opened up to the more public glare of the newspaper, a shift captured by Austen in *Northanger Abbey* (completed in 1803, but published posthumously in 1817), where Henry Tilbey asks if his fears about his father's crime could be possible in a country 'where roads and newspapers lay every thing open?'[90]

7

The Creation of the Modern Press

There is a gentle slope in Virginia at the foot of which is a small river and a stone farmhouse. It can be reached by car from central Washington, DC, in about half an hour and would have taken half a day to reach by horse or carriage in the nineteenth century. And it was here on 21 July 1861 that crowds gathered to watch what became known, variously, as the 'Picnic Battle', the First Battle of Bull Run or the First Battle of Manassas, the opening land battle of the U.S. Civil War. Although many believed it would quickly settle the conflict with decisive defeat for the insurgency, it instead presaged the lengthy war and the intensity and bloodiness of the many battles of the next four years. The exact number of gawkers is not known, but there are many accounts of visitors – a 'throng of sightseers', wrote one Union captain – from Washington and elsewhere picnicking or setting up stalls to sell food and drinks to the observers. Many of the viewers were politicians, drawn out to witness the battle that they had supported.

Among them were also journalists and sketch artists, either attending speculatively or sent by their papers to record the battle. These included William Howard Russell, the war reporter, and the photographer Mathew B. Brady and his assistants, who were able to record the bloodshed and inconclusive nature of the battle. Perhaps no other battle had been as closely observed by the press, or as swiftly transmitted. President Lincoln received news of the outcome by telegraph message, a technology at that time twenty years old, and depending on electrical pulses of Morse code sent along fixed lines. Reporters similarly could send to their papers their headlines. As the stories were filled out in more detail, copy was quickly disseminated simultaneously around the country among the hundreds of local titles, and thence around the world.

Like the battles of the Crimean War, the Bull Run stands as one of the earliest episodes of what might be termed 'media wars', and the immediacy of the news and its methods of being gathered became the subject of discussion in its own right. Directly observed and recorded by more than just the military, it elicited commentary about how it was witnessed and reported, and how it affected the national psyche more broadly. For example, in 1861 the *Boston Herald* published the verse 'Civilians at Bull Run' by H. R. Tracy:

> Have you heard of the story so lacking in glory,
> About the Civilians who went to the fight,
> With everything handy, from sandwich to brandy,
> To fill their broad stomachs and make them all tight.
> There were bulls from our State street, and cattle from
> Wall street,
> And members of Congress to see the great fun;
> Newspaper reporters (some regular shorters)
> On a beautiful Sunday went out to Bull Run.

The sentiments capture something of the discrepancy between popular narratives of war, which stressed its noble purpose, virtuous sacrifice and the glory of battle, and its reality: indecisive, inconclusive, bloody and confused. Newspapers contributed to the popular fervour for the cause of the Union or Confederacy and continued to be full of reports contributing to romantic notions of war, while also beating a constant, if quieter, drum that revealed these realities, with 'incomplete information, inaccurate statements, and artificial heightening of the dramatic effect of the narrative'.[1] Among the highfalutin prose celebrating victories and the hopes of ultimate triumph were lists of casualties, the names of the dead, the costs to trade and the uncertainty of grand strategy. Papers combined a national (or even international) voice and viewpoint, while also offering a parochial take reporting broader events through a neighbourly lens and helping to form the invisible webs that united the concerns of a local community. Technological advances and elite concerns about the rhetoric of news and its role in shaping politics came most forcibly to the fore in the mid-nineteenth century during the great conflict, both rhetorical and real, over the issue of slavery in the United States of America.

Propaganda, News and Slavery

Arguments about slavery had burned brightly in the pages of the American press in the years before the Civil War. Such was its influence that the Southern states sought to suppress it, not without some success: various Gag Rules, tabled repeatedly in Congress between 1836 and 1840, were designed to restrict Congress and the States discussing the question. Introduced during the period 1836–40, they were repealed in 1844. Abolitionist voices could be found within certain parts of the press, but antebellum (that is, pre-war) racial politics were dominated by assumptions of white superiority. Those papers that advocated abolition, such as *The Liberator* (Boston, 1831–65), were suppressed in the South, with the *Richmond Enquirer* reporting that a vigilante group offered a reward of $1,500 (roughly $51,000 in today's money) for the 'apprehension and prosecution to conviction, of any white person' distributing the paper.[2] The press's more general racism is pointedly unpicked in Lydia Maria Child's story 'Slavery's Pleasant Homes: a faithful sketch' (published in 1843 in the anti-slavery gift book *The Liberty Bell*), which is concerned with the upsetting affair of George, an enslaved worker and half-brother of Frederic Dalcho, who is also his owner. In the tale, George marries an enslaved women, Rosa, who is then raped by Dalcho. In response, George kills Dalcho, who then admits his actions when another man is about to hanged for the crime. George is beaten and hanged. Maria Child closes her fictional tale with a juxtaposition of the between two sets of 'factual' newspaper reports:

> The Georgian papers thus announced the deed: 'Fiend-like Murder. Frederic Dalcho, one of our most wealthy and respected citizens, was robbed and murdered last week, by one of his slaves. The black demon was caught and hung; and hanging was too good for him.'

The Northern papers, the narrator observed, copied this version; merely adding, 'These are the black-hearted monsters, which abolition philanthropy would let loose upon our brethren of the South.'

While the press should not be seen as a bastion of abolitionism, it increasingly gave room to the fractious debates between the political parties as the issue of slavery dominated the political stage. Fierce questions of the status of the new states joining the Union, partly as a consequence of the lands won in the war against Mexico in 1848, such as California, Nevada, Utah or New Mexico, exploded the fragile consensus between the slave-owning and the free-states that had been maintained since the 1820. Would they be free states, or not? Would slavery, and the influence these future states had in Congress, upset the balance of power? In 1854 the Kansas-Nebraska Act, orchestrated by the Illinois senator Stephen Douglas, constructed a second fragile compromise, allowing the slavery question to be settled by 'popular sovereignty' when these territories became states. The Act inflamed opinion, as well as paving the way for further destruction of the Native Americans on the territories. Newspapers played a crucial role in informing, and stoking up, public opinion. In 1854 the *Burlington Free Press* gave a flavour of the range of opinion in newspapers, with its front page presenting 'The Press on Nebraska', offering 'specimens of the sentiments which the passage of the Nebraska bill is calling forth from leading journals'. The Whig *Commercial Advertiser* cast the Act as

> a compact violated . . . the deed is done. The wrong to the North is consummated. A solemn compact is violated. The South, having pledged itself that slavery should never cross a certain line of latitude of Missouri was admitted into the Union as a Slave State, has broken its pledge.

The newpaper stated that the compromises that the North 'had acquiesced for the sake of peace has been abused and perverted'. The Democrat *Evening Post* believed it represented an abuse of power by the southern states that would punish the party in power. It argued that the annexation of Cuba would likely soon follow as another slave state, and the 'renewal of the African trade'. It noted the influence of the press, suggesting that the 'southern journals already speak of [the annexation of Cuba and the renewal of the trade] as familiarly and flippantly as they do of an ordinary appropriation bill'. The bill, the *Post* thought, was ushered through Congress in part through the support of the *Washington Star* and a few other journals. Newspapers also contained the rumours that the friends of those who supported the Bill would be conferred clerkships in public office. The *New York Tribune* urged calmness 'in the presence of a great peril', a reminder of how newspapers had taken the role as a leading public voice. The *New York Times* reporter had been, he claimed, travelling through the country districts of the North and noted that 'we are surprised at the depth of . . . discontent among men who once opposed Slavery agitations, and were once friends of the Compromise.' Newspapers partly reflected, partly confirmed and informed public opinion hardening views in both the North and the South. Papers on both sides were crucial in demonizing those groups who became the opponents of their readers, creating an 'other' that could be hated. As the *New York Times* revealed,

> [A] Southern paper has lately scattered all through the country an ingenious and insulting analogy, in which the Northerners are pictured as holding the place of the Greeks in the Roman Empire: supplying their chivalric masters at the South with school-masters, pimps, and books, bearing their insults of oppression, but revenging themselves by the petty over-reaching of bargain and trade.[3]

This calumny became the means to further discredit the South and its propaganda methods, as the *Richmond Enquirer*'s May front page editorial was reprinted in other papers such as the *National Era*.[4]

In 1858 the 'Great Debates', a series of seven debates between the candidates for the Illinois Senate, Abraham Lincoln and Douglas, created rivers of ink, with each debate transcribed in shorthand by competing papers. Interest was not limited to Illinois but was reported across the nation, thanks to press that now relied on the telegraph, railroad and postal system to share news. Such was the intensity of feeling in the debates that the shorthand typists themselves became the focus of political attention.[5] The two Chicago papers, the Democrat *Times* and the Republican *Press and Tribune*, employed James B. Sheridan, assisted by Henry Binmore, and Robert R. Hitt respectively. Lincoln subsequently helped to find Hitt employment in Washington as secretary to several government commissions, noting he was 'about the only man he had ever known in his life connected with newspapers in whose honesty he fully believed'. Each paper accused the other of doctoring the candidates' language, with *The Times* suggesting that a 'council of "literary" men' improved his words, since 'they dare not allow Lincoln to go to print in his own dress . . . he cannot speak five grammatical sentences in succession.' The *Press and Tribune* claimed: 'If mutilating public discourses was a criminal offence, the scamp whom Douglas hires to report Lincoln's speeches would be a ripe subject for the Penitentiary.' Lincoln's rhetoric had been 'disemboweled, and chattering nonsense substituted in their stead'. The accusations continued: the Republican paper charged that *The Times*'s stenographer 'defaced and garbled' Lincoln's text at Douglas's behest. A comparison of the text certainly shows Lincoln's speeches in *The Times* to contain less felicitous prose than when reported in the *Press and Tribune*. Sheridan and Binmore undoubtedly lacked Hitt's skills in shorthand; there is also evidence that Binmore was later employed by Douglas to 'occupy himself with writing letters to various papers throughout the state and managing others into silence, to assist in every possible way the election of Douglas'.[6]

Along with being reported in the press across the American nation, the debates also travelled across the Atlantic. *The Times*'s New York correspondent included mention of them in his account of events in September 1858, reporting that 'the contest for Senatorship in Illinois goes on with as much acrimony as ever. Mr Douglas and Mr Lincoln call each other hard names' and noting that the public's interest was turning to the New York race. British readers were also informed that 'The Niagara has left for Charleston, to take the negroes from the Echo to deliver them on the coast of Africa'; readers were expected to know that this referred to the two hundred Black people rescued and freed from a slaving ship off the coast of Cuba.[7]

The Civil War continued for four more years. In both America and Europe it covered thousands of pages of the press. *The Times* had dispatched William Howard Russell, famed for his reporting in the Crimea, who filled lengthy dramatic reports of the campaign. The European press also presented the conflict through the lens of its own concerns: a mixture of geopolitical possibilities and threats, concerns about trade, and debates about the institution of slavery and the 'new' American republic. Regional concerns also amplified interest in the conflict, notably in the northwest of Britain, which relied heavily on U.S. cotton for its dominant weaving industries and was also the focus of a pro-abolitionist boycott of Confederate cotton. In the U.S., of course, the war dominated all other news and, rather than damaging the newspaper industry, helped to transform the fortunes of press, at least in the North. Successful papers could hardly keep up with the demand for their content, which they kept supplied with a massive investment in their product. Two of the main papers spent several billion dollars, in today's terms, much of it on the telegraph wires. When these were destroyed by war, other methods were used. In early 1861 the New York *Herald*'s reporter Henry Villard wrote to *The Tribune*, which he also supplied with news that

> after a few days' interruption, I am again able to supply you with news from Washington. I am obliged to do this in a rather roundabout way owing to the cutting off of all telegraph and railroad facilities between the capital and the north . . . I have started a courier-line . . . In order to insure expeditiousness, I established six relay stations, working as many horses once daily each way. – The expense is of course heavy. But the *Herald* will bear by far the largest portion of it.[8]

A Media Age?

The war took place in what might be termed the modern media age. Although, as earlier chapters have explored, the press played a significant role in the shaping of public and political opinion, as well as being closely linked in terms of individual actors, in the English Civil Wars and the American and French Revolutions, the world of news and newspapers had been transformed before the first shots had been fired at Fort Sumter. In every aspect of the newspaper industry, a transformation had taken place in terms of scale, the technologies involved in creation and dissemination, and the nature of its readership. These innovations were also allied to other changes in taxes on papers, shifts from the rural towards urban and industrial society, and demands for wider political participation. Literacy was by no means universal, but was extensive, particularly in the United States. The second half of the nineteenth century would build on these changes to found great newspaper empires, but the seeds of this transformation had been sown – and germinated – in the years of relative European and North American peace following the Napoleonic Wars and the War of 1812.

The number of newspaper titles had increased dramatically, and debates about the institution of slavery, the nature of U.S. politics and the relative sovereignty of states and the federal government took place in an expanded public sphere. The concept of the press had also solidified. Newspapers as a format had settled into more established patterns of appearance, with a common language of textual columns, mastheads, headings and accepted typography. Their language and range of registers had become more defined. The press as a fourth estate was confirmed, as was freedom of speech in the U.S., at least theoretically. During the nineteenth century the concepts of a newspaper proprietor, editor and journalist took on a clearer form, and might be seen to be careers of sorts, with a range of defined roles in the gathering of news, publishing, distribution, illustration and advertising, as the editors and journalists Sheridan, Binmore and Hitt showed. A job as a 'newspaper writer' or 'newspaper carrier' was seen as part of the printing trade.[9] Politicians, always alert to the

Spurred on by antiwar newspapers, a mob attacks the Republican and pro-war *New York Tribune* newspaper office in Printing House Square during the racially charged Draft Riots of 1863.

press, explored new ways of using it as a promotional or propaganda tool, as Binman's later puff pieces for Douglas demonstrated. As a contemporary noted, the 'influence of the newspaper press is great and wide spread; it gives a voice to public complaint, and must necessarily have a powerful influence on the public mind'.[10] The market had matured enough to produce papers for a range of groups, with papers increasingly aimed at different political persuasions, religious affinities or trades. Agricultural periodicals and newspapers were another important part of the sector, notably, *Bell's Weekly Messenger*, first published in 1796, with many competitors founded in the 1820s and '30s.[11] In New York, the *Colored American*, printed at 2 Franklin Street, catered to the city's large community of Black citizens from 1836 to 1842. Growing class consciousness was also reflected in titles aimed at workers, the commercial or middle classes, and the establishment. The importance of location and locality was also underscored by the press, with nearly every town in the U.S., Britain and much of continental Europe having a local paper by the mid-nineteenth century, and often with a couple of competing titles.

It was a time of fierce competition between papers, and many failed to reach financial security or last more than a few issues. Numerous others also folded after a few years. While the papers of the late 1700s were run out of a printer's office, which took on a range of other work as well as publishing the newspaper, the large city papers of the mid-nineteenth century primarily concerned themselves with the production of their papers. Special issues and other printing tasks might occupy the press and tradespeople some of the time, but the focus of the operation was on the news. In this way, significant capital was directed at investment in presses, machinery, acquiring news and securing a distribution network.[12] In contrast to the smaller presses of the earlier era, the great metropolitan papers rarely owned their premises and instead rented their offices and printing shop, although these could be considerable in size. In large cities, such papers tended to cluster together near the centres of power and traditional site of print shops: in New York, this led to the creation of 'Newspaper Row', clustered around Park Row.[13]

By 1850 the United States would boast thousands of newspaper titles, with a total annual circulation of some 500 million. European visitors, such as the Hungarian intellectual Sándor Farkas, were struck by the extent to which newspapers were read: 'remote from civilization and poor as he may be,' the traveller noted, 'every settler reads a newspaper.' The finances of production and dissemination were undergoing a process of transformation. In the first third of the century, many of these Americans would have subscribed, paying between $4 and $10 annually (around $130 to $330 today, but also representing $2,540 in labour costs) for titles such as *The Columbian* (New York) or the *Independent Chronicle and Boston Patriot*.[14] But just as the tone of the press in America had been transformed from the journalism of the Republican era – a time when the press was noted for its partisan debate between political factions into a more commercially focused endeavour with an eye to the sensational – entrepreneurial publishers saw the opportunity to reach a mass market. By 1830 the population of the U.S. had increased to nearly 13 million, almost five times the size of population at the time of Independence, and the first waves of mass immigration had begun. In 1833 the *New York Sun*, published by Benjamin H. Day, was sold for the remarkable – and low – sum of one cent. In 1835 James Gordon Bennett founded the *New York Herald*, and the 'penny press' was established, dramatically undercutting existing papers, which tended to be priced at six cents or more, and were often sold in advance by subscription. In 1841 it established a Sunday edition, much to the dismay of many clerics who disavowed its sensational nature and its violation of the Sabbath.[15] Following the creation of the *Sun* (which also developed a network of news boys to sell the paper on the sidewalks), *The Herald* and *The Tribune*, the newspaper business attracted further investment and business interest. Confidence in the future of the press could be seen in the investment of $69,000 in 1851 in the *New York Daily Times*, which was founded by a former editor of *The Tribune* and aimed to offer a more informed, less populist approach than the other papers of the 'penny press'. In 1857 it became the *New York Times*, taking a corner building at the intersection of Spruce, Park and Nassau Streets.

The English novelist Charles Dickens first visited New York in 1842, where he was the subject of public fascination. His *American Notes* record his distaste for much of what he found, and he got his revenge a year later in his novel *Martin Chuzzlewit*, one section of which contains a parody of American life. The young Chuzzlewit's first encounter of New York is on the packet-ship *The Screw* as it comes into port, where it is met by the 'shrill yell of newsboys' and 'boarded and overrun by a legion of those young citizens':

> 'Here's this morning's New York Sewer!' cried one. 'Here's this morning's New York Stabber! Here's the New York Family Spy! Here's the New York Private Listener! Here's the New York Peeper! Here's the New York Plunderer! Here's the New York Keyhole Reporter! Here's the New York Rowdy Journal! Here's all the New York papers! Here's full particulars of the patriotic locofoco movement yesterday,

in which the whigs was so chawed up; and the last Alabama gouging case; and the interesting Arkansas dooel with Bowie knives; and all the Political, Commercial, and Fashionable News. Here they are! Here they are! Here's the papers, here's the papers!'

'Here's the Sewer!' cried another. 'Here's the New York Sewer! Here's some of the twelfth thousand of to-day's Sewer, with the best accounts of the markets, and all the shipping news, and four whole columns of country correspondence, and a full account of the Ball at Mrs White's last night, where all the beauty and fashion of New York was assembled; with the Sewer's own particulars of the private lives of all the ladies that was there! Here's the Sewer! Here's some of the twelfth thousand of the New York Sewer! Here's the Sewer's exposure of the Wall Street Gang, and the Sewer's exposure of the Washington Gang, and the Sewer's exclusive account of a flagrant act of dishonesty committed by the Secretary of State when he was eight years old; now communicated, at a great expense, by his own nurse. Here's the Sewer! Here's the New York Sewer, in its twelfth thousand, with a whole column of New Yorkers to be shown up, and all their names printed! Here's the Sewer's article upon the Judge that tried him, day afore yesterday, for libel, and the Sewer's tribute to the independent Jury that didn't convict him, and the Sewer's account of what they might have expected if they had! Here's the Sewer, here's the Sewer! Here's the wide-awake Sewer; always on the lookout; the leading Journal of the United States, now in its twelfth thousand, and still a-printing off: – Here's the New York Sewer!'

'It is in such enlightened means,' said a voice almost in Martin's ear, 'that the bubbling passions of my country find a vent.'[16]

Technological advances, notably steam printing and mechanical paper production, helped to create this 'vent', enabling the development of a relatively cheap mass market for newspapers. Paper could still be expensive, particularly those based on linen-cotton mixes (or, on occasion, straw, in the case of a short-lived experiment in 1829 by *Niles' Weekly Register* and the *Philadelphia Bulletin*) rather than wood pulp, but its price dropped dramatically from the 1800s. Rather than relying on linen, cotton rag could be used, which was far cheaper.[17] In this period a series of technological developments in paper-making transformed production from a slow, manual task to a more industrial process. Joshua Gilpin of Wilmington, Delaware, illicitly obtained details of the British patent for the cylinder-wire paper machine, and in 1817 his new factory began manufacturing paper on the Brandywine river. To mark the occasion, he presented the American Philosophical Society with a 300-metre (1,000 ft) roll of paper. This technology was itself superseded in the late 1837 with the introduction of the Fourdrinier moving wire machine in Connecticut. This advance increased production tenfold. Experiments in additives also played a role: from 1806 it was understood that the addition of rosin soap and alum helped to make the fibres in paper smoother and stronger, allowing for faster and cheaper production. Other developments included methods of washing or bleaching the stuff to increase the quality of paper from cheaper rags. By the 1830s paper was relatively cheap, allowing for the production of spelling books at a price that meant not only did every American schoolhouse have a copy, but each student did, too, laying the base for future readers and consumers of print culture.[18]

Printing technology and print-shop organization transformed the potential output from a night's printing. In Britain *The Times* had acquired a machine developed by a German resident, Friedrich Koenig: a steam-driven press, which used cylinders that were automatically inked by rollers for the impression of ink on paper. Thousands of sheets could be produced overnight at the rate of 1,100 per hour, and on 29 November 1814 John Walter, the editor, declared 'the greatest improvement connected with printing since the discovery of the art itself. The reader of this paragraph now holds in his hand one of the many thousands of impressions of *The Times* newspaper, which were taken off last night by a mechanical apparatus.' The technology continued to be improved, and by the 1850s machinery could produce

40,000 copies of the paper overnight. While Walter noted, perhaps optimistically, that 'little more remains for man to do, than to attend upon, and watch this unconscious agent in its operations,' the new processes opened up further employment and specialist roles in the printing press, such as inkers, feeders and, later, the brush beating of paper moulds.[19] The *Manchester Guardian* introduced a steam press in 1828.

A flurry of patents and innovations continued to improve the efficiency and output of the presses, with a host of engineers across Europe and America finding new methods, competing, copying and learning from one another. In America Richard Hoe, who began to work for his father's company R. Hoe & Co., revolutionized the printing press in terms of speed of printing. The *Philadelphia Public Ledger* deployed his firm's rotary press in 1846 – a 'wilderness of wheels, and cylinders, and straps, and . . . a deafening thunder', and, with the addition of further mechanical feeders, upped the output to 20,000 sheets per hour. In 1851 *The Times* purchased its own pair of ten-feeders, based on Hoe's designs but manufactured by the British firm of Whitworth.[20]

The press was also built on the back of the vast networks of canals, telegraph systems and, increasingly, railroads created largely by immigrant – or, in the United States, enslaved – labour. It thrived on the development of postal services, through which news could be sent in the form of letters from friends, business associates, relatives and, increasingly, networks of stringers, informers and journalists. Newspapers, pamphlets and other texts could be sent through these networks. Such routes helped to shorten the distances across land, and the Atlantic Ocean, English Channel and Mediterranean and Indian Oceans were gradually shrunk by the development of regular shipping lines and maritime technology, such as iron hulls, improved navigation and steam ships: by 1840 the *Morning Herald* in New York listed the London and Liverpool steamers *British Queen*, *Great Western*, *President*, *Columbia*, *Britannia* and *Acadia*, ahead of the older sail-borne packets. The *Britannia*, which carried passengers as well as mail and cargo, became a news item in its own right. In July 1840, the newspapers reported that the vessel arrived in Boston with 85 passengers, including Samuel Cunard, shipping magnate and founder of the Cunard Line, after beating the *British Queen* in the run down from Halifax. These arrivals, combined with 'overland news from China', informed the reader that the empress of China had died and that the Queen's Consort, Prince Albert, was very ill. The *Herald*'s readers were cautioned that the London packet had not yet arrived, which would bring further news (those seeking escape from such matters were directed to 'amusements, etc.' on the final page). The paper also noted that the Boston papers 'are filled with descriptions' that were 'copied word for word from what we published'. It gave due credit to the arrival of European news from 'Mr Harden, of the Boston Express Line' for 'our files of English papers' at the head of its first page (31 July 1840). The news flagged, with an editor's irony, as 'Most Important' also related to the Consort: 'It is not true,' says a correspondent from a London paper, 'that Prince Albert has shaved off his moustache.' It is uncertain what readers were to make of Albert's health and upper lip, but the Chinese news meant that 'American merchants had all left Canton on account of the trouble betwixt the Chinese and the English.' This would have had repercussions for commerce.[21]

Newspapers brought tidings from around the globe at an increasing pace through the nineteenth century, drawing attention to national and ethnic differences as well as connections. While the main newspapers presented a metropolitan, white viewpoint, they also sometimes occasioned the dissemination of other voices, including those descended from the peoples living in the lands occupied by the European colonists. Between 1828 and 1834 the first indigenous paper, the *Cherokee Phoenix* (ᏣᎳᎩ ᏧᎴᎯᏌᏅᎯ), was printed in a mixture of English and the newly designed Cherokee 'syllabary' – a typeface created by Sequoyah representing over 85 syllables of his language. It offered the Cherokee, who survived their forcible removal from their homelands along what became the 'trail of tears' to lands west of the Mississippi, a community focus, combining details of the new constitution of the Cherokee Nation, news and pieces highlighting their loss of land and threats from white settlers. Distributed free to those who could read Cherokee, and read across most of the Nation's townships, it was also sold more widely on subscription (starting at $2.50, around $68 today). The editor Elias Boudinot (Galagina Oowatie (ᎦᎴᎩᏅ ᎤᏩᏘ)) had a broader audience in mind, and as well as penning editorials on the loss of native land, he undertook tours of the United States and the United Kingdom, attracting subscriptions beyond the Cherokee lands and ensuring that the paper was predominantly printed in English. In 1829 the paper was renamed the *Cherokee Phoenix and Indian Advocate*. Boudinot's conversion to the Removal Party, which believed that a move beyond the Mississippi offered the best hope to the Cherokee people, brought its own retribution. With others, but crucially not the Principal Chief, he signed the Treaty of New Echota with the U.S. Government, which agreed to the Removal and the confiscation of Cherokee lands in Georgia. Boudinot had resigned the editorship in 1832, and the paper ceased publication two years later. In 1839 Boudinot, along with several of his relatives, was assassinated in retribution by an unknown group of Cherokee in Indian Territory.

Other indigenous newspapers were established in Dakota in 1850 (*Dakota tawaxitku kin; or, The Dakota Friend*, although this was a Christian missionary activity rather than a production by members of the tribe). Owned and published by a Mississauga Anishinaabe, George Copway, the *American Indian* (1851) was founded with a white American and European audience in mind, collating information about Native American life in newspaper form.[22] It would not, however, be until the late nineteenth century that Native American newspapers would be established in any number (this would also prove to be short-lived, as official policies of acculturation discouraged their production, a policy that lasted until after the Second World War).

Native Americans were also rarely far from the contents of newspapers: since colonial times, conflict with settlers had filled the column inches, and the press continued to rely on and reinforce racist images of vanishing, backward and savage peoples. Just before the outbreak of the Civil War, the first transcontinental railroad had been completed, and the New York *Tribune* journalist and future statesman Horace Greeley travelled across the Continent sending back reports to the paper in order to promote the railroad.[23] A reformer and abolitionist, Greeley was nonetheless not immune to the widespread racism and harsh views in relation to Native Americans. Both reflecting generations of stereotypes and reinforcing them through his influence as a leading figure in the press (the *Tribune*'s readership at this time reached some 40,000), Greeley's accounts of Native Americans cast the remaining communities as a relic of a bygone age, and as a question to be solved by destruction at worst or acculturation at best. Since colonial times, the press had portrayed Native Americans in the worst possible way, an image that was solidified and even intensified in the 1800s, cast as a 'noble savage' at best and more usually as an 'ignoble savage', both barbaric and violent.

Such reports were passed, largely unfiltered, into the British and continental European press. In January 1859, for example, *The Times* of London carried the usual news in its 'America' column: diplomatic arrivals at Southampton, and 'further reports of fresh troubles in Kansas, and this time in a shape which warrants some faith in their correctness', with accounts of violence undertaken by a pro-slavery band, and the activities of John Brown's 'Jayhawks'. News had also arrived from San Francisco (where the weather was 'colder than ever before') on the overland mail, which reported threats from the Comanche. To counter these perils, the company was building 'strong station-houses', which were 'to be well provided with arms and ammunition'.[24] In such ways, newspapers fed off stereotypes and reinforced the image of indigenous life within European and white American society. And, rather than unpicking or challenging such simplistic depictions of Native Americans as violent and only appearing on the press when 'on the warpath', the brevity of telegraph reports led journalists and newspapers to resort to a 'set of standardized ways of writing about Indians'.[25] Violent encounters in the West, without any contextualization or explanation, framed the way native peoples were seen. In contrast, massacres of Indians never became major news stories. In an analogous way, perhaps, the Welsh, Gaelic and Cornish regions of Britain were romanticized in the press, while their languages were repressed as a matter of policy. Newspapers published in these languages were rare. The first successful Welsh-language paper, *The*

Cambrian, was founded in 1804, with a few other examples appearing in the following half century. The relaxation of stamp duty in 1855 provided the impetus for the launch of several titles in west and north Wales. A more fraught analogy might be found in Britain's colonial territories, where the colonial and commercial authorities established papers in English: *Hicky's Bengal Gazette* (1780), the *India Gazette*, the *Calcutta Gazette*, the *Madras Courier* (1785) and the *Bombay Herald* (1789) all carried news from the British perspective. Weekly papers in Gujarati were founded in 1822 (Fardunjee Marzban's *Bombay Samachar* મુંબઈ સમાચાર, which became a daily in 1832 and is still in print as the *Mumbai Samachar*) and in 1826, Hindi (*Udant Martand*, which lasted until 1827). Both focused on advertisements, the price of goods, such as opium, London court and political news, and local administrative affairs; little room was given to local news. News, of course, existed before the arrival of these European papers, and had what the scholar Julie Codell describes as 'long-standing indigenous traditions of information collecting and dissemination which co-existed with the modern press'.[26] From the 1830s to the 1850s English and vernacular papers began to appear in considerable numbers, partly as a result of the Liberal Press Act (1835), which reduced press restrictions and enabled their cost to drop to around two *annas* (1/8 of a rupee). Many of these began to devote space to political commentary, notably the English periodical *Hindoo Patriot* (1853). Following the Great Rebellion of 1857–8, the press received considerable scrutiny and censorship.

As well as misrepresentations, newspapers could also give a voice to other groups. The *Cherokee Phoenix* was one such case. The ethnic salad-bowl of American society also provided for a range of non-Anglophone immigrants, whether from the colonial period or during the great waves of immigration that reached the United States during the nineteenth century. By 1850 perhaps one in ten of those living in the U.S. was an immigrant. The immigrant populations of New York and Boston offered a potential market for non-English papers, as did the Chinese and Spanish populations of California. And since the mid-eighteenth century German and Dutch papers had catered to those communities in Pennsylvania and elsewhere. Unlike the early Hispanic newspapers, which tended to be produced by exiled patriots writing with a non-U.S. audience in mind, the German papers spoke to an American audience. In 1848, Chicago could boast the weekly *Illinois Staats-Zeitung*, which became a daily in 1855; by the time of the Civil War, it was the second-largest daily paper in the city. A Republican-supporting paper, it opposed slavery and played an important role in the Illinois newspapers' opposition to the Kansas-Nebraska Act, which allowed these new entities to decide whether to be free or slave states. Newspapers, perhaps more than other printed forms, were a flag bearer for identity, whether political, ethnic or national.

The Burden of News

The political effects of such a mass media has long been considered by historians, whether for the manufacture of consent or the focus for dissent, as well as the shaping of party factions. Newspapers also had a cultural, even emotional, impact. They may have created a sense of community, but they also brought worrisome news, reinforced political divisions and were fraught with questions of veracity. Could this story be trusted? What information was missing, or might arrive in the next issue? Underscoring all these concerns was the unrelenting nature of the news, arriving daily and seemingly never-ending, filling up conversations and individuals' thoughts.

The poet Emily Dickinson read the newspaper every day, perhaps undercutting her subsequent reputation for reclusiveness and withdrawal from society. Her household regularly took the pro-abolition *Springfield Daily Republican*, bringing with it bulletins of news and updates on the progress of the war. Her writings suggest the tension between the incursions of the outside world into the inner life, and the unavoidable nature of news. 'The Only News I Know' (1864) economically contrasts her poetic, personal knowledge of truth and God with the 'bulletins' of the press. The poem captures her concerns with time, with knowledge of the world, and with truth were expressed in numerous works, but were possibly best distilled into the four short stanzas.

The Only News I know
Is Bulletins all Day
From Immortality.

The Only Shows I see –
Tomorrow and Today –
Perchance Eternity –

The Only One I meet
Is God – The Only Street –
Existence – This traversed

If Other News there be –
Or Admirable Show –
I'll tell it You –

The prevalence and cultural impact of the news press can perhaps be measured by the response of poets such as Dickinson. The shape of writing and the forms of its publication reacted to the daily appearance of pages of news and writing in noticeable ways. In a move intensified by the lead up to the war and the conflict itself, writers, editors and publishers shifted their outputs towards a more self-consciously literary mode – one that was more considered, less inflammatory and less populist than the news and magazine press that had come to dominate the public realm. Such works eschewed language or themes that might be considered melodramic and shifted rhetorical modes into a more symbolic or allusive register. There was a renewed interest in the appearance of the written word, in its typefaces, quality of paper and artistry of binding. Rather than necessarily seeking a wider audience, focus was placed on writing for the more restricted audience of the cognoscenti. It was a withdrawal from the popular world of newspapers in an attempt to find a more considered, artistic and finer way of being in the world.

Dickinson and other writers, editors and publishers reacted against the bustle of the news, its melodramatic register and journalistic sentences, by shifting to a literary mode that sought a more limited and sensitive audience, and emphasized the beauty of the text, the paper and even its binding. But literature and the newspaper in many ways also came ever closer together during the war. Dickinson, John Greenleaf Whittier, Herman Melville and others who deliberately explored a more aesthetic way of experiencing and communicating their understanding of the world, in the words of the critic Eliza Richards, also interrogated 'the difference between writing news and writing poems in a time of national crisis'.[27] Poetry drew on the language, style and publishing rhythms of the press, a tacit acknowledgement of its cultural predominance, as well as a critique of its consequences. Melville, for example, ransacked reports from the reprint of ephemeral publications (mostly newspapers) *The Rebellion Record* for his post-war collection of poetry, *Battle-pieces and Aspects of the War* (1866). Melville not only drew on the events recorded within this huge collection, but in poems such as 'Donelson (February, 1862)' made use of the forms of newspaper reporting, a collage of headlines, stock phrases and bulletins, with the reader's attention drawn towards the newspaper audience's responses to these texts. The newspaper – in this case a bulletin board around which the town gathers – is a mediated conduit for information and the creator of a community, with the phrase '*We Learn*' introducing the staccato set of bulletins from the front. Melville also carefully contrasts the press's hysterical discourse of sacrifice, which is consumed by the community as a whole that gathers in front of the bulletin board with that of the 'wife and maid' who return to it to read the names of their loved ones, their tears dissolving the letters on the page.

While the world of the newspaper and popular magazine also create an aesthetic reaction, with some writers and publishers responding to this 'cultural din' by an escape into more rarefied publishing, the worlds of the press and the literary strongly overlapped. Newspapers were full of poetry; it had long been used to editorialize on current events, such as wars with Native Americans, the long-running question of slavery and abolition, and various forms of social reform, such as prison reform or women's rights. Poetry provided a welcome contrast to the staccato prose of the newspaper column, and filled in the emotional blanks behind the purportedly more objective reporting of the press, especially following the outbreak of the war. Newspaper and magazine poetry, as Richards summarizes, 'urged men to join, fight, and die for the sake of the Union; they urged civilians to support the soldiers and to accept the sacrifice of loved ones; and they insisted that soldiers' deaths would sanction and promote the growth of a stronger democratic nation purged of the sin of slavery.'[28] The huge numbers of poems written and published during the Civil War era helped to form a 'national ideology' in the North, translating the sacrifice of the war dead into a moral purpose and helping to create a unified vision of a national community, bound by their sacrifice in blood.[29]

Beyond this personal clamour, the press also affected – or afflicted – popular politics. In a knockabout democracy such as the United States, the press could play a powerful role in elections. It could not be ignored. Instead, the political machine took steps to ameliorate or manipulate its influence. Reporters travelled in the train that took Lincoln to the White House following his election in 1860, and, in the days before the Battle of Manassas, it was in part the 'clamour of the press', as the historian of the press during the Civil War J. Cutler Andrews notes in his *The North Reports the Civil War* (1955), that led Lincoln to decide to attack the Confederate forces at that early point. Such was the importance of the press that Lincoln's administration saw the ability to control the Associated Press's telegraph network as a vital component of its military strategy.

Wallpaper, Stereotypes and the Modern Press

As in other conflicts, the American Civil War occasioned a dearth of everyday objects, including paper. Newspapers clearly suffered from the lack of printing stock; as a consequence of this lack some enterprising publishers turned to other materials at hand, including rolls of wallpaper, which had begun to be produced in a relatively new machine-made roll format out of rag and straw in the 1860s. As well as covering or decorating walls, such papers were manufactured to line drawers or cover boxes and trunks, a fashion in the States since the turn of the nineteenth century. Since the back of wallpaper was largely plain, except for the paste or glue used to attach it, desperate writers turned to material at hand when plain paper could no longer be obtained. There are accounts, for example, of women ripping paper from the walls in Richmond in an effort to write to their sons and husbands fighting in the war. At the outbreak of the war, the States could boast only 55 paper mills, with the majority in the North (24 were in the South, with none in Mississippi; paper was instead often purchased from the North, or even, in the case of cotton rag for Confederate banknotes, from Britain). The paper these mills produced was not based on wood pulp, which had only begun to be manufactured in the States in 1867, but on cotton – the very crop produced with the labour of the enslaved African American workers, the central cause of the Civil War. In an attempt to use the economic might of 'King Cotton', the South burned some 2.5 million bales of cotton to create a shortage that they hoped would force Britain and perhaps France to declare themselves for the Confederacy.

As the conflict continued the South ceased supplying the North with bales of cotton, the army drained the plantations of men and inflation on paper was remarkable, rising tenfold by late 1862. Other demands were placed on the cotton that could be had, from uniforms to bandages and paper for musket rifle cartridges. Newspaper proprietors were forced to turn to other materials, including wrapping paper, tissue paper, blue ledger paper and wallpaper, as their publications shrunk in size and length.[30]

Over 35 newspapers are known to have been printed on wallpaper, including the *Vicksburg Daily Citizen*, published by J. M. Swords during the town's siege by General Grant's Union Army. As the siege continued, the paper was reduced to a single sheet, having been printed on wrapping paper, blank pages torn from books and – for six editions – wallpaper. Following the surrender of Vicksburg, Union troops found the 2 July edition set in type, and added a postscript dated 4 July:

> Two days bring about great changes, The banner of the Union floats over Vicksburg. Gen. Grant has 'caught the rabbit:' he has dined in Vicksburg, and he did bring his

> dinner with him. The 'Citizen' lives to see it. For the last time it appears on 'Wall-paper.' No more will it eulogize the luxury of mule-meat and fricassed kitten – urge Southern warriors to such diet never-more. This is the last wall-paper edition, and is, excepting this note, from the types as we found them. It will be valuable hereafter as a curiosity.[31]

As the Union intervention suggests, such papers might primarily be seen as curios, with a limited readership or influence. In many ways, this is surely the case, but the efforts taken to print papers during such a time of crisis underscores the social and cultural importance of newsprint and the functions that it could satisfy. It combined the domestic space of the decorative paper with the public realm of news, encapsulating the boundary-crossing nature of the newspaper.[32] Its existence testified to a very real set of desires. Information and news during a time of war was crucial, not just for politicians and the military, but for the civilians who were likely to be caught up in the violence and, because of the size of the armies on both sides, would be desperate for news of their family, relatives, friends and neighbours in uniform. At a time of civil war, news from elsewhere was a psychological prop for both sides, helping to create the 'imagined community' of either the North or the South, in all their complexities. Perhaps even more pressingly, news reinforced local and provincial ties, bringing information that was both useful, such as reports of supplies arriving or damaged railroads, and reinforced communal identities. Newspapers could also bring moments of personal distraction at a time of national crisis.

The concern with news and paper at such a time is a reminder of the centrality of the press. News, 'tydings', intelligences, insider gossip and informed, authoritative information had also been sought, as the earlier chapters showed, but by the mid-nineteenth century, the technologies of print, the spread of various forms of literacy, the development of journalism and newspaper production as careers (which could be made by daring reporting on the Crimean or U.S. Civil War), and sophisticated distribution networks responded to and shaped this desire, making newspaper the central cultural and textual

Portrait daguerreotype of a blind man and his reader holding the sensationalist *New York Herald*, *c*. 1850.

artefact in European and American society – something that one could include in a photographic portrait to demonstrate how much one is part of that society. Novels, magazine, primers, religious works and the Bible were inseparable textual objects of the age, but the frequency of publication, broad geographical and social spread of newspapers, along with their close connections to loci of power and the social ties that formed communities, gave them an agency and vitality perhaps like no other cultural form. Newspapers helped to provide the backdrop to everyday life: the wallpaper of informed society.

Their materiality also played a role here. As the wallpaper newspapers of the Civil War showed, their ephemerality and immediacy relied on the stuff from which they were made. The technologies and supply chains that produced the paper were at once complex and crude, with papers able to adjust to the availability and supply of different types of paper – changing their size, colour and texture to suit. The simplicity of columns of text on one, two or a dozen pieces of paper, simply folded, ensured that the newspaper could find its niche in nearly any environment, adapting to fit the political situation, responding to taxation on print or paper and adjusting its price to fit. And, by the Civil War, newspapers were also manufactured not just from paper, but by paper. In 1829 a Lyonnaise printer, Claude Genoux, did away with the metal type fixed in rectangular forms that had provided the means of printing papers from the early days of *corantos* and *gazettes*. Instead of this flat form, the Lyonnaise's flexible *papier-mâché* mould could be shaped into a curved form, allowing the creation of casting of thin, curved metal plates. Drawing on the stereotyping techniques developed in England and Germany in the early eighteenth century, which largely fell out of use, this new method allowed for quick and relatively cheap production of duplicate plates that could be attached to a rotary press, allowing for faster production on several presses. The central innovation of the French method was the use of *papier-mâché* to create a fine mould called a 'flong' rather than clay, plaster of Paris or other material, such as bitumen. These moulds were then used to case a number of metal plates for rotary press. Vast numbers of pages could now be printed without the difficulty of adding type to the cylinder. Genoux's method for making paper moulds was used to print *La presse* in Paris.

The method began to be used by the 1840s in Europe. In 1848 the influential literary and liberal French newspaper *Le constitutionnel* helped to promote the election of Louis Napoleon, but this caused two of its printers, James and Tommaso Bartolomeo Dellagana, to flee to England, bringing with them their knowledge of the stereotype process. Creating a flong large enough for a newspaper, *The Times* began to be printed by this method in 1857, and in 1863, it had created a curved casting box allowing for a rotary press to be used. In America a number of printers and engineers experimented with the stereotype method, with one London-born engraver, Charles Craske, able to make use of the *New York Tribune*'s offices for his experiments in 1854.[33] Richard Hoe travelled to London to observe *The Times*'s press in action, which made use of knowledge gained from a Philadelphia printing machine agent, whose firm had observed and brought the foreign rights to Genoux's method. Hoe later sold his sheet-fed rotary machines to the *Lloyd's Weekly Newspaper* and the *Manchester Guardian,* which replaced its slower British steam feeders at a cost of £10,000 and brought the ability to vastly increase their output. Despite early enthusiasm, stereotype's practical implementation took several years in the States, and it was not until 1861 that *The Tribune* was printed using the stereoscopic method developed by Craske. By 1864 Craske had won contracts for all four of the New York papers, the *Sun*, *Herald*, *Times* and *Tribune,* before the papers created their own stereotyping departments, increasing the number of papers produced to meet the demand for war news – as well as the new demand for Saturday baseball scores.[34] These new stereotype rooms were soon known for their smells, smoke and steam. Metal was routinely melted to make the plates, the wet mats of the paper flongs emitted steam and were dried in wooden blankets, while scrapings of all kinds of waste were thrown into the metal pot, which was heated by burning coals and wood. Craske was known for his taste for chewing the end of his cigars, and his colleagues recorded his habit of spitting tobacco juice onto the mould to remove the broken pieces of flong from the hot plate. The proprietor of the *Sun* complained that 'you stereotypers make more noise and stink than any other department in the office.'[35] Printing a newspaper was tough work, as the New York Typographical Society declared at its founding in 1833: 'Scarcely any employment can be more laborious that that of publishing a daily morning newspaper . . . it requires the united exercise of the mental and bodily labor of the persons employed, for nearly the whole night, and a considerable portion of the day; being seldom able to allot more than seven hours to rest and refreshment.'[36]

The men – moulders, foremen, brushers – and presumably women (since many of the newspaper unions devoted the 1860s to keeping women, who were paid less, out of their shops) working in such foundries were skilled workers, who had expertise in judging how wet to make the mixture, to balance how dry the mould had to be, and a thousand other small judgements, all made at speed to make the pages of the paper appear early in the morning for delivery the next day. When the *New York Herald* acquired its own Dellagana rolling machine from London the paper shipped a gang of men used to operating it. The crew largely remained in America, where they became founder members of the New York Stereotypers Union No. 1.

By 1860 the newspaper had taken on an unmistakably modern form. By 1890 the U.S. had more than 1,600 daily newspapers, which could boast a combined circulation of 8.4 million, and nearly 9,000 weekly papers in 1880, ensuring that nearly every town or village had its own paper. At the start of the century, hand presses could produce perhaps two hundred sheets an hour; steam rotary machines using

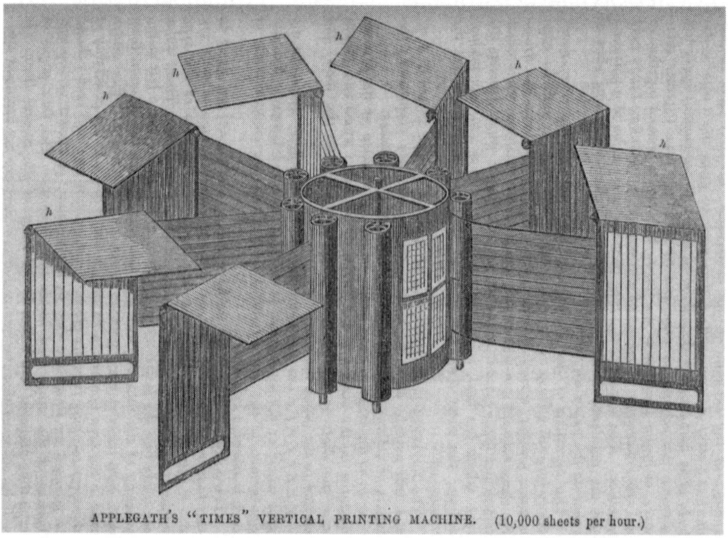

APPLEGATH'S "TIMES" VERTICAL PRINTING MACHINE. (10,000 sheets per hour.)

Applegarth's *Times* vertical printing machine capable of producing 10,000 sheets per hour; illustration in John Weale, ed., *London Exhibited in 1851*.

stereotyped plates could produce fifty times as much. In Britain the rolling back of 'taxes on knowledge', notably in 1855 with the removal of the 1d stamp tax, which allowed the *Daily Telegraph* to appear as Britain's first 'penny daily', achieving a circulation of 270,000 by early 1856. The press represented not just the sharing of information, or the skill and aptitude of a local printer or witty journalist, but a vast, interconnected web of knowledge. It operated within the framework of patent law, but also drew on advances made by industrial espionage, engineering entrepreneurship and experiment. Demand for the press came from an interest in politics, whether radical or conservative, but also a fascination with the operation of the world and what was happening locally, nationally and globally. The proportion of space devoted to political news decreased as the size of papers expanded, with readers seeking amusement, social news, advice and entertainments as much as 'tydings', unless they related to crime or accidents, sensational subjects that continued to fascinate readers and writers.[37] Celebrity and sports reporting vied with coverage of religious assemblies, convocations and special services, or literary criticism. Journalism as a literary form was recognized as offering both an attempt at accuracy and even authoritativeness, while also being obsessed with the novel, the amusing and the entertaining. Truth could well be sacrificed in the search for a story and the need to entertain the readership; calm, measured language certainly was in the interests of enjoyable sensationalism and entertainment. Papers chased different audiences, tailoring their products to different classes and political tastes, from the yellow journalism of Joseph Pulitzer's *New York World* and William Randolph Hearst's *New York Journal* of the 1890s to the more staid, if reforming, *New York Times* or *The Times* or *Daily Telegraph* in London. Newspapers were aimed at, and to some extent produced by, different classes: working, middle and upper. They were also consumed in different places and in different ways. Some were taken in private homes or gentleman's clubs, while others were purchased by groups of working-class men, or for reading rooms aimed at women.[38] The press also had an important local or provincial dimension, which was only reinforced by the maturation of the newspaper industry and the centrality of newspaper reading to everyday life.

The vast geographic size of the United States ensured that the local press had a central role in American society.

A similar picture was true in Britain and the European Continent, with regional and city-based titles playing a profound role in their local community. In 1857, for example, the conservative rival of *The Guardian*, the *Manchester Courier*, was billed as the champion of 'provincial aggrandizement'.[39] Journalism, newspaper production, advertising and selling and distribution offered employment and a professional ethos to thousands in towns and cities outside of the capital, while every village, town and city provided places for the consumption of news, whether a bar, café or pub, which would take at least one newspaper, or a reading room or news room, often in a hotel or other semi-public building.[40] 'Ask the landlord why he takes the news-paper; he will tell you that it attracts people to his house and in many cases its attractions are much stronger than those of the liquor there drunk,' the pamphleteer and journalist William Cobbett had maintained in 1807, while other, public houses could be famed for their newspaper readers.[41] Andrew Hobbs, a historian of the powerful provincial press in nineteenth-century Britain, draws our attention to figures such as Sloppy from Dickens's *Our Mutual Friend* (1865), 'who do the Police in different voices', reminding us of a world where 'skilled public readers brought the newspaper alive in crowded pubs'.[42] Reading rooms were constructed across the land, sometimes provided for by benevolent mill owners such as John Goodair in Preston, catering for a desire for news that seemed to outstrip the demand for novels or other books.[43] We can glimpse something more of the place newspapers played in the routine of everyday life in the diary of John O'Neil, a weaver in Clitheroe, Lancashire: 'I went up to Clitheroe and got my Christmas glass. It was the best whiskey I ever got in my life, it nearly made me drunk. It made me so that I could not read the newspaper, so I had to come home without any news.'[44] The habits of the wealthier sort had taken root. Earlier in the century, Benjamin Robert Haydon's painting *Waiting for the Times* (1832) depicts an interior with a gentleman reading the paper, with his companion next to him waiting his turn along with decanters of wine; the newspaper dominates nearly all of the composition. It was reproduced as a print and formed the

Bagging for the Great Towns, 1845. Newspapers relied heavily on the postal network for distribution.

basis for cartoons such as *Punch's Waiting for the Railway Times*, which satirized the railway boom.

When O'Neil was not reading the newspaper (or taking a sip of his Christmas whisky), he was weaving cotton, a product that deeply tied Victorian Britain into an international and imperial system of trade. Indeed, few aspects of commercial life or material production were exempt from these links, and newspapers also played their role in the shaping of empire, whether directly colonial or commercial. They carried news of events at home and abroad, helped to inform a concept of what empire was, and, as the nineteenth century continued, 'court[ed] the loyalty' of readers. Imperfect, and delayed and degraded by time and distance, reports on home and abroad nonetheless linked home and away.[45] In 1842 the East India Rooms in St Martin's Place, Charing Cross, offered a 'commodious reading room', with 'the Latest Intelligence and Indian Journals by every overland dispatch'. By the 1850s it offered a wide selection of titles from across India, including the *Bombay Hurkaru*, *Bombay Government Gazette*, *Bombay Gazette*,

Bombay Telegraph, *Bombay Herald*, *Bombay Guardian*, *Calcutta Government Gazette*, *Colombo Observer*, *Delhi Gazette*, *Madras Government Chronicle* and *Kurrachee Advertiser*. The company also helped to ship *Home News*, *Indian News*, *United Service Gazette*, *Allen's Indian Mail*, *Civil Service Gazette* and the *Naval and Military Gazette*.[46]

From the 1820s through to the 1850s, newspapers in Britain were involved, as Hannah Barker reminds us, in a 'huge variety of political campaigns and sustained a series of heated public debates'. All the major newspapers, including *The Times*, and a good number of provincial ones, were largely pro-reform. From the Queen Caroline Affair to Chartism and the British establishment's incompetence and mismanagement of the Crimean War, newspapers acted to amplify and disseminate reformist sentiment. During the campaign for political reform in the 1830s, in particular for the extension of the franchise to more of the male propertied classes, *The Times* urged its readers to undertake 'the solemn duty of forming themselves into political societies throughout the whole realm', and when the House of Lords rejected the bill in October 1831, it, in common with other London papers, printed a black border around its pages as a sign of mourning.[47] Newspapers did not, however, represent a united front. Local papers such as the *Cambridge Chronicle* or the *Kentish Gazette*, as Barker notes, worried that reform went too far and too fast; as the *Kentish Gazette* warned, 'the inhabitants of this great nation are rapidly dividing themselves into two classes', namely the 'the friends of order' and 'the lovers of change'.[48] While newspapers as a rule supported the Whiggish reform, there were also attempts by conservative politicians to court the press, such as *The Courier* in 1840. When approached with a suggestion that their friends might acquire shares in the paper, Robert Peel worried that 'I have such a horror of money transactions with Newspaper Proprietors – and have had experience of much embarrassment arising from them – that perhaps I am unduly prejudiced against such a negotiation.'[49] Eventually, it was concluded that too close a relationship would be counterproductive, as Sir Thomas Fremantle MP noted that it might cause jealousy among the other papers supporting them, and that the paper would be considered 'as the organ of the Party & we should be considered (however unjustly) as responsible for the tone & language which it may hereafter adopt on every public question'.[50]

While newspapers could give voice to opposition or help to create class-consciousness, as a mass media, with a complicated and expensive technical infrastructure, they could be the voice of capital as much as protest. Division became particularly apparent during the agitation for factory reform and for the ten-hour day in the 1830s. The industrial reformist Richard Oastler wrote to the editors of the *Leeds Mercury* that in the worsted mills in and around Bradford 'Thousands of our fellow-creatures . . . are at this moment existing in a state of slavery *more horrid* than are the victims of that hellish system, "*colonial slavery*".' As one of the reformers phrased it in an 1866 history of the struggle, it sparked a 'newspaper controversy' among the proponents and opponents of reform, along with transporting 'new courage and gleam of hope' to the exhausted Manchester committee for factory reform when the *Leeds Mercury* containing Oastler's letter was produced at one of their meetings.[51] In general, the *Mercury* took the view of the manufacturers, who feared that reform would damage industry. In 1832 the *Manchester Guardian* also believed that the ten-hour day constituted 'an act of suicidal madness'.[52]

Despite the repeal of stamp and other duties campaigned for by campaigners such as Richard Cobden and Charles Bright, *The Times* remained the biggest-selling paper, with a circulation of around 60,000 in 1855. Although newspapers, including *The Times*, could be proponents for reform or political change, and indeed that paper took the credit for the fall of the Aberdeen administration in 1855, they could also represent the voice of the establishment. Proprietors similarly wielded influence, and John Walter MP saw that his paper, *The Times*, opposed the New Poor Laws, in this case going against the grain of public opinion. The paper continued to receive secret-service money up until the 1840s, and in 1848, confronted with the mass Chartist protests demanding a vote for all men, warned its readers that the movement, which it conflated with unrest in Ireland, 'wish[ed] to make as great a hell of this island as they have made of their own'. While radical movements, such as the Chartists, could produce their own broadsides and smaller papers, such as the *Northern Star* (which did

The *Illustrated London News* being taken to Somerset House for stamping, 1842.

reach sales of 50,000 at its peak in 1839, and was perhaps read twenty or fifty times more in pubs, coffee houses and workplaces), truly mass-produced papers required an investment in skilled workers, machinery and distribution infrastructure. The *Star* briefly flourished in part because of its ability to capitalize on its use of paid newspaper agents to become Chartist organizers, and to use organizers as agents.[53] To thrive, newspapers needed to attract advertisers, subscribers and readers willing to purchase the paper on the street. Enthusiasm for a cause could only overcome these restrictions to a limited extent; in a crisis, a state's legal, police and military powers could easily disrupt opposition papers and their presses. Newspapers' content also affected social attitudes, often in reactionary ways. The dramatic increase in crime reporting from the middle of the nineteenth century created a heightened fear of violent crime, which the historian Christopher Casey concludes 'halted the march towards the abolition of capital punishment that had seemed inexorable'.[54] Such shifts in opinion were also encouraged by the development of a more popular press, which drew on technological developments and relaxations in print taxation to create more entertaining publications, such as Henry Ingram's weekly *London Illustrated News* (founded in 1841, by 1855 it was selling some 200,000 copies a week), which helped to inculcate a culture of celebrity and offered to an eager public melodramatic tales of criminality, among other news.

It is hard to escape the many complaints about the liberties journalists took, and the lack of truth that newspapers contained compared to their traffic in falsehoods and misrepresentations. In 1834 a Forrest Gump-like fictional character, Major Jack Downing, warned his readers, 'don't you believe any thing you see in the papers.' His creator, the journalist and humourist Seba Smith, knew something of how newspapers were put together. He also knew that they 'were dreadful *smoky* things, and any body couldn't read 'em half and hour without having their eyes so full of smoke they couldn't tell a pig sty from a meeting house'. Newspapers may well be 'bewitching things', but they certainly could be deceptive. Searching further for a simile, Downing alighted on liquor: 'You know rum will sometimes set quite peaceable folks together by the ears, and make them *quarrel* like mad dogs – so do the newspapers. Rum makes folks act very *silly* – so do the newspapers. Rum makes folks *see double* – so do the newspapers. Rum, if they take tu much of it, makes them sick to the stomach – so do the newspapers.'[55]

But for all of the smoke, rum and Dickinson's 'burden of news', there was also a profound belief in the importance of the newspaper press. Charles Mitchell's *Newspaper Press and Directory for 1846*, which played a profound role in enabling advertisers to engage with newspaper proprietors, argued that 'the press is the corrector of abuses; the redressor of grievances; the modern chivalry, that defends the poor and helpless, and restrains the oppressor's hand.' It quoted with approval a piece in the *Shilling Magazine*, 'the true mission of the press, its very soul, is to gather and diffuse truth'.[56] Over time, and with strenuous efforts, the press had established itself as a fourth estate, an important check and balance within the civil fabric of most Western nations. It stood as a bulwark against the abuse of power, seeking neither favour nor fortune: 'We care not for the smiles or frowns of those in authority,' wrote Mitchell.[57] He was writing the truth, but like much in the newspapers, there was also a certain spin. Mitchell had begun his career as an apprentice on the *Manchester Courier* before he founded C. Mitchell & Co, one of the first advertising agencies in the world. From an office in Red Lion Court, off Fleet Street, London, he knew all the leading journalists of the day, including Charles Dickens, Stirling Coyne – the drama critic of the *Sunday Times* – and Shirley Brooks of *Punch*, the comic journal printed by Mitchell (and, Mitchell claimed, had been created by him). In 1846 he began his newspaper directory, establishing it by 1856 as an annual trade directory for the British press, with mostly impartial coverage of tone, religious 'advocacy', political leanings and practical details. It also, of course, reflected the networks that Mitchell had developed: the *Daily Mail*, edited for a period by Dickens, was described by the directory as 'an organ which includes so eminently the men who at once guide and represent the public mind'. Mitchell had found a role as an advertising agent, promising to guide advertisers towards a paper 'suitable for their announcements', a form of what today would be termed media planning.[58] It was a rich market. Medical suppliers such as Thomas Holloway were spending £40,000 per annum by the 1860s. In 1847 Mitchell's *Punch* complained that England had become a 'Nation of Advertisers'.[59] Commerce and the press were almost inextricably linked: an inky business, indeed.

Afterword

The popularity of the press and the opportunities of mass media in the industrial age meant that unparalleled fortunes could soon be gained, along with political power. Those who amassed enough capital to acquire the newly developed technological means to produce enough papers to satisfy a mass market, and had the editorial savvy to discover the popular tone and content that the people wanted, could become very rich indeed. Within a few generations, a new term, 'press baron', was deployed to describe the handful of men who dominated the newspaper business: Joseph Pulitzer and William Randolph Hearst created media empires and architectural landmarks, and indulged in politics both through their newspapers and in person. In Britain in the twentieth century, Lords Northcliffe, Beaverbrook, Rothermere, Camrose and Kemsley became rich and powerful figures on the national stage. These barons had their predecessors in the nineteenth century. In the United States men such as Gordon Bennett Sr and Jr and Manton Marble were able to carve influential roles as a result of their presses, and in Britain Edward Lloyd, who began as a melodramaticist and plagiarist, created the mass-selling *Lloyd's Weekly Newspaper*, which boasted the 'Largest Circulation in the World'. We now have politicians who worked as journalists, and who, in the case of Boris Johnson, found that sensationalism and untruths could be a route to an entertaining rise to prominence.[1] In America, the 45th president demonstrated a natural talent for grasping power and shortcutting established patterns of media behaviour, and in so doing created a new language of 'fake news', with the media seemingly unable to find an effective way to report, analyse and critique the person and position of the president. He never seemed to be as happy as when he was firing zingers such as this one about the Gray Lady, the *New York Times*:

> Wow! The Deputy Editor of the Failing New York Times was just demoted. Should have been Fired! Totally biased and inaccurate reporting. The paper is a Fraud, Zero Credibility. Fake News takes another hit, but this time a big one![2]

Benedict Anderson's 1983 depiction of the practice of newspaper reading in creating national identity has been hugely influential among scholars of news, print and nationalism. He argues that daily consumption of newspapers is an 'extraordinary mass ceremony', involving 'almost precisely simultaneous consumption . . . each communicant is well aware that the ceremony he performs is being replicated simultaneously by thousands (or millions) of others of whose existence he is confident, yet of whose identity he has not the slightest notion'.[3] Such a formulation certainly needs a reconsideration in the age of the daily – or hourly – presidential tweet. But the content, structure and consumption of newspapers, as the preceding chapter suggests, also undercut these national communities, forming international and international bonds.[4] Newspapers could undermine the national, helping to disassemble national ties as in the American Civil War, or enforce and undercut national boundaries, as in the Empire. The 'daily ritual' of newspaper reading might also be subverted by the specialisms of the press and the seeking out of reading rooms, creating associations and imagined communities of a power equal or different to that of the nation. And now, as forces which we are only just apprehending, finding our mostly digital feed or stream of news manipulated and bellowing as never before, we find the hints of other civil wars, of divisions and emotional intensities that echo the tumults of the past, and are intensified by the language, tone and speed of information's online forms. The media is now 'social' and compounded by armies of 'bots', innocent retweets, Facebook likes, tracking cookies and the mysteries of big data and AI algorithms. We have seen how these amplify rumours, fears and false hopes in the 'infodemic' that has accompanied the COVID-19 crisis.

It is not necessarily an optimistic place to end. In 2013, Wikipedia's article 'Future of Newspapers' was renamed 'Decline of Newspapers'.[5] In part, this may reflect the online encyclopaedia volunteer editors' comfort with online resources, but the traditional newspaper industry has undoubtedly been through a period of profound change, with the business models that had sustained it since the end of the hand press – advertising and wholesale distribution – destroyed by Google, Facebook and the other giants of the Internet. On the same day that the U.S. president tweeted his complaint about the *New York Times*, a media commentator (from BuzzFeed, one of the new breed of online news and entertainment sites) noted that UK newspaper circulation figures had declined by 5 per cent (*The Guardian*) to 12 per cent (*Daily Telegraph*), even at a period of political tumult.[6] Consolidation, online subscriptions and reader-sponsored support have shown a route to a future, but one that looks to be predominantly digital for serious papers, though free sheets continue to find a place in the commute of many in the modern world. Even more seriously, perhaps, city, local and provincial newsrooms have been shuttered and journalists made redundant. In many towns and even states, the authorities find themselves without the scrutiny of the fourth estate. We may have 'bulletins all day', and shouting all around us, but a suspicion that truth is not the thing that is being diffused. Perhaps that is our choice.

References

Preface

1 Robert Lynam, ed., *The Works of Samuel Johnson, LL.D*, vol. V (London, 1825), p. 189.

Introduction

1 J. Greer and D. Mensing, 'The Evolution of Online Newspapers: A Longitudinal Content Analysis, 1997–2003', in *Internet Newspapers: The Making of a Mainstream Medium*, ed. Xigen Li (New York, 2006), p. 13.
2 Roy Greenslade, '166 U.S. Newspapers Stop Printing in Two Years', *The Guardian*, www.theguardian.com, 6 July 2010; Clay Shirky, 'Last Call: The End of the Printed Newspaper', https://medium.com, 19 August 2014.
3 Michael M. Grynbaum, 'Trump Calls the News Media the "Enemy of the American People"', *New York Times*, www.nytimes.com, 17 February 2017.
4 Michael Harris and Alan J. Lee, *The Press in English Society from the Seventeenth to Nineteenth Centuries* (Rutherford, 1986), p. 15.
5 Shannon E. Martin and David A. Copeland, *The Function of Newspapers in Society: A Global Perspective* (Westport, CT, 2003), p. 4.
6 Harris and Lee, *The Press in English Society*, p. 19.
7 Fielding, however, did not necessarily approve of this body, which he termed 'The Mob' (*Covent Garden Journal*, quoted in *'Estate, n'*, www.oed.com, March 2020).
8 Robert E. Park, 'The Natural History of the Newspaper', *American Journal of Sociology*, XXIX (1923), p. 277.

1 Origins

1 'Đa wearþ se cing swyþe bliðe þissere tidunge' (*Anglo-Saxon Chronicle*) in 'tiding, n.1', www.oed.com, accessed March 2020.
2 Arthur der Weduwen, *Dutch and Flemish Newspapers of the Seventeenth Century, 1618–1700*, vol. I (Leiden and Boston, MA, 2017), pp. 81–2.
3 Joad Raymond, *The Invention of the Newspaper: English Newsbooks, 1641–1649* (Oxford, 1996), p. 5.

4 Quoted in Eileen Reeves, *Evening News: Optics, Astronomy, and Journalism in Early Modern Europe* (Philadelphia, PA, 2014), p. 12.
5 See P. M. Handover, *A History of the London Gazette, 1665–1965* (London, 1965), p. 7, no. † for details of the dating of the first issue.
6 Ibid., p. 2.
7 Harold Love, 'L'Estrange, Sir Roger', Oxford Dictionary of National Biography, http://oxforddnb.com, accessed 9 December 2020.
8 C. Y. Ferdinand, *Benjamin Collins and the Provincial Newspaper Trade in the Eighteenth Century* (Oxford, 2008), p. 7.
9 Handover, *History of the London Gazette*, p. 6.
10 'Courant uyt Italien, Duytslandt, &c', in Weduwen, *Dutch and Flemish Newspapers*, vol. I, p. 182.
11 Weduwen, *Dutch and Flemish Newspapers*, vol. I, p. 81.
12 'Story, n', www.oed.com, accessed March 2020.
13 W. G. Bell, *The Great Fire of London in 1666* (London, 1951).
14 William Bray, ed., Diary and Correspondence of John Evelyn, vol. II (London, 1859), p. 12.
15 Thomas Blount, *Glossographia; or, A Dictionary Interpreting all such Hard Words* (London, 1656).
16 Jack Avery, 'Book-women after the Great Fire of London', https://blog.nationalarchives.gov.uk, accessed 11 December 2020.
17 Fred Hunter, 'Women in British Journalism', in *The Encyclopedia of the British Press, 1422–1992*, ed. Dennis Griffiths (London, 1992), p. 686.
18 Adam Fox, *The Press and the People: Cheap Print and Society in Scotland, 1500–1785* (Oxford, 2020), p. 208.
19 Brian Cowan, *The Social Life of Coffee: The Emergence of the British Coffeehouse* (New Haven, CT, and London, 2005), p. 173.
20 Ibid.
21 Ibid., pp. 173–4.
22 Ibid., pp. 105–6.
23 Quoted ibid., p. 108.
24 Ibid., pp. 110–11.
25 Ibid., pp. 157, 175–6.
26 Ibid., p. 167.
27 Ibid., p. 172.
28 W. E. Knowles Middleton, trans. and ed., *Lorenzo Magalotti at the Court of Charles II: His Relazione D'Inghiltera of 1668* (Waterloo, 1980), p. 124.
29 Jeremy Black, 'The Eighteenth Century British Press', in *Encyclopaedia of the British Press*, ed. Griffiths, p. 13.
30 Louise Craven, 'The Early Newspaper Press in England', in *Encyclopaedia of the British Press*, ed. Griffiths, p. 11.
31 Jonathan Swift, *Letters, Written by Jonathan Swift, D. D. Dean of St Patrick's, Dublin. And Several of His Friends: From the Year 1703 to 1740*, vol. I (London, 1767), p. 180.
32 Handover, *History of The London Gazette*, p. 47.

2 Reporting Parliament

1 'Topography', www.historyofparliamentonline.org, accessed 2 May 2020.
2 Mr Rigby, 'Debate on Mr Luttrell's Motion for the Admission of Strangers into the Gallery' in *Cobbett's Parliamentary History of England* (London, 1808), vol. IV, p. 210.
3 Andrew Pettegree, *The Invention of News: How the World Came to Know about Itself* (New Haven, CT, and London, 2014), p. 220.
4 David Jones, *A Compleat History of Europe . . . for the year 1702* (London, 1703), preface.
5 Quoted in Ann C. Dean, 'Court Culture and Political News in London's Eighteenth-century Newspapers', *ELH*, LXXIII (2006), p. 633.
6 Fredrick Seaton Siebert, *Freedom of the Press in England, 1476–1776: The Rise and Decline of Government Controls* (Champaign, IL, 1952), p. 348.
7 Randall P. Bezanson, *Taxes on Knowledge in America* (Philadelphia, PA, 1994), p. 25.
8 *Mirror for the Multitude*, p. 24, quoted in John Sainsbury, *John Wilkes: The Lives of a Libertine* (London, 2017), p. xxi.
9 Elsewhere Potter and Wilkes made use of the following formulation: 'Prick, cunt, and bollocks in convulsions hurl'd'.
10 Stanley Morison, *The English Newspaper: An Account of the Physical Development of Journals Printed in London, 1622–1932*, reprint (Cambridge, 2009), p. 167, n. 2.
11 *A Letter to the Right Hon. Thomas Harley, Esq; Lord Mayor of the City of London* (London, 1768), p. 19, quoted in Sainsbury, *John Wilkes*, p. xxi.
12 Morison, *English Newspaper*, p. 167.
13 John Ingamells, *National Portrait Gallery: Mid-Georgian Portraits 1760–1790* (London, 2004). A copy hangs in the Palace of Westminster; Woodfall himself is buried in St Margaret's, next to the Palace of Westminster, 'William Woodfall', www.npg.org.uk, accessed 2 May 2020.
14 Hannah Barker, *Newspapers, Politics and English Society, 1695–1855* (Harlow, 2000), pp. 95–7.
15 British Library (BL), MSS EUR F 617. William Woodfall to Richard Twining, 22 December 1794.
16 Quoted in Hannah Barker, 'William Woodfall', www.oxforddnb.com, 23 September 2004.
17 Vicesimus Knox, *Essays Moral and Literary*, vol. II (London, 1782), p. 20.

3 Colonial Papers

1 John McCusker, *Essays in the Economic History of the Atlantic World* (London, 1997), p. 109.
2 See https://franklinpapers.org, accessed 2 May 2020; Charles E. Clark, 'Boston and the Nurturing of Newspapers: Dimensions of the Cradle, 1690–1741', *New England Quarterly*, LXIV (1991), pp. 243–71.

3 Clark, 'Boston and the Nurturing of Newspapers', p. 270.
4 *Pennsylvania Journal*, 17 January 1765.
5 Benjamin Franklin, 'Autobiography, part 8', https://franklinpapers.org, accessed 2 May 2020.
6 As the subtitle suggests, Andrew Pettegree, *The Invention of News: How the World Came to Know about Itself* (New Haven, CT, and London, 2014), combines the twin concepts of news and self-identity.
7 Daniel O'Quinn, *Entertaining Crisis in the Atlantic Imperium, 1770–1790* (Baltimore, MD, 2011), p. 12.
8 John Adams, *Diary*, 20 August 1774, www.masshist.org, accessed 2 May 2020.
9 See James Green on competition for accuracy in the American newspaper market in the Hugh Amory and David D. Hall, eds, *History of the Book in America*, vol. I: *The Colonial Book in the Atlantic World* (Chapel Hill, NC, 2009).
10 Joseph M. Adelman, *Revolutionary Networks: The Business and Politics of Printing, 1763–1789* (Baltimore, MD, 2019), p. 38.
11 *Daily Gazetteer* 17 November 1739; Catherine Armstrong, *Landscape and Identity in North America's Southern Colonies from 1660 to 1745* (London, 2016), pp. 162–3.
12 Benjamin Franklin, *Autobiography*, part 10, https://franklinpapers.org, accessed 2 May 2020.
13 John Adams, *Diary*, 3 September 1769, www.masshist.org, accessed 2 May 2020.
14 *Philadelphia Journal*, 8 Aug 1765; Quoted in Mary Lou Lustig, *Privilege and Prerogative: New York's Provincial Elite, 1710–1776* (Madison, MN, 1995), p. 125.
15 Carol Sue Humphrey, *The American Revolution and the Press: The Promise of Independence* (Evanston, IL, 2013), p. 36.
16 *Boston Gazette*, 17 March 1766.
17 W. David Sloan and Lisa Mullikin Parcell, eds, *American Journalism: History, Principles, Practices* (Jefferson, NC, 2002), p. 146; 'Postage Rates for Periodicals: A Narrative History', www.about.usps.com, accessed 2 May 2020.
18 *Boston Evening-Post*, 13 January 1766.
19 *Ibid.*, 23 September 1765.
20 Pettegree, *Invention of News*, p. 359.
21 Charles E. Clark, 'Boston and the Nurturing of Newspapers: Dimensions of the Cradle, 1690–1741', *New England Quarterly*, LXIV (1991), p. 253.
22 See for example, Kariann Akemi Yokota, *Unbecoming British: How Revolutionary America Became a Postcolonial Nation* (Oxford, 2010), p. 321.
23 Library Company of Philadelphia, Bradford Papers, folder 2. Wm Burns to Thomas Bradford, May 1762.
24 Clark, 'Boston and the Nurturing of Newspapers', p. 254.

25 Adelman, *Revolutionary Networks*, p. 30.
26 *New York Gazette*, 17 January 1765; *Pennsylvania Journal*, 25 April 1765 and 19 September 1765; *Philadelphia Journal*, 17 January 1765.
27 *Pennsylvania Journal*, 3 January 1765.
28 Library Company of Philadelphia, Bradford Papers, Folder 3, James Askey to William Bradford, March 1766.
29 *Boston Gazette and Country Journal*, 8 April 1765.
30 *Virginia Gazette*, 1 December 1768, quoted in Adelman, *Revolutionary Networks*, p. 33.
31 Ibid.

4 News and the American Revolution

1 The date and name of the ship is disputed. See Frank Smith, 'New Light on Thomas Paine's First Year in America, 1775', *American Literature*, I (1930), pp. 347–71; Albert Matthew, *Proceedings of the Massachusetts Historical Society*, XLIII (1909), p. 245, no. 1. Smith, however, graciously later admitted that the earlier date of 1774 was the accurate one: Frank Smith, 'The Date of Thomas Paine's First Arrival in America', *American Literature,* III (1931), pp. 317–18. The confusion, however, is a reminder of the imperfect nature of information supplied by contemporary newspapers.
2 Robert Olwell and Alan Tully, eds, *Cultures and Identities in Colonial British America* (Baltimore, MD, 2015), p. 10.
3 Gerald D. McDonald, Stuart C. Sherman and Mary T. Russo, *A Checklist of American Newspaper Carrier's Addresses, 1720–1820* (Worcester, MA, 2000), p. 188.
4 On what advertisements reveal about the lives of enslaved peoples of America, see David Waldstreicher, 'Reading the Runaways: Self-fashioning, Print Culture, and Confidence in Slavery in the Eighteenth-century Mid-Atlantic', *William and Mary Quarterly,* LVI (1999), pp. 243–72.
5 *Freedom on the Move Database,* www.freedomonthemove.org, accessed 2 May 2020.
6 Jean B. Russo, '"The Fewnesse of Handicraftsmen": Artisan Adaptation and Innovation in the Colonial Chesapeake', in *Cultures and Identities in Colonial British America*, ed. Robert Olwell and Alan Tully (Baltimore, MD, 2006), p. 176.
7 John C. Miller, *Origins of the American Revolution* (Stanford, CA, 1943), p. 119, quoted in Randall P. Bezanson, *Taxes on Knowledge in America* (Philadelphia, PA, 1994), p. 58.
8 Joseph S. Tiedemann, *Reluctant Revolutionaries: New York City and the Road to Independence, 1763–1776* (Ithaca, NY, 1997), p. 110.
9 Ibid., pp. 161–2.
10 Moncure D. Conway, ed., *The Writings of Thomas Paine* (New York, 1894) vol. I, p. 1.

11 James V. Lynch, 'The Limits of Revolutionary Radicalism: Tom Paine and Slavery', *Pennsylvania Magazine of History and Biography*, CXXIII (1999), pp. 177–99.
12 Worthington Chauncey Ford, 'Franklin's *New England Courant*', *Massachusetts Historical Society Proceedings*, LVII (1923–4), pp. 336–53.
13 Thomas C. Pears Jr, 'The Story of the Aitken Bible', *Journal of the Presbyterian Historical Society*, XVIII (1939), pp. 225–41.
14 On the dating of publication, see Albert Matthews, *Proceedings of the Massachusetts Historical Society*, XLIII (1909), p. 243, no. 1.
15 Trish Loughran, 'Disseminating *Common Sense*: Thomas Paine and the Problem of the Early National Bestseller', *American Literature*, LXXVIII (2006), p. 2.
16 Ibid., p. 17.
17 Tiedemann, *Reluctant Revolutionaries*, p. 246.
18 Harry M. Ward, *The War for Independence and the Transformation of American Society: War in Society in the United States, 1775–83* (London, 1999), p. 60.
19 Massachusetts Historical Society (MHS) Adams Family Papers, *Diary of John Adams*, 16 September 1777, www.masshist.org, accessed 2 May 2020.
20 David Ramsay, *The History of the American Revolution* [1789], https://archive.org, accessed 2 May 2020.
21 Ward, *War for Independence*, p. 62.
22 Daniel O'Quinn, *Entertaining Crisis in the Atlantic Imperium, 1770–1790* (Baltimore, MD, 2011).
23 See Todd Andrlik, 'Breaking News 1776: First Reports of Independence', www.allthingsliberty.com, 28 August 2013.
24 MHS Adams Family Papers, *Diary of John Adams*, 14 January 1780.
25 Ibid., 27 August 1774.
26 Hugh T. Harrington, 'Propaganda Warfare: Benjamin Franklin fakes a newspaper', https://allthingsliberty.com, 10 November 2014.
27 See https://franklinpapers.org, Benjamin Franklin to David Hartley, Philadelphia, 27 July 1786.
28 MHS Adams Family Papers, John Adams, letter, 5 March 1777.
29 MHS Adams Family Papers, *Diary of John Adams*, 14 September 1782.
30 Ibid., 19 May 1783.
31 See Isaiah Thomas, *The History of Printing in America, with a Biography of Printers, and an Account of Newspapers* (Worcester, MA, 1810).

5 The French Revolution

1 Literary and scholarly periodicals that also held similar privileges included the *Mercure de France* and the *Journal des sçavans*.
2 Although detailed studies by Simon Burrows have cautioned against taking at face value the assumption that materials seized by the censor or produced in the expatriate *libelliste* capitals of London

or Neufchatel really reached a wider audience; Robert Darnton, *The Literary Underground of the Old Regime* (Cambridge, MA, 1982), p. 143.

3 Robert Darnton has tracked in his account of how an anti-Royal ditty circulating among the students and professors of Paris' Left Bank was curtailed by effective and heavy-handed policing. Robert Darnton, *Poetry and the Police: Communication Networks in Eighteenth-century Paris* (Cambridge, MA, 2011).

4 Colin Jones, 'The Great Chain of Buying: Medical Advertisement, the Bourgeois Public Sphere, and the Origins of the French Revolution', *American Historical Review*, CI (1996), p. 36.

5 Quoted in Jeremy Popkin, 'Journals: The New Face of News', in *Revolution in Print: The Press in France, 1775–1800*, ed. Robert Darnton and Daniel Roche (Berkeley, CA, 1989), p. 145.

6 Jones, 'Great Chain of Buying', p. 18.

7 Elizabeth Andrews Bond, 'Circuits of Practical Knowledge: The Network of Letters to the Editor in the French Provincial Press, 1770–1788', *French Historical Studies*, XXXIX (2016), pp. 535–65.

8 Simon Burrows, 'The Cosmopolitan Press', in *Press, Politics and the Public Sphere in Europe and North America, 1760–1820*, ed. Hannah Barker and Simon Burrows (Cambridge, 2002), p. 26.

9 Jeremy D. Popkin, *News and Politics in the Age of Revolution: Jean Luzac's 'Gazette de Leyde* (Ithaca, NY, 1989), pp. 52–3. See also Jeremy D. Popkin, *Revolutionary News: The Press in France, 1789–1799* (Durham, NC, 1990).

10 Popkin, *News and Politics*, p. x.

11 The German states had the largest readership for newspapers, with perhaps 300,000 copies a week printed (Popkin, *News and Politics*, p. 2).

12 Popkin, *News and Politics*, p. 15.

13 Burrows, 'The Cosmopolitan Press', p. 29.

14 Ibid., p. 25.

15 Popkin, *News and Politics*, pp. 215–16.

16 Darnton, *Literary Underground*, p. 221.

17 Dominique Godineau, *The Women of Paris and the French Revolution*, trans. Katherine Streip (Berkeley, CA, 1998), p. 216.

18 Ibid., p. 12.

19 Ibid., pp. 68–9.

20 Jeremy Black, 'The Eighteenth Century British Press' in *Encyclopedia of the British Press*, ed. Dennis Griffiths (London, 1993), p. 13.

21 Popkin, 'Journals', p. 145.

22 Godineau, *Women of Paris*, p. 10.

23 Hugh Gough, 'The Provincial Jacobin Club Press during the French Revolution', *European Historical Quarterly*, XVI (1986), p. 49.

24 Quoted in Ruth Scurr, *Fatal Purity: Robespierre and the French Revolution* (London, 2007), p. 270.

25 *Gazette de Leyde*, 29 January 1790 (Paris 22 January), quoted in Popkin, *News and Politics*, p. 210.

26 Nigel Ritchie, 'An Anglo-French Revolutionary? Jean-Paul Marat Channels the Spirits of Wilkes and Junius', *French History*, XXX (2016), pp. 181–96.

27 *Histoire parlementaire de la révolution française* (Paris, 1834), vol. VIII, pp. 299–300.

28 Samuel Bernstein, 'Marat, Friend of the People', *Science and Society*, V (1941), pp. 310–35.

29 Godineau, *Women of Paris*, p. 67.

30 *Histoire parlementaire de la révolution française*, vol. VIII, p. 298; Godineau, *Women of Paris*, p. 68.

31 According to some accounts, his slipper tub was sold to a journalist, and it then passed to a royalist, M. de Saint-Hilaire, finally making its way to the Musée Grevin waxworks.

32 Harvey Chisick, 'Pamphlets and Journalism in the Early French Revolution: The Offices of the *Ami Roi* of the Abbé Royou as a Center of Royalist Propaganda', *French Historical Studies*, XV (1988), p. 640.

33 Harvey Chisick, *The Production, Distribution and Readership of a Conservative Journal of the Early French Revolution: The Ami du Roi of the Abbé Royou* (Philadelphia, PA, 1992); Chisick, 'Pamphlets and Journalism', p. 630.

34 Ibid., pp. 628–37.

35 Quoted in Albert Soboul, *The Sans-culottes: The Popular Movement and Revolutionary Government*, trans. Rémy Inglis Hall (Princeton, NJ, 1980), p. 227.

36 'Reawakening of Père Duchesne', www.marxists.org, accessed 7 April 2019.

37 Quoted Popkin, *Revolutionary News*, p. 154.

38 Gough, 'Provincial Jacobin Club Press', pp. 47–76.

39 Ibid., p. 57.

40 Ibid., pp. 66–7.

41 Ashli White, 'The Politics of "French Negroes" in the United States', *Historical Reflections*, XXIX (2003), pp. 103–21.

42 Matthew Rainbow Hale, 'On Their Tiptoes: Political Time and Newspapers during the Advent of the Radicalized French Revolution, circa 1792–1793', *Journal of the Early Republic*, XXIX (2009), pp. 191–218.

43 Popkin, *News and Politics*, p. 254.

6 Scandal

1 William St Clair, *The Reading Nation in the Romantic Period* (Cambridge, 2004), p. 576.

2 Nikki Hessell, 'News and Newspapers: Readers of the Daily Press in Jane Austen's Novels', *Persuasions*, XXXI (2009), p. 250.

3 A. Francis Steuart, ed., *The Diary of a Lady-in-waiting, By Lady Charlotte Bury* [née Campbell], vol. I (Bodley Head, 1908), p. 19.
4 Christopher Hibbert, *George IV, Regent and King, 1811–1830* (London, 1976); Thea Holme, *Caroline: A Biography of Caroline of Brunswick* (London, 1979); Flora Fraser, *The Unruly Queen: The Life of Queen Caroline* (New York, 1996).
5 The National Archives (TNA), London, TS 11/106 and HO 126/3.
6 Fraser, *Unruly Queen*, p. 188.
7 See Elizabeth Eger and Charlotte Grant et al., ed., *Women, Writing and the Public Sphere, 1700–1830* (Cambridge, 2001).
8 Hannah Barker, *Newspapers, Politics and English Society, 1695–1855* (Harlow, 2000), p. 80.
9 Growing advertising revenues could also provide the 'material base of the change in attitude from subservience to independence', Ivon Asquith, 'Advertising and the Press in the Late Eighteenth and Early Nineteenth Centuries: James Perry and the Morning Chronicle 1790–1821', *Historical Journal*, XVIII (1975), pp. 703–24.
10 A. Aspinall, *Politics and the Press* (Brighton, 1973), p. 306.
11 *Burke's Peerage and Baronetage* (London, 1915), p. 729.
12 Fraser, *Unruly Queen*, p. 191; Edwin Gray, ed., *Papers and Diaries of a York Family* (London, 1927), pp. 125–6.
13 Robert Huish, *Memoirs of Her Late Majesty Caroline, Queen of Great Britain*, vol. I (London, 1821), p. 440.
14 'Memorial Respecting the Present State of the British Press', 17 September 1812, quoted in *Letters of George IV*, ed. A Aspinall, vol. I (Cambridge, 1938), p. 146.
15 Steuart, ed., *Diary*, vol. I, pp. 99–102.
16 British Library (BL), Add. 61986, f. 42. Lady C. Lindsay to H. Douglas, 19 January 1813. Ashe claimed that Carlton House paid for its publication. See Fraser, *Unruly Queen*, p. 234.
17 TNA, HO 126/3, part 5; Huish, *Memoirs*, p. 441.
18 TNA, HO 126/3, part 5. Lord Liverpool to Caroline, Princess of Wales, 14 February 1813.
19 Steuart, ed., *Diary*, vol. I, p. 127.
20 Huish, *Memoirs*, pp. 446–8; Steuart, ed., *Diary*, vol. I, p. 136. The princess's cause could be a rallying point for Whig politicians in Parliament and the City.
21 Steuart, ed., *Diary*, vol. I, p. 162; ibid., vol. II, p. 388. The princess denied involvement with the 'Regent's Valentine'. See Fraser, *Unruly Queen*, p. 231.
22 BL, Loan 72/3 (Liverpool Papers). Lady Anne Hamilton to Lord Liverpool, 15 February 1813, f. 37.
23 Lady Charlotte Lindsay to Henry Brougham [10 March 1813?], quoted in Aspinall, *Politics and the Press*, p. 306; BL, Add. 78704, ff. 67–8. Letter to Lady Perceval from [Edward Fitzgerald?].

24 The paper wrote to Lady Perceval, noting that 'you will perceive some of your ladyship's own ideas', BL, Add. 78704, f. 68.
25 John Mitford, *The King (On the Prosecution of Viscount and Viscountess Perceval) Against John Mitford, Esq. For Perjury* (London, 1814).
26 Ibid.
27 Redesdale allegedly paid £300 for nine months' sojourn at Warburton's Madhouse.
28 Mitford, *The King;* Aspinall, *Politics and the Press*, p. 307; BL, Add. 78704, f. 69.
29 TNA, HO 126/3.
30 Thomas Ashe, *Memoirs and Confessions of Captain Ashe, Author of 'The Spirit of the Book'*, vol. III (London, 1815), pp. 246–7.
31 Iain McCalman, *Radical Underworld: Prophets, Revolutionaries and Pornographers in London, 1795–1840* (Cambridge, 1987), p. 163.
32 Ashe, *Memoirs*, vol. III, pp. 227, 230; BL, Add. 78703, f. 45v; Steuart, ed., *Diary*, vol. I, p. 136.
33 Steuart, ed., *Diary*; Fraser, *Unruly Queen*, p. 233.
34 Ashe, *Memoirs*, vol. III, pp. 235–6.
35 John Wilkes, *Memoirs of Her Majesty Queen Caroline Amelia Liz* (London, 1822), vol. I, p. 289; Steuart, ed., *Diary*, vol. I, p. 136.
36 Fraser, *Unruly Queen*, p. 235.
37 Ibid., p. 189.
38 Aspinall, *Politics and the Press*, p. 307.
39 Fraser, *Unruly Queen*, 234; TNA HO 126/3. Minutes of cabinet.
40 Mitford, *The King*, p. 25.
41 Ibid.; TNA, HO 126/3.
42 BL, Add. 78703, March 1813, ff. 125–34v.
43 Ibid., f. 138; McCalman, *Radical Underworld*, p. 41.
44 *Letters of George IV*, vol. I, p. 194.
45 Steuart, *Diary*, vol. I, p. 360.
46 Ibid., pp. 118–19.
47 BL, Add. 78703, f. 143, 8 April 1813.
48 Arthur D. Morris, *The Hoxton Madhouses* (March, 1958).
49 Aspinall, *Politics and the Press*, p. 308, suggests that Mitford 'escaped'. Mitford, *The King*, records that 'Mr Mitford was actually attended at his house in Crawfurd-Street, on Friday 9 April, by one of the gentry from Hoxton madhouse. The man, however, was *no restraint* upon him, and in a *day or two*, on Mr Mitford desiring him, he "quietly took his leave".'
50 The *News*, 6 June 1813; Aspinall, *Politics and the Press*, p. 309.
51 *The Times*, 22 June 1813; Aspinall, *Politics and the Press*, p. 307.
52 HC Deb 05 March 1813, vol. XXIV, cc1131-55, Hansard 1803–2005, https://api.parliament.uk, accessed 11 December 2020.
53 Edward Law, *Dictionary of National Biography* (London, 1892), vol. XXXII, p. 219; Fraser, *Unruly Queen*, p. 185.

54 Steuart, *Diary*, vol. I, 117.
55 V.A.C. Gatrell, *The Hanging Tree: Execution and the English People, 1770–1868* (Oxford, 1994), p. 515.
56 BL, Add. 78703, ff. 142–70v.
57 IBID., ff. 26.
58 Ashe, *Memoirs*, p. 46.
59 Aspinall, *Politics and the Press*, p. 306.
60 BL, Add. 78704, f. 69, Francis Ludlow Holt to Lady Perceval, 14 April 1814.
61 G. C. Boase, revised by Pam Perkins, 'Bury [née Campbell], Lady Charlotte Susan Maria', www.oxforddnb.com, 23 September 2004.
62 Steuart, *Diary*, vol. I, p. 168.
63 Mitford, *The King*, p. 11.
64 John Mitford, *Description of the Crimes and Horrors in the Interior of Warburton's Private Madhouse at Hoxton* (London, 1825), p. 16; Ashe, *Memoirs*, p. 255.
65 Ashe, *Memoirs*, pp. 236, 254.
66 Mitford, *The King*, pp. 10–11.
67 Ibid., pp. 158–9.
68 Ibid., p. 108.
69 Steuart, *Diary*, vol. II, p. 220.
70 Ashe, *Memoirs*, p. 244.
71 Ibid., p. 241.
72 Mitford, *The King*, p. 84.
73 Fraser, *Unruly Queen*, p. 140; BL, Add. 78704, f. 79v; Add. 78704, f. 69v, Francis Ludlow Holt to Lady Perceval, 14 April 1814.
74 *'Lady P Aragraph championizing.- Vide Letters'* (London, 1814); Mitford, *The King*.
75 Mitford, *Crimes and Horrors*, p. 17.
76 BL, Add. 78704, f. 70. F. L. Holt to Lady Perceval [aft. 1814].
77 *Letters of George IV*, p. 521.
78 Ashe, *Memoirs*, pp. 255–6, 294.
79 BL, Add. 78704, ff. 76–8.
80 Ashe, *Memoirs*, vol. II p. 3.
81 Aspinall, *Politics and the Press*, p. 309
82 BL, Add. 78702, f. 157; Steuart, *Diary*, vol. II, p. 371.
83 BL, Add. 78703, f. 8.
84 Charles, Lord Colchester, *The Diary and Correspondence of Charles Abbot, Lord Colchester, Speaker of the House of Commons, 1802–1817* (London, 1861), vol. II, p. 144.
85 J. Gilliland, 'John Mitford', www.oxforddnb.com, 23 September 2004; McCalman locates him 'at the old waterworks near St Giles' (McCalman, *Radical Underground*, p. 166).
86 McCalman, *Radical Underworld*, pp. 165–7.
87 BL, Add. 78703.

88 Linda Colley, *Britons: Forging the Nation, 1707–1837* (London, 1996); Steuart, *Diary*, vol. I, p. 127.
89 Mitford, *The King*.
90 Hessell, 'News and Newspapers', p. 254.

7 The Creation of the Modern Press

1 J. Cutler Andrews, *The North Reports the Civil War* (Pittsburgh, PA, 1955), p. 77.
2 Brian Gabrial, *The Press and Slavery in America, 1791–1859: The Melancholy Effect of Popular Excitement* (Columbia, SC, 2016), p. 162.
3 *Burlington Free Press*, 2 June 1854.
4 *Richmond Enquirer*, 12 May 1854; the comparison was also reported in the *National Era*, 25 May 1854.
5 Walter Barlow Stevens, *A Reporter's Lincoln*, ed. Michael Burlingame (Lincoln, NE, and London, 1998), p. 240.
6 Ibid., pp. 230–31.
7 *The Times*, 27 September 1858.
8 Quoted in *The North Reports the Civil War*, p. 80.
9 *Public Documents of Massachusetts for 1835* (Boston, MA, 1835), p. 105.
10 *The Apprentice: A Journal of the Mechanics' Institutes and General Education*, vols I–II (London, 1844), p. 109.
11 Nicholas Goddard, 'The Development and Influence of Agricultural Periodicals and Newspapers, 1780–1880', *Agricultural History Review*, XXXI (1983), pp. 116–31.
12 Alfred McClung Lee, *The Daily Newspaper in America* (New York, 1937), pp. 165–7.
13 Lisa L. Lynch, 'Mapping Newspaper Row', https://arcgis.com, accessed 2 May 2020.
14 Mark Canada, *Literature and Journalism: Inspirations, Intersections, and Inventions from Ben Franklin to Stephen Colbert* (New York, 2013), p. 31.
15 Jeffery A. Smith, 'Sunday Newspapers and Lived Religion in Late Nineteenth-century America', *Journal of Church and State*, XLVIII (2006), p. 136.
16 Charles Dickens, *The Life and Adventures of Martin Chuzzlewit* [1843], ch. 16. www.gutenberg.org; Robert McParland, *Charles Dickens's American Audience* (Minneapolis, MN, 2011), pp. 71–2.
17 A. E. Musson, 'Newspaper Printing in the Industrial Revolution', *Economic History Review* [new series], X (1958), pp. 411–26.
18 A. J. Valente, 'Changes in Print Paper During the 19th Century',*Proceedings of the Charleston Library Conference* (2010)
19 *The Times*, 29 November 1814 (dated 20 November 1814 in *The Times Digital Archive*).
20 Musson, 'Newspaper Printing', p. 416.
21 *Morning Herald*, 31 July 1840.

22 David Shane Wallace, 'From Native to Nation: Copway's American Indian Newspaper and Formation of American Nationalism' (2011). LSU Doctoral Dissertation, p. 796.
23 Horace Greeley, *An Overland Journey from New York to San Francisco in the Summer of 1859* (New York, 1860).
24 *The Times*, 22 January 1859.
25 John M. Coward, *The Newspaper Indian: Native Identity in the Press, 1820–90* (Champaign, IL, 1999), pp. 101–2.
26 Julie F. Codell, 'Introduction: The Nineteenth-Century News from India', *Victorian Periodicals Review*, XXXVII (2004), pp. 107, 111.
27 Eliza R. Richards, '"How News Must Feel When Traveling": Dickinson and Civil War Media', in *A Companion to Emily Dickinson*, ed. Martha Nell Smith and Mary Loeffelholz (Oxford, 2008), p. 157.
28 Ibid., p. 158.
29 Timothy Sweet, *Traces of War: Poetry, Photography, and the Crisis of the Union* (Baltimore, MD, 1990).
30 Clarence Brigham, 'Wallpaper Newspapers of the Civil War' in *Bibliographical Essays: A Tribute to Wilberforce Eames* (Cambridge, MA, 1924); Susan Campion, 'Wallpaper Newspapers of the American Civil War', *Journal of the American Institute for Conservation*, XXXIV (1995), pp. 129–40.
31 'The Daily Citizen Vicksburg, Mississippi', *Information Circular*, III (1967), www.loc.gov.
32 Sari Edelstein, *Between the Novel and the News: The Emergence of American Women's Writing* (Charlottesville, VA, 2014), pp. 120–21.
33 Two patents were issued between 1840 and 1850, eleven patents were granted for stereotyping methods between 1850 and 1860, and eighteen were granted between 1860 and 1870. George A. Kubler, *A New History of Stereotyping* (New York, 1841), p. 180.
34 Swen Kjaer, *Productivity of Labor in Newspaper Printing* (Washington, DC, 1929), p. 90; Philip Gaskell, *A New Introduction to Bibliography* (Oxford, 1979), pp. 201–6; Jeffrey Makala, 'The Early History of Stereotyping in the United States: Mathew Carey and the Quarto Bible Marketplace', *Papers of the Bibliographical Society of America*, CIX (2015), pp. 461–89.
35 Kubler, *History of Stereotyping*, p. 178.
36 *Constitution of the New York Typographical Society* (1833), quoted in E. B. Dietrich, 'National Arbitration in the Balance: The Newspaper Publishers Versus the Compositors', *Social Forces*, VIII (1929), p. 284.
37 Jeffery A. Smith, 'Sunday Newspapers and Lived Religion in Late Nineteenth-century America', *Journal of Church and State*, XLVIII (2006), p. 136.
38 Andrew Hobbs, *A Fleet Street in Every Town: The Provincial Press in England, 1855–1900* (Cambridge, 2018), p. 76; Chris Baggs, '"In the Separate Reading Room for Ladies Are Provided Those Publications

Specially Interesting to Them": Ladies' Reading Rooms and British Public Libraries, 1850–1914', *Victorian Periodicals*, Review, XXXVIII (2005), pp. 280–306.

39 Simon J. Potter, 'Webs, Networks, and Systems: Globalization and the Mass Media in the Nineteenth- and Twentieth-century British Empire', *Journal of British Studies*, XLVI (2007), p. 623.

40 Historic England, *Listing Selection Guide: Culture and Entertainment Buildings* (London, 2017), p. 16.

41 *Cobbett's Political Register*, 25 September 1807.

42 Hobbs, *Fleet Street*, p. 76.

43 Ibid.

44 Andrew Hobbs, 'Local Newspapers in Victorian Era: Early "Rolling News" and Reading as Pub Activity', www.pressgazette.co.uk, 27 December 2018.

45 Potter, 'Webs, Networks, and Systems', p. 622.

46 *The India Office and Burma Office List* (London, 1842); Amelia Bonea, *The News of Empire: Telegraphy, Journalism, and the Politics of Reporting in Colonial India, c. 1830–1900* (Oxford and New York, 2016), p. 169.

47 Hannah Barker, *Newspapers, Politics and English Society, 1695–1855* (Harlow, 2000), pp. 206–7.

48 *The Times*, 27 October 1831, quoted in Barker, *Newspapers and English Society*, p. 206.

49 Ibid., p. 350.

50 Robert Stewart, 'The Conservative Party and the "Courier" Newspaper, 1840', *English Historical Review*, XCI (1976), pp. 348, 350.

51 Philip Grant, *The History of Factory Legislation* (Manchester, 1866), pp. 19, 21.

52 Barker, *Newspapers, Politics, and English Society*, p. 209.

53 Thomas Milton Kemnitz, 'Chartist Newspaper Editors', *Victorian Periodicals Newsletter*, XVIII (1972), pp. 1–11; D. G. Wright, *Popular Radicalism: The Working Class Experience* (London, 2014).

54 Christopher A. Casey, 'Common Misperceptions: The Press and Victorian Views of Crime', *Journal of Interdisciplinary History*, XLI (2010), p. 369.

55 Seba Smith, *The Life and Writings of Major Jack Downing of Downingville: Away Down East in the State of Maine* (Boston, MA, 1834), p. 86.

52 Charles Mitchell, *The Newspaper Press Directory and Advertisers' Guide* (London, 1846), p. 29.

57 Ibid., p. 33.

58 Liz McFall and Elizabeth Rose McFall, *Advertising: A Cultural Economy* (London, 2004), p. 144.

59 *Punch*, XII (1848), p. 31; Nicholas Daly, *The Demographic Imagination and the Nineteenth-century City* (Cambridge, 2015), p. 114.

Afterword

1 Editorial Board, *'Donald Trump Too Tame for You? Meet Britain's Boris Johnson'*, www.nytimes.com, 29 June 2019.
2 Donald Trump (@realDonaldTrump), www.twitter.com, 15 August 2019.
3 Benedict Anderson, *Imagined Communities: Reflections on the Origin and Spread of Nationalism* (London, 1991), p. 35.
4 Simon J. Potter, 'Webs, Networks, and Systems: Globalization and the Mass Media in the Nineteenth- and Twentieth-century British Empire', *Journal of British Studies*, XLVI (2007), pp. 623–4.
5 'Decline of Newspapers', https://en.wikipedia.org, 17 March 2009.
6 Mark Di Stefano (@MarkDiStef), www.twitter.com, 15 August 2019.

Further Reading

Adelman, Joseph M., *Revolutionary Networks: The Business and Politics of Printing the News, 1763–1789* (Baltimore, MD, 2019)

Andrews, J. Cutler, *The North Reports the Civil War*, paperback reprint (Pittsburgh, PA, 1985)

Aspinall, Arthur, *Politics and the Press, c. 1780–1850* (London, 1949)

Barker, Hannah, *Newspapers, Politics, and Public Opinion in Late Eighteenth-century England* (Oxford, 1998)

—, *Newspapers, Politics and English Society, 1695–1855* (Harlow, 2000)

—, and Simon Burrows, ed., *Press, Politics and the Public Sphere in Europe and North America, 1760–1820* (Cambridge, 2002)

Bezanson, Randall P., *Taxes on Knowledge in America: Exactions on the Press from Colonial Times to the Present* (Philadelphia, PA, 1994)

Black, Jeremy, *The English Press, 1621–1861* (Stroud, 2001)

Bleyer, Willard Grosvenor, *Main Currents in the History of American Journalism* (Boston, MA, 1927)

Coward, John M., *The Newspaper Indian: Native American Identity in the Press, 1820–90* (Urbana and Chicago, IL, 1999)

Darnton, Robert, and Daniel Roche, ed., *Revolution in Print: The Press in France, 1775–1800* (Berkeley, CA, 1989)

Frasca, Ralph, *Benjamin Franklin's Printing Network: Disseminating Virtue in Early America* (Columbia, MI, 2006)

Handover, P. M., *A History of the London Gazette* (London, 1965)

Harris, M., *London Newspapers in the Age of Walpole: A Study in the Origins of the Modern Press* (London, 1987)

—, and Alan Lee, eds, *The Press in English Society from the Seventeenth to Nineteenth Centuries* (London and Toronto, 1986)

Hobbs, Andrew, *A Fleet Street in Every Town: The Provincial Press in England, 1855–1900* [2018], www.openbookpublishers.com

Humphreys, Carol Sue, *'This Popular Engine': New England Newspapers during the American Revolution* (Newark, DE, 1992)

Morison, Stanley, *The English Newspaper: An Account of the Physical Development of Journals Printed in London 1622–1932*, reprint (Cambridge, 2009)

Pettegree, Andrew, *The Invention of News: How the World Came to Know about Itself* (New Haven, CT, and London, 2014)

Popkin, Jeremy, *News and Politics in the Age of Revolution: Jean Luzac's 'Gazette de Leyde'* (Ithaca, NY, and London, 1989)

—, *Revolutionary News: The Press in France, 1789–1799* (Durham, NC, 1990)

Raymond, Joad, *The Invention of the Newspaper: English Newsbooks, 1641–1649* (Oxford, 1996)

St Clair, William, *The Reading Nation in the Romantic Period* (Cambridge, 2004)

Sommerville, C. John, *The News Revolution in England: Cultural Dynamics of Daily Information* (New York, 1996)

Sutherland, James, *The Restoration Newspaper and Its Development* (Cambridge, 1986)

Williams, Kevin, *Read All About It! A History of the British Newspaper* (Abingdon, 2010)

Acknowledgements

Part of the research for this book was undertaken at the Library Company, Philadelphia. I am grateful to the William Reese Company for the fellowship that enabled this to take place, and to Jim Green and his colleagues for their hospitality and deep wells of generously shared knowledge. I am also grateful to the British Library for granting me research leave for that trip, and the support of the head of the Americas section, Carole Holden. Ben Hayes, then at Reaktion Books, suggested that there might be something worth pursuing in a piece that *History Today* published, and Michael Leaman gracefully continued to support the project to its conclusion.

I am particularly thankful to colleagues in research libraries, notably the Americas and Australasian Collections and the Department of Manuscripts at the British Library, the superintendents of the special materials reading room at the National Archives, and the librarians and others behind the scenes working with Google Books, the Internet Archive and the HathiTrust. Colleagues at the Institute of Historical Research have provided helpful encouragement at all times. I am pleased that Christie's delivered the final tranche of the Egmont Papers to the British Library, full as they were with the trials and tribulations of Lady Perceval. I started making a catalogue of them and ended up some time later with a book. As Ambrose recently noted, cycling past the Reaktion offices, this time has been longer than he has been alive. I hope that the dedication makes up for this in some way.

Photo Acknowledgements

The author and publishers wish to express their thanks to the below sources of illustrative material and/or permission to reproduce it:

Collection of the author: pp. 73, 142, 172, 173, 183, 205, 208; Carol M. Highsmith Archive, Library of Congress, Prints and Photographs Division, Washington, DC: p. 104; courtesy the Institute of Historical Research, School of Advanced Study, University of London: pp. 40, 41, 128; collection of the Massachusetts Historical Society, Boston: p. 79; The Metropolitan Museum of Art, New York: pp. 29, 150–51, 199; courtesy Thomas Fisher Rare Book Library, University of Toronto: p. 65; © The Trustees of the British Museum: pp. 10, 47, 169; from John Weale, ed., *London Exhibited in 1851* (London, 1851), photo courtesy Library of Congress, Washington, DC: p. 202.

Index

Page numbers in *italics* indicate illustrations

Acta diurna 23
Adams, John 81, 103, 107, 110–11
advertising
    affiches 114, 120
    Charles Mitchell and the *Newspaper Press and Directory* 209–10
    colonial newspapers 77–8, 92–3
    first advertisements 50
    free papers 11
    of newspapers 71, 211
    online 12–13
    payment for 86
    reflection of society 87–9, 210
Affiches de Toulouse 121
Aitken, Robert 97–9
Almon, John 70, 109
Anderson, Benedict 19, 114, 212
Applegarth's *Times* vertical printing machine *202*
Ashe, Thomas 147, 158–60, 166
Associated Press 196
Austen, Jane
    Mansfield Park 150–51
    Northanger Abbey 174
Austin, William 152, 170

Bagging for the Great Towns *205*
Balzac, Jean-Louis Guez 31
Bell, Robert 99–100
Bennett, James Gordon 185, 211
Bennett Jr, James Gordon 75, 211
Binmore, Henry 180, 182
blackmail and threats 119, 153, 160–61
Boudinot, Elias 190
Boyer, Abel 57–59
Bull Run, First Battle of *see* Manassas, First Battle of
Brady, Mathew B. 175
Brissot, Jacques Pierre 118, 145
Brooks, Shirley 210
Burney, Charles 32
BuzzFeed 213

Calonne, Charles-Alexandre de 116, 118
Campbell, lady Charlotte 155, 156, 165, 167
Canada 92, 108
Caroline of Brunswick 147, 151–2, 154–5, 164, 168, 170, 171, 173
Catholic Church 24–6, 28, 31, 135
celebrity 203, 208–9
censorship 16, 29, 45, 33–4, 102, 113, 118, 119, 123, 124, 144–5
Chartism 207–8
Child, Lydia Maria, 'Slavery's Pleasant Homes: a faithful sketch' 177–8
China 23, 28, 189
Civil Wars, English 20–22
Clive, Lord 99
coffeehouses 15, 18, 44–50, 58, 81, 97, 136

Colombe, Anne-Félicité 132–3
competition 127–9, 176
Condorcet, marquis de 129
content
affiches 120
colonial papers 78
eclectic 14–15
Martin Chuzzlewit 186
of *Oxford Gazette* 33
political and financial news 28
political influence of 51
profitability 50–51
relationship with society 150
satirized in Thomas Rowlandson's *The News Paper* 148–9, 150
sensationalism 203
Copway, George 190
Corday, Charlotte 133
Cordeliers Club 131
couriers 24–7
cosmopolitan press 113–14, 121–5
COVID-19 213
Coyne, Stirling 210
Cracow, Tree of 113
Craske, Charles 201
crime, reporting on 208–9
Cromwell, Oliver 20–21

Danton, Georges 131
Deane, Silas 107
decline 13, 213
definition 14
design 34–7, 50, 86, 92, 127, 129–30, 194, 200
Desmoulins, Camille 130–31, 145
Discours de la lanterne aux Parisiens 130, 145
Dickens, Charles 210
Martin Chuzzlewit 185–6
Our Mutual Friend 204
Dickinson, Emily 193–5, 209, 213
'The Only News I Know' 193–4
disability 42, 199
distribution networks 88, 135, 213
domestic space 29, 30, 126, 151
Douglas, Stephen 178, 180
Draft Riots 183, *183*
Drogheda 20–21
Dumas, Charles 109

Egmont, Lady *see* Perceval, Viscountess Bridget
Ellenborough, Lord 163–4
An Englishman's Delight; or, News of All Sorts 10
Evelyn, John 39, 49

Facebook 8, 212
Fielding, Henry 16
Fleet Street 11–12
foreign news
early newsgathering 28
Gazette de Leyde 124
identity 93, 189
transatlantic exchange of 75–6, 80–82, 85, 105, 110, 180–81
Ford, Charles 51
fourth estate 16, 30, 112
Franklin, Benjamin 78, 83–4, 87, 90–91, 96, 107–10
Franklin Court *104*
freedom of the press 45, 53, 67–8
Fremantle, Sir Thomas 206–7
Fréron, Elie-Catherine 133
Fréron, Mme 133, 134

Galagina *see* Boudinot, Elias
Gentleman's Magazine 60–61
Google 213, 232
gossip 37, 44, 50, 54, 60, 113
Greeley, Horace 190–91
Grub Street 57, 114, 119, 153, 157, 174
The Grumblers of Great Britain 47
guilds 127, 137

Habermas, Jürgen 17–18, 120
habit 13, 30, 126
Hearst, William Randolph 203, 211
Hébert, Jacques-René 137–40

Hitt, Robert R. 180, 182
Hoe, Richard 188, 201
Hooke, Robert 48

information networks
Atlantic world 82–5, 93, 97, 103, 105, 107
coffeehouses 48
early networks 28, 30–31
print shops 136
India 99, 143, 192, 205–6
ink 58, 127, 187, 188
intelligence and espionage 110
Ireland 20–21, 22, 45, 70, 72, 105–6, 153, 207

Jay, John 109
Jefferson, Thomas 101, 111–12
job printing 58, 77, 87
Johnson, Samuel 9
Jones, David 54–6
Secret History of White-hall 54–6, 57
Jones, John Paul 103, 105, 108
journalists
as a career 16, 119, 131, 182, 198
in classical world 23
Père Duchesne 140
and the public sphere 119
reputation 9
and revolution 114–15
Woodfall, William 69–72
Journal de Champagne 121
journals 98–9

Kant, Immanuel 17
Koenig, Friedrich 187
Knox, Vicesimus 72–4

L'Estrange, Roger 34, 43
letters
fake 107, 161
from readers 121
news 23–8, 30, 80–81, 83, 85–6
libel 119
Lincoln, Abraham 175, 180, 196
local identity 18, 78, 82, 88, 93, 177, 193, 203
London, Great Fire of 38–43, 50
London Magazine 60–61
Loudon, Samuel 102
Luzac, Jean 123, 144

Manassas, First Battle of 175–6
manuscript news and news sheets 28, 31, 34, 85–6
Marat, Jean-Paul 126, 131–3
Marble, Manton 211
materiality 15–16, 77, 78, 200
Maxwell, Robert 75
Melville, Herman 195
Battle-pieces and Aspects of the War 195
Donelson (February 1862) 195
merchants 24, 28–9, 85, 97, 116
Mercury Women 42–3, 127
Mirabeau, comte de 130
Mitchell, Charles 209–10
Mitford, John 147–50, 157–8, 161, 166, 171
The Adventures of Johnny Newcombe in the Navy 171
Description of the Crimes and Horrors 157, 158
A Peep into W-r Castle, after the Lost Mutton 171
'The Vampyre' 171
Morande, Charles Théveneau de 124
Lettres d'un voyageur 124
Moxon, Joseph 36
Muddiman, Henry 34

national identity 78–80, 88–9, 105–6, 111–12, 141, 193, 212
Native Americans 81, 108–9, 178, 189–91, 195
Necker, Jacques 116, 131
Neufchâteau, François de 121
Newcombe, Thomas 37

news
- burden of 193–5
- business of 11–13
- as commodity 44, 46, 48, 54, 76, 109–10, 114
- desire for 115, 125–6, 198–9
- fake 9, 107, 124, 209
- idea of 7–9, 23, 30–31
- oral 31, 44, 105

news sheets 34, 53, 124
newsbooks 36, 37
newsboys 11, 88
newspapers
- *20 minutes* 12
- *Actes des Apôtres 130*
- *L'Ami du people* (*Publiciste Parisien*) 125, 131
- *L'Ami du Roi* 133–5
- *amNewYork* 12
- *Annual Register* 16
- *Avisa* 28
- *Bell's Weekly Messenger* 183
- *Bombay Herald* 192
- *Bombay Samachar* 192
- *Boston Evening-Post* 78, 85
- *Boston Gazette* 85, 103
- *Boston Independent Chronicle* 108, 109
- *Bouche de fer* 129
- *British Gazette and Sunday Monitor* 44
- *Burlington Free Press* 178
- *Calcutta Gazette* 192
- *Cambrian* 192
- *Cambridge Chronicle* 206
- *Cherokee Phoenix* 189–90, 192
- *Chronique de Paris* 124, 127
- *Club des observateurs* 141
- *Colored American* 183
- *Courante* (Amsterdam) 28, 35
- *Courant* (Edinburgh) 44
- *Courier* 147
- *Courrier d'Avignon* 122, 141
- *Courrier de l'Europe* 123
- *Courrier du Bas-Rhin* 122, 123
- *Current Intelligence* 37
- *Daily Mail* 11, 76, 210
- *Daily Gazetteer* 83
- *Daily Post* 83
- *Dakota tawaxitku kin* 190
- *Diary; or, Woodfall's Register 73*
- *European* 75
- *Les Événements du jour* 141
- *Evening Post* 179
- *Evening Standard* 12
- *Express* 11
- *Feuille politique, littéraire et commerciale de la Gironde* 143
- *Financial Times* 12
- *Gazette de Cologne* 122
- *Gazette de France* 29, 113, 139
- *Gazette de Leyde* 107, 122, 123, 131, 144
- *Gazette* (Edinburgh) 44
- *Gazette nationale, ou le monituer universel 128*
- *Gazette Universelle* 127
- *Gazetteer* 80
- *Guardian* (and *Manchester Guardian*) 12, 13, 76, 188, 201, 204, 207
- *Herald* 181
- *Hicky's Bengal Gazette* 192
- *Hindoo Patriot* 192
- *Histoire des revolutions de France et de Brabant* 130
- *Illinois Staats-Zeitung* 193
- *Illustrated London News 208*
- *Independent Chronicle and Boston Patriot* 184
- *India Gazette* 192
- *International Herald Tribune* 75
- *Journal de Paris* 126
- *Journal de la société de 1789* 129
- *Journal des frontières* 142
- *Journal du club national de Bordeaux* 143
- *Journal du département de Marne-et-Loire* 141
- *Le Junius français* 131

Kentish Gazette 206
Ladies Mercury 44
Leeds Mercury 207
Liberator 177
L'Orateur du Peuple 125, 133
Lloyd's Evening Post and British Chronicle 106
Lloyd's Weekly Newspaper 201, 211
London and Country Journal 83
London Chronicle 106
London Gazette 39–44, *40*, *41*, 50, 54, 106
London General Advertiser and Morning Intelligencer 109
London Evening Post 70, 80, 83, 106
Manchester Courier 204, 209
Massachusetts Spy 103
Metro New York 12
Metronews 12
Middlesex Journal 80
Morning Chronicle 70, 71, 106, 147, 156
Morning Herald (London) 70, 71, 160
Morning Herald (New York) 188
Morning Post 71, 157, 160
National Era 179
New-England Courant *79*
New Jersey Gazette 109
New York Daily Times 185
New-York Gazette 80–81, 84
New York Herald 185, *199*, 201, 202
New York Journal 95, 203
New-York Packet 102
New York Sun 185, 201
New York Times 12, 13, 75, 123, 179, 201, 203, 212
New York Tribune 179, 183, *183*, 190, 201
New York World 203
News 158, 162, 165, *173*
Niles' Weekly Register 187
North Briton 64, *65*, 80
Northern Star 207–8
Notizie scritte 28
Ordinari Post Tijdender (*Post- och Inrikes Tidningar*) 29–30
Oxford Gazette 32–6
Paris Herald see International Herald Tribune
Pennsylvania Evening Post 106
Pennsylvania Gazette 87, 90
Pennsylvania Journal and the Weekly Advertiser 95
Le Père Duchesne 137–40
Philadelphia Bulletin 187
Philadelphia Journal 84
Philadelphia Herald 88
Philadelphia Public Ledger 188
Pilot 156, 173
Press and Tribune 180
Le Publiciste *142*
Publick Occurences both Forreign and Domestick 30
Relation aller Fürnemmen und gedenckwürdigen Historien 28
Richmond Enquirer 179
Springfield Daily Republican 193
Star 71, 147, 158
Sun 147, *172*
Sunday Times 210
Telegraph 12, 203
Tijdinghen (*Antwerp Gazette*) *35*
Times (Chicago) 180
Times (London); audience 203; circulation 207; financial value 71; Lady Perceval affair 158; New York correspondent 180–81; online 12; opposition to Poor Laws 207; printing technology 187, 188, 201, 202; reform 206; U.S. Civil War 175, 181
Today 11
Udant Martand 192
Vicksburg Daily Citizen 197

Vieux cordelier 130
Virginia Gazette 89, 101
Washington Post 13
Washington Star 179
Weekly Newes from Italy, Germanie, Hungaria, etc. 29
Weekly Journal; or, British Gazetteer 60
Worcester Post-man 44
York Courant 71

Oastler, Richard 207
objectivity 34, 36, 38, 81–2, 86, 209
online publishing 12–13
Ostade, Adriaen van, *Reading the News at the Weavers' Cottage* *29*, 30

Paine, Thomas 90–91, 95–102
Common Sense 99–102
'The Magazine in America' 98
pamphlets 22, 35–6, 99–102, 110, 118, 130, 135
The Snowdrop 99
paper
additives 187
difficulty of obtaining 127, 134, 196
flong 200–201
Fourdrinier Machine 187
lack of rags for 101
mechanical production of 186, 187
mills 197
moulds 188, 200–202
papier-mâché 15, 200
pulp 187
protections from thieves 136
quality 127
wallpaper 196–8
Park, Robert E. 6, 18
Pennsylvania Magazine; or, American Monthly 97–9
Pepys, Samuel 36, 37, 48
Perceval, Viscountess Bridget 147–50, 153, 158, 162–3, 165–6, 167–71
Phipps, Thomas 158, 162, 163, 165, 164, 166
pirated works 113, 131, 171
plague 32–3
poetry 15, 99, 120, 150, 176, 193–5
political influence 51, 69
post 54, 58, 84–6, 105, 122, 205
press barons 13, 211
print runs 100–101, 126, 127, 134, 135, 143, 160, 188, 211
print shops 77, 102, 104, *104*, 127, 135–6, 138, 187–8, 201–2
printers 126–7, 132, 134, 135
printing
costs 51
job *see* job printing
labour 127, 201–2
methods 11–12, 30, 127, 129, 186–8, 198, 202
quality 101
rotary press 188, 201, 202
steam 186, 187
stereotype 201, 203
trades 78, 135
propaganda 31, 100–101, 104, 107, 111, 124, 158, 171, 182–3
provincial press 60, 71, 94, 105, 120, 140–43, 150, 203–4, 205
public houses 30, 105, 204, 208
public opinion 51, 104, 145, 160–61, 166, 171, 207
public sphere 17, 44–50, 114, 119–21, 130
Pulitzer, Joseph 203, 211

Ramsay, David 104
reading and readership
appetite for scandal 160
cheap print 187
community 82–3
during the French Revolution 125–6

expense 58
habit of 30, 126
influence 98–9, 103–4
literacy 28
in London 150
online 13, 213
stereotypes 72, 150
war excitement 176
reading rooms 124, 203, 204, 205
reform 67–9, 206–7
Regent's Valentine 147, 152, 156–7
Robespierre, Maximilien 127, 131, 140, 142
Roman Empire 23–4
Rowlandson, Thomas, *The News Paper 148–9*, 150
Royou, Abbé 133–4
rumour 27, 54, 60, 113–15, 125, 152, 179, 213
Rush, Benjamin 96, 99
Russell, William Howard 175, 181

Saint Domingue 144
sans-culottes 136–7
Say, Mary 74
scissors and paste journalism 83–4, 86–7, 101–2, 109
Shah, Eddy 11
Sheridan, James B. 180, 182
slavery
advertisements 93, 95
Atlantic economy 77, 93
Child, Lydia Maria, 'Slavery's Pleasant Homes: a faithful sketch', 177–9
classical world 23
enslaved printers 78
labour 188
sports 201, 203
Stamp Act Crisis 18, 85, 94
Stationers' Company 32
Stono River rebellion 83
subscriptions 86, 88, 89, 120, 124, 134, 142, 150, 184, 213

taxation
in American Revolution 91
in French Revolution 117
on newspapers 61, 208
Stamp Acts 94–5
stamp duty (1757) 61
stamp duty (1855) 192, 203
telegraph and telegram 13, 175–6, 181, 196
theatre 14, 80, 105, 138
Thomas, Isaiah 103, 104
time 19, 31, 32, 105, 127, 135
tipau 23
town criers 27
Tracy, H. R., 'Civilians at Bull Run' 176
transport 12, 24–5, 49, 76, 77, 85, 105, 188–9
Trump, Donald 13, 211–12, 213
Twitter 8, 212
type 36, 127
typesetters 126, 127
typography *see* design

unionization 12, 201–2

vendors 13, 15, 16, 39, 42, 71, 127
see also Mercury Women
Voltaire 133, 123

Wales 191–2
Wales, Prince of 147, 151
Wales, Princess of *see* Caroline of Brunswick
Walter, John 187
Washington, George 102, 111, 123
Whittier, John Greenleaf 195
WikiLeaks 75
Wikipedia 213
Williams, Charles, *Lady P aragraph Championizing.– Vide Letters 169*
Williamson, Joseph 34, 37
Wilkes, John 62–9, 131
Witherspoon, John 107
Woodfall, William 69–73